The Modern Mystic's Wheel of the Year

A Multi-Faith Path to Living in Harmony

Rev. Dr. Tracey L. Ulshafer

Copyright © 2025 Rev. Dr. Tracey L. Ulshafer 2025 & Zen Barn Publishing, LLC. All rights reserved. For personal use only and not for distribution or reproduction purposes without the written permission of the author. No part of this book may be used or reproduced by any means, graphic, electronic, or mechanical, including photocopying, recording, taping, or by any information storage retrieval system, without the written permission of the authors, except in the case of brief quotations embodied in articles and reviews. The licensed decorative elements and fonts sourced from Canva are under the Commercial Use license.

www.OneYogaCenter.net

www.TraceyUlshafer.com

ISBN: 978-1-969009-04-4

The Triad of Transformation

The Book:
Modern Mystic's Sacred Map

A sacred guide weaving ancient wisdom into today's world, this map and its keys unlock your Eternal Timeless True Self using chakras, astrology, ceremony, and more.

The Workbook:
Journey Journal

The book's companion offers exercises to explore all of the components of the book, serving as a key to unlocking your highest potential.

The Oracle Deck:
Celestial Insights

A radiant bridge to divine guidance, this 55-card deck uses celestial phases and mystic wisdom as a key to illuminate your spiritual path.

PERMISSIONS & FAIR USE NOTICE

This work is adapted from the author's Doctor of Ministry thesis. It is a scholarly and spiritual exploration intended for educational and inspirational purposes.

Quotations from published works have been carefully attributed to their original authors and sources. These quotations are included under the doctrine of fair use (U.S. Copyright Law, Title 17, U.S. Code), which permits limited use of copyrighted material for commentary, criticism, scholarship, teaching, and research.

The author does not claim copyright ownership of any material quoted herein. All rights remain with the original copyright holders. If any material has been inadvertently used without proper acknowledgment, please notify the author so corrections may be made in future editions.

DISCLAIMER

Take a deep breath, and align with your Highest Self, the True You, the One. You already possess within you the answers to everything you seek, and only you can make the best decisions for your overall health and well-being.

Take another deep breath, and receive the information contained within these pages for that Highest Self, using all that you need, and leaving the rest, respectfully, behind.

The information provided in this book and its accompanying Workbook is for educational and informational purposes only and not intended as a substitute for professional medical advice, diagnosis, or treatment. Always consult your physician or other qualified healthcare provider with any questions you may have regarding a medical condition or treatment. The views expressed in this book are the authors' own and should not be a substitute for any medical advice or training given to you by a qualified professional.

Yoga practices in the Book and Workbook are created for all levels; however, as with any new exercise, it is best to consult with your doctor before starting any new exercise regimen. Although many modifications and expert instructions are provided, by partaking in the yoga practices, you are accepting responsibility for your own body and actions, and releasing Rev. Dr. Tracey L. Ulshafer, One Yoga and Wellness, and any other names it is known by from any liability.

Essential oils are powerful and should be used with care. Always dilute before topical use, and consult a qualified healthcare professional before using essential oils if you are pregnant, breastfeeding, have epilepsy, high blood pressure, or other medical conditions. Keep out of reach of children and pets and avoid contact with eyes.

The use of any information from this book is solely at your own risk.

Take a third deep breath, inviting in all the wisdom contained within these pages for the Highest Good of All. And so it is.

DEDICATION

To the radiant souls who heed the sacred summons to awaken the Divine spark within, this book is for you. You, Modern Mystics, rise each dawn to weave the timeless threads of love, kindness, and interconnectedness into the tapestry of this living Earth. Through the alchemy of your inner work, you embody a high-vibrational existence, igniting others to ascend in your wake. For you, life pulses with magic, mysticism, and the ceaseless rhythm of natural energies.

Though many of you walk solitary paths—sometimes misunderstood, cast out, or set apart by the brilliance of your gifts—you challenge the shadows of dogma and the confines of convention.

Whether you call yourself an empath, an alchemist, mystic, pagan, Hindu, Shaman, Starseed, Divine Being, or something else, no label can contain your boundless essence. You are limitless, a mystery beyond definition, and seated in your authenticity, you reshape the world.

This book is dedicated to you and to those you will awaken with your unwavering truth. I honor your journey and the luminous legacy you forge.

In Eternal Love & Radiant Light,

Rev. Dr. Tracey

WHAT THEY'RE SAYING

"To stand fully and securely vested in authenticity, one must undertake a journey within and discover their truth...the truth that is yours alone, expressly formed for you directly from The Divine Mind and Heart. This truth is your unique contribution to humanity. In this book, Rev. Dr. Tracey Ulshafer shares her unique insights and tools from her journey to self-discovery and leadership as she navigated her path to her higher self. It's a gift to those who seek to discover their truth and share it with the world."

~ Rev. Dr. Jay Speights

"When Rev. Dr. Tracey Ulshafer's 'Wheel of the Year' turns, it brings along a plethora of elements, tools, and rituals to satisfy the mystic calling in virtually everyone. Her multi-faith approach is inclusive of all paths and honors traditions both ancient and modern. Addressing these sacred events with both the discipline of a scholar and the open heart of a very wise woman, she welcomes the reader to embrace these teachings from either perspective. *The Modern Mystic's Wheel of the Year* is a precious guide that belongs among the sacred books of all time. Bless you, Dr. Tracey, for this truly amazing and dedicated work!"—Rev. Dr. Victor Fuhrman, Doctor of Spiritual Direction, Author, and Podcast Host of OmTimes "Destination Unlimited."

~ Rev. Dr. Victor Fuhrman, Author, Podcast Host & Producer: *Destination Unlimited, Vox Novus*

"Tracey's rich writing style, infused with depth of knowledge and years of study, offers a guiding light to self-discovery. As you navigate these pages, you'll be challenged to uncover the profound truths within while gaining a wealth of knowledge. Your inner teacher is waiting, and Tracey's wisdom serves as a powerful catalyst to help you tap into it."

~ Sarah Stevenson, Mindful Educational Services, Yoga Teacher

"I'm so excited that Rev. Dr. Tracey has written this gorgeous book, *The Modern Mystic's Wheel of the Year: A Multi-Faith Path to Living in Harmony*! And not just a book, which would have been more than enough, but also a workbook and a deck of cards to accompany it. This collection is a treasure house of wisdom and esoteric teachings, and it couldn't have come at a better time. In a world that is caught up in narcissism and divisiveness, we need each individual to take personal responsibility for nourishing the seed of harmony within so it can blossom into the flower of greater harmony that shines in the world, and become love and light in action. Tracey has provided a wonderful resource, containing something for everyone. I know I will be using this book for years to come!"

~ Rev. Dr. Mimi Kate Munroe

"Tracey brings a deep well of wisdom and experience that speaks to spiritual seekers of all paths. Whether you're rooted in a long-standing tradition or just beginning your journey, this book offers guidance to help you explore and expand your spiritual practice. With an open heart and mind, you'll be inspired to reach the full potential of your path—whatever form it may take."

~ Allyson Baglieri, Earth-Based Practitioner

"There are mystics in every faith tradition, those people who have a deep, inner connection to the mystery of God. In this remarkable book, Dr. Ulshafer shares some of the multitude of practices, rituals, and rites of many varied traditions that have been followed by those mystics through the ages. From this presentation, we have an opportunity to expand our repertoire, to create personal practices to enhance our spiritual life and connection to The Divine. Month by month, in harmony with nature and the great mystics and philosophers of the past, she teaches and exhorts us to find our own best practices. Sharing her numerous personal experiences, travel, and extensive research, there is something here for everyone who is seeking something more."

~ Rev. Dr. Stacy Lee Goforth

"Having had the honor of both learning from and creating alongside Dr. Tracey, I can say without hesitation that her work carries a rare kind of magic—rooted in integrity, experience, and deep spiritual truth. *The Modern Mystic's Wheel of the Year* is more than a book; it's a living transmission of wisdom that invites us to remember our connection to the sacred cycles of life. Dr. Tracey's words guide us home—to harmony, to wholeness, and to the divine rhythm within all things."

~ Suzi Zappile, Yoga Teacher, Creative Guide + Founder of Zen Barn Publishing

* * *

Contact Zen Barn Publishing:

Zen Barn Publishing is a sacred space where creativity becomes ceremony. Suzi offers energetically aligned design and soulful support for authors, healers, and visionaries who are ready to bring their wisdom into the world.

With deep intuition and artistic devotion, Suzi helps shape books, decks, and sacred tools that carry frequency, intention, and truth—each one a ripple of your light in the collective field.

Give your vision wings!

www.zenbarnpublishing.com

ZEN BARN PUBLISHING
Elmer, New Jersey

ACKNOWLEDGEMENTS

In 2020, I completed my Doctor of Ministry at The New Seminary for Interfaith Studies (TNS), the oldest worldwide interfaith seminary, which was officially founded in 1981. The pandemic was raging, and I had a spiritual community that needed my presence. Although I completed my capstone project, I didn't publish it. What transpired over the few years after changed the world as we knew it, and my thesis slipped out of my mind—until 2025.

I awoke one morning knowing that I needed to publish, but so much had changed, and I needed to revisit the concept. Well, here we are. I want to formally thank Rev. Dr. Jay Speights of TNS for his support, generosity, and understanding throughout this process. I also wish to thank my fellow seminarians, Rev. Dr. Stacy Goforth and Rev. Dr. Victor "The Voice" Fuhrman, for taking time out of their busy lives and schedules to read over my thesis and provide me with valuable feedback, many times over.

To my family, for constantly giving me the space to do my solitary research and writing, how can I translate what your support means to me? I promise, it is all for a good cause!

To my friends and extended family who continue to support me in all my endeavors, thank you, thank you, thank you. My tribe has become smaller over the years, but much more "True." I sincerely appreciate you all.

To the One Yoga & Wellness community, thank you for helping me discover my dharma: assisting people in healing their body, mind, and spirit. I've always said, I learned way more from you than you did from me.

To the many great authors and teachers who have shared their wisdom and inspiration through their books, a heartfelt bow of gratitude is extended—for you have inspired me to share this work and my own inspiration with others.

Someone once asked me what my Grandmother's belief system was. It was to her Highest Self. There was no entity outside of herself to whom she put her faith. This woman was a guiding light to me growing up, and I learned very early on that I, too, needed to acknowledge and appreciate that same Divine spark within me.

I would be forever lost in a meaningless world without my faith that there is a Divine architecture running through all that is, all that has ever been, and all that will be, and that I am also a part of that current of energy.

I am especially grateful to my parents, who had the wherewithal to understand that it was essential for me to figure out for myself what I believed in without forcing their own faith systems on me. The echo of these words inspired me to constantly stretch myself in determining what Spirit was to me. Frankly, I don't personally like the word God. It feels like an outdated and underwhelming idea of an old white man on a billowy cloud as the source of all. What I have come to realize is that there is not solely one name that expresses all that is the Universal Consciousness that I believe in. But I will acknowledge this energy, this essence, in the many ways that it has come to be known, by the many cultures all over the world, to whom I've found a passionate appreciation.

So, thank you. Thank you, Yahweh, Elohim (Judaism), Allah (Islam), Holy Spirit (Christianity), Brahman, Devi (Hinduism), Ahura Mazda, Angra Mainyu (Zoroastrianism), Amaterasu (Shinto), Amun-Ra, Osiris (Kemetic), Zeus, Athena (Ancient Greek), Odin, Freyja (Norse), Tengri, Ülgen (Turkic-Mongolian), Wakan Tanka (Lakota, Native American), Great Spirit (Native American), Quetzalcoatl (Aztec), Itzamná (Maya), Waheguru (Sikhism), Enki, Inanna (Sumerian), Dagda, Morrígan (Celtic), Damballah (Haitian Vodou), Anansi (Akan-Ghana), Diwata (Tagalog-Philippine), Kāne (Hawaiian), Amma (Dogon-Mali), Chukwu (Igbo-Nigeria), Pangu (Chinese Mythology), Viracocha (Inca), Mungu (Swahili-East African), Ngai (Kikuyu-Kenya), Makemake (Rapa Nui), Pachamama (Quechua-Andean).

Thank you for your All-Presence.

Thank you for allowing me to find my spiritual path to you through all the many ways you appear around the world. Thank you for never giving up on us humans, even after it seems that many have long given up on each other.

TABLE OF CONTENTS

Introduction..1
Treasure Map Cipher 4
Key 1: The Mystic Path 6
Key 2: Numerology..13
Key 3: Gregorian Calendar..22
Key 4: Solar Calendar 26
Key 5: Sankalpa 30
Key 6: Moon Phases...34
Key 7: Zodiac Wheel 39
Key 8: Elements 46
Key 9: Altars and Sacred Space..59
Key 10: The Multi-Faith/ Interfaith Approach.............................63
Key 11: Archangels & Ancestors...69
Key 12: Chakras & Yoga 73
January..85
February 109
March 130
April..151
May...174
June..196
July...218
August..242
September 264
October..288
November..309
December...330
Moving Forward 355
Bibliography...372
Other Books By Tracey..377
"The Vault" Yoga 378
About the Author...379

INTRODUCTION

Welcome to *The Modern Mystic's Wheel of the Year — a Multi-Faith Path to Living in Harmony*. Yes, that's certainly a mouthful, but wait until you see all the information inside, gathered from decades of personal and professional work in mysticism, holistic healing, study of religious and spiritual practices, and sacred travel around the globe, unraveling the connective tissue between cultures and religions.

As one journeys through life, eventually he/she pause to reflect on the meaning of it all. The age-old questions of "Why am I here?" "What did I come here to accomplish?" And "Is there a Higher Power?" Become gleaming headlights that we're unable to escape. Therefore, we are fated with only one option: to stare into the light and find the truth we seek.

For some, this journey begins earlier in life than for others. But age is of no matter or consequence, as eventually we all find ourselves seeking wisdom. It should come as no surprise to hear that the road to enlightenment comes with many bumps, roadblocks, dead ends, and potholes in which to maneuver around, along with many sprints on the Audubon and even some "Sunday Morning Drives." That's life. And as many have said in one way or another, it's not the destination that matters, but the journey.

This book serves as an enormous guide map to those on a continuous mystical spiritual path. As with any map, there is a map key. This book contains 12 keys:

1. The Mystic Path
2. Numerology
3. The Gregorian Calendar
4. The Solar Calendar
5. Sankalpa
6. Moon Phases
7. Zodiac Wheel
8. Elementals

9. Altars and Sacred Spaces
10. The Multi-Faith Approach
11. Angels & Ancestors
12. Subtle Energy and Yoga

Once we unlock the keys to the map, we begin to traverse the landscape through a wheel-of-the-year, following the energies of the twelve months of our modern calendar system, and linking them to religious or spiritual paths. Each path will allow the Modern Mystic to enjoy an extended staycation for the month, offering insights into the connections of the monthly theme, ceremonies and rituals, and yoga and meditation practices to embody the energy completely. The separate Workbook will assist in personalizing the ongoing practices and chronicling your journey.

The beauty of the wheel is that it is an unending circle. Each month, we follow the moon's journey around the Earth. Each year, we follow the Earth's journey around the sun. And month after month, year after year, we can return and refine the energy for as long as we want or need to. And for those who believe that they've mastered this particular path, the final chapter, titled "Moving Forward," gives you a glimpse of where new destinations lie when there are no more maps for where we are going, because there are no longer the traditional roads upon which to journey.

If you're ready to dive in, just be open. There is no one way. There are many paths, and they all lead to the same place. For those who feel lost, don't despair. We've all been there. You may not resonate with every month's theme or spiritual path. It's okay. You need to be authentic to yourself.

For those wondering if this book is for you or why you should follow this roadmap, let me be clear: you were called to this book for a reason. While there are no guarantees in life, you can rest assured that as part of the One Consciousness pervading all that is, was, and ever will be, you already have all the answers to those and any other questions that you seek. All too often, we have been taught to seek answers outside of ourselves, and unfortunately, that's like riding in a cart that went off the rails. True answers are found once we turn inward—something that all mystics, modern or ancient, understand. This book, this "Treasure Map," and its keys assist you on that inward journey to knowing.

So while this Treasure Map bears an "X" to mark the spot, the treasure we seek lies not in distant lands but in the sacred depths of our heart's eternal knowing. Whether you wander lost or stand found, the cosmic wheels turn for us all, weaving destinies through the tapestry of time. Embrace the journey with mindful courage, and the ride will unveil the truth of all truths—there's a radiant unity that pulses within you, binding your soul to the infinite dance of the Divine. Allow the Modern Mystic path to guide you, and all will be revealed.

In love, service, and wisdom,
Rev. Dr. Tracey L. Ulshafer

TREASURE MAP CIPHER

What would a Treasure Map be without a cipher to unlock its sacred treasures? Within the hallowed pages of *The Modern Mystic's Wheel of the Year - a Multi-Faith Path to Living in Harmony*, especially in Part 2's monthly odyssey, ancient wisdom unfurls through exclusive yoga practices and mystical videos woven into each chapter's heart. For those who hold this sacred guide, a hidden realm awaits—a private sanctuary on my website, brimming with yoga and other class videos, Oracle Card readings, and esoteric revelations. To cross the threshold, you must unravel the cipher, a cryptic key etched in cosmic glyphs, pulsing with the promise of divine secrets. Seek the cycle that turns through twelve sacred moons, harmonized by the multi-faith path, and let its number and essence guide you to the code that unlocks this veiled domain.

1. Go to: https://www.oneyogacenter.net/enter-cipher-from-book

2. Wield the following cipher to unlock this sacred page:

<u>Solve this Riddle:</u>
Name the mystic wheel that spins through the year's twelve moons, echoed in its twin gates of cosmic harmony.

<u>Hint</u>: There are 15 characters in the cipher's code

Fear not, seeker of sacred truths. Should the cipher's cosmic glyphs elude your grasp, venture to the end of Part 1, where the secret code awaits to unlock your treasures.

Part 1

KEY 1: THE MYSTIC PATH

Webster's dictionary describes the word mystical as: "having a spiritual meaning of reality that is neither apparent to the senses nor obvious to the intelligence…having the nature of an individual's direct subjective communion with God or ultimate reality."[1] Webster's therefore describes the mystic as a "follower of a mystical way of life." There are obvious links to one having magical or supernatural inclinations, and a direct link to Universal energy. But is this a full description of all things mystical?

In Andrew Vidich's book *Love is a Secret*, he explains: "Unlike Western psychologies, which are more or less understandable to the average person, mystic psychology describes levels of transcendent experience that are virtually impossible to compare with commonly understood modes of behavior. It is often difficult to clearly define and articulate in ordinary language the experience of the mystic."[2]

With this description, it is apparent that the mystics and their paths are experiential wisdom, rather than being born of academia and its focus on mental faculties, as we have been taught to seek knowledge in the West. In truth, mystics often recount methods to cease the mind in their various paths. Therefore, many of these methods of experience and practice will be presented in this book.

In the past, mystics stood out as individuals from the norm, offering philosophies and theologies that are still studied worldwide today. Some well-known ancient mystics are the Buddha (480 BCE), who founded the spiritual path of Buddhism, followed by over 500 million people worldwide today, Lao Tzu (6th century BCE) Taoism founder of which approximately 20-30 million people (a mid-range number often used but some research suggests as much as potentially 170 million) follow, and Confucianism founder Confucius, born in 551 BCE, whose work shaped East Asian culture for over two millennia. Today, 6-10 million people follow Confucianism, while 100–350 million practice Confucian-influenced traditions worldwide. That's nearly one billion people practicing mystic paths founded by these three avatars alone.[3]

---

[1] Merriam Webster's Collegiate Dictionary, 10th Edition, Merriam-Webster, 1993

[2] Love is a Secret, Andrew Vidich, PhD, Energy Psychology Press, 2015

[3] Various sources, including: https://www.thearda.com/world-religion and https://www.pewresearch.org/

The 13th-century Persian poet Rumi's mysticism, rooted in Sufism, emphasizes the heart's role in connecting to universal truth. His poems have influenced millions globally, from spiritual seekers to Modern Mystics. Rumi's work is a cornerstone of Sufi mysticism, which seeks direct, experiential union with the Divine (Allah in Islam) through love, devotion, and inner transformation. His poetry and teachings align with mystical traditions across cultures, making him a true bridge between numerous traditions on this mystic path.

The Catholic Saint Padre Pio, known for his deep piety, miraculous gifts, and intense suffering, embodied the Christian mystical path characterized by a direct, transformative encounter with God through prayer, suffering, and supernatural experiences. He was born in Italy more recently (May of 1887), but this is not surprising, as Christianity/Catholicism is one of the more recent world religions.

Another candidate for Christian mysticism that dates back to the beginning of this faith tradition is Mary Magdalene, a figure often misunderstood by mainstream theologians who do not typically provide her with the formal mystic title. However, Mary Magdalene has strong mystical credentials, particularly in her visionary encounter with the risen Christ, with her reported transformative exorcism, and her elevated role in Gnostic texts as a bearer of esoteric wisdom. In The Gospel of Mary (2nd century), she is a favored disciple with esoteric knowledge, receiving visions and teachings from Jesus that others did not understand. She describes the soul's ascent through spiritual realms, a hallmark of mystical theology. Most Modern Mystics place her role next to Christ, aligned with him in ministry and healing practices.

The famous Judaic mystic, Rabbi Isaac Luria (1534–1572), also known as Ha'Ari ("The Lion") or the Arizal, is a pivotal figure in Kabbalah, the mystical tradition of Judaism. His teachings, particularly the Lurianic Kabbalah, revolutionized Jewish mysticism with profound insights into the nature of God, creation, and the soul's role in cosmic redemption.[4]

A famous Hindu mystic, Sri Ramakrishna Paramahamsa (1836–1886), a 19th-century Indian saint, priest, and spiritual teacher, is a pivotal figure in modern Hinduism. His teachings, popularized by his disciple Swami Vivekananda,

---

[4] https://www.jewishvirtuallibrary.org/isaac-luria

emphasize the unity of all religions and the direct experience of the Divine, resonating deeply with the Modern Mystic. His teachings are preserved in works like *The Gospel of Sri Ramakrishna* by Mahendranath Gupta, and his key works are *The Life Divine*, Savitri (epic poem), and *Synthesis of Yoga*.

The prominent Celtic or Druid mystic, Myrddin Wyllt (540–584 CE), also known as Merlin Sylvestris or Merlin the Wild, is a legendary figure in Welsh tradition who embodies the mystical essence of Druidry and Celtic spirituality. Myrddin is celebrated as a bard, prophet, and nature mystic, whose life and visions in the wild forests of Tweeddale (Scottish Borders) reflect the Druidic connection to nature, prophecy, and the Otherworld. This semi-historic figure appears in Welsh texts such as the *Black Book of Carmarthen* and Geoffrey of Monmouth's *Vita Merlini* (1150), which blends Celtic lore with Arthurian legend, portraying him as a Merlin-esque figure distinct from the later Arthurian wizard.[5]

Born in present-day Wyoming, North America, Black Elk was a Lakota healer and spiritual leader during a time of immense upheaval, as U.S. policies disrupted Native life. At age 9, he experienced a profound vision of the "Great Spirit" (Wakan Tanka) and the interconnectedness of all beings, which shaped his role as a Shaman. He participated in the Battle of Little Bighorn (1876) and survived the Wounded Knee Massacre (1890). Later, he converted to Catholicism, blending Lakota and Christian spirituality, and shared his visions to preserve the Lakota traditions. Although practiced by a small number of people (100,000-200,000), his teachings shaped Western Shamanism and are studied in Universities and spiritual communities globally. His legacy is written down in *Black Elk Speaks*.

The Völva of the Völuspá, a mythological Norse seeress from the *Poetic Edda* (1000 CE), is a renowned Norse mystic embodying the visionary and Shamanic traditions of *seiðr*. Through ecstatic trances, she prophesies the cosmos's creation, destruction (Ragnarök), and renewal, revealing divine truths to Odin. Her wisdom, connection to nature, and feminine spiritual power continue to influence Norse mythology, with her legacy preserved in the *Völuspá*, resonating in a global pagan revival. The actual number of Norse and pagan practitioners is challenging to pinpoint due to the decentralized, non-dogmatic nature of these practices,

---

[5] https://en.wikipedia.org/wiki/Myrddin_Wyllt

varying definitions, and limited formal membership records. However, the implications of the potential impact should not be underestimated.

A notable Kemetic mystic is Imhotep (27th century BCE), an ancient Egyptian high priest and sage revered as a mystic in Kemetic spirituality, the ancient Egyptian religion. Serving as high priest of Ptah under Pharaoh Djoser, Imhotep designed the famous Step Pyramid at Saqqara, blending practical genius with spiritual insight. His mystical status stems from his reputed communion with gods like Ptah and Thoth, channeling divine wisdom, *heka,* or magic, for healing and architecture. Later deified as a god of medicine and wisdom, his cult endured for centuries, with devotees and spiritual seekers connecting to his legacy through temples and pyramids throughout Egypt.

Mesoamerican mystic from the Toltec, Ce Acatl Topiltzin Quetzalcoatl (947–1047 CE) was a semi-historical priest-king of the Toltec capital, Tollan in Tula, Hidalgo, Mexico. He was revered as a mystic and cultural hero whose legacy profoundly influenced Aztec and Mayan cultures, particularly through the worship of Quetzalcoatl, the Feathered Serpent deity. Like Imhotep, Topiltzin practiced magic and rituals to commune with Quetzalcoatl, achieving visionary states akin to shamanic trances. His teachings emphasized spiritual enlightenment, cosmic harmony, and balance. Aztec codices such as the *Codex Chimalpopoca* and oral traditions depict him as a mystic who accessed divine knowledge, similar to the Völva's prophecies or Imhotep's wisdom.[6]

We can easily name mystics for every religion or spiritual tradition on Earth, past or present, seeing the connections with each. What, then, is a "Modern Mystic?"

In Linda Silk's book, *Survival Manual for the Modern Mystic*, she defines these people as having qualities such as "everyday, common people in different stages of their spiritual quests" who "strive to become a stellar example of the unconditional love and compassion exemplified by the Dalai Lama," and being "genuine humanitarians."[7]

---

[6] https://www.mexicolore.co.uk/aztecs/ask-us/ce-acatl-topiltzin-quetzalcoatl

[7] Survival Manual for the Modern Mystic, Linda Silk, Balboa Press, 2012

Linda continues to define the Modern Mystic as those who are inclined to be drawn to sacred sites on the planet, participate in a variety of healing modalities, have personal mystical experiences, and have an inner calling to find their true selves. Based on this criterion, if you feel aligned, know that you are in good company.

We all have personal journeys, including mystical experiences—we may not always realize that what is happening in our lives is just that. Maybe you have a regular yoga practice that's produced various "A-Ha" moments when on the mat. You may have been introduced to Reiki and greatly benefited from the healing modality, so that you became a Reiki Master who feels God's grace present while working with clients. You might have traveled on vacation and visited an ancient temple, only to have a direct experience with the Goddess while there. Or perhaps during a dangerous moment, you were suddenly spirited away by an angel. If you stop to look around, you will notice that mystical experiences are constantly happening in your life.

Perhaps you're asking questions, like, "Is it important to travel a mystical path?" Or, "If I read this book, will I become a Modern Mystic?" And even, "Will seeing life through the eyes of a mystic make me a better person?" These are interesting questions that one might have. First, this book does not claim to make anyone anything that one is not already. If you're called to follow the mystic path, you will know, and that may be why you chose this book. Having said that, if you long to have a deeper understanding of the Divine in your daily life and are looking for guidance, then this book can be an assistance in your quest. And for those already on the path, this book can also open the doors more as you explore mysticism through the lens of different faith traditions that you may not be familiar with.

In response to the question posed earlier, the material presented in these pages offers strong potential for fostering personal growth and improvement. With a focus on expanding individual consciousness to Divine Consciousness and Oneness, we unleash a vast potential that exceeds everyday expectations, advancing one into a space where everyday miracles are commonplace and the extraordinary becomes the ordinary. Of course, the mystical path is not for everyone. Some are meant to be warriors or advocates, workers or caregivers, and other archetypal souls on the earth. There is a place for all of it—for all of us. No role is greater or less than another, as long as we are fulfilling our destiny in this life and performing our tasks with deep integrity. And, of course, love and mutual respect.

We are living in exciting times. Many agree that we are transitioning into an era of expanded light and love on our planet. And yet, we are still in the gap preceding these times. Hindus believe that we are transitioning out of the *Kali Yuga*, an era of war and strife on the planet, and into an era of peace. This doesn't mean that we will not see more challenges as the end times of *Kali Yuga* wane; instead, perhaps, the opposite, as this old, dying paradigm still encompasses many on the planet.

The Ancient Mayans predicted this time shift to begin in 2012, with the famous end of their solar calendar. Most spiritual traditions prophesied this time, this "Age of Aquarius," that is upon us. Unsurprisingly, more Modern Mystics are awakening by the thousands. Why? We are most needed for global healing, the continuation of humanity, and the creation of a true heaven on earth.

The time to stop thinking and living in outdated patterns is now.

The time to claim our abilities as shepherds of Mother Earth is now.

The time to usher in our superpowers is now.

What is a Modern Mystic? You, the reader, are a Modern Mystic. And it is time for you to awaken fully!

KEY 2: NUMEROLOGY

Each month, the energetic meaning of the number corresponding to the month of the year and the chakra associated with the month will be brought to light. Numerology is the belief in a mystical or divine relationship between numbers and events, people, or objects, often used to interpret character, predict the future, or gain spiritual insight. It has roots in ancient Greece, with Pythagoras, who discussed the energy behind numbers. But it was not until 1907 that Dr. Julian Stenton first coined the actual term.[8]

There is historical evidence to support that many cultures believed numbers had an energetic or spiritual significance. Ancient Babylonians viewed numbers as keys to the Divine Order in astrology. The ancient Egyptians attributed magical properties to numbers, using them in rituals, pyramid architecture, and religious texts. In Jewish mysticism, *Kabbalah*, numbers reflect the presence of God's creative energy, linking words and events. Hindu *Vedic* texts view them as cosmic vibrations aligning human life with the universe. And for the Chinese, the I Ching uses numerical patterns (hexagrams) for divination, reflecting cosmic forces, and Chinese numerology assigns auspicious or inauspicious energies to numbers, influencing cultural practices like naming and architecture.[9]

A basic guide to the meaning of numbers based on Numerology is:

1. Leadership, new starts
2. Partnership, balance
3. Creativity, expression
4. Structure, stability
5. Adventure, change
6. Love, nurturing
7. Spirituality, reflection
8. Success, abundance
9. Completion, wisdom
10. Renewal (1+0=1)
11. "Master Number" (retains its original number), intuition
12. Harmony (1+2=3)

---

[8] Times of India, "Origins and History of Numerology," July 3, 2024

[9] Encyclopedia of Religion (2005): Babylonian, Greek, Hebrew, Chinese numerology, and Times of India, "Origins and History of Numerology"

The 12 Astrological Houses

Another aspect of numerical energy refers to the 12 Astrological "Houses" representing different areas of life, each influenced by the planets in a natal chart. They describe how and where energies manifest.

First House: Self and Identity relates to personal appearance, personality, self-expression, and how others perceive you

Second House: Money and Values relates to personal finances, possessions, self-worth, and material security

Third House: Communication and Learning relates to siblings, short trips, communication, and early education

Fourth House: Home and Family relates to roots, home life, parents (especially mother), and emotional foundations

Fifth House: Creativity and Pleasure relates to romance, children, creativity, hobbies, and self-expression

Sixth House: Work and Health relates to daily routines, jobs, health, and service to others

Seventh House: Partnerships relate to marriage, business partnerships, and one-on-one relationships

Eighth House: Transformation and shared Resources relates to intimacy, shared finances, inheritance, death, and rebirth

Ninth House: Philosophy and Travel relates to Higher education, long-distance travel, spirituality, and beliefs

Tenth House: Career and Public Life relates to career, reputation, public image, and ambitions

Eleventh House: Friendships and Goals relates to friends, social groups, aspirations, and collective causes

Twelfth House: Subconscious and Spirituality relates to dreams, intuition, hidden matters, and spiritual retreat[10]

Chinese Numerology

Chinese Numerology Numerical Meanings:

1. Yī: Unity and Beginnings symbolize independence, leadership, & new starts
2. Èr: Harmony and Balance representing partnerships, cooperation, & duality
3. Sān: Growth and Creativity signify life, vitality, & expansion
4. Sì: Death and Misfortune represent stagnation or loss
5. Wǔ: Change and Versatility symbolize transformation, freedom, & the five elements (wood, fire, earth, metal, water)
6. Liù: Smoothness and Success represent ease, flow, and good fortune
7. Qī: Spirituality & Mystery are associated with introspection, spirituality, and the unknown
8. Bā: Wealth and Prosperity, considered the most auspicious number, symbolizing abundance & success
9. Jiǔ: Eternity and Completion represent longevity, permanence, & fulfillment[11]

Vedic

Vedic Cosmic Meanings for Numbers:[12]

1. Leadership & Initiation
1. Harmony & Sensitivity
2. Creativity & Expression
3. Stability & Discipline
4. Freedom & Versatility

---

[10] *Astrology: A Guide* (2021) and *The Complete Astrologer* by Parker (2007)

[11] *Journal of Chinese Studies* (2023), *Times of India* (2024)

[12] *The Journal of Vedic Studies* (2023)

5. Love & Responsibility
6. Spirituality and Introspection
7. Power & Ambition
8. Compassion & Completion

Kabbalistic

In Jewish mysticism, *Kabbalists* believe that numbers correspond to a *Sefirah* (divine attribute) on the Tree of Life, a central Kabbalistic diagram, and are used to uncover mystical connections in texts by assigning numerical values to Hebrew letters. According to the *Journal of Jewish Studies* (2023), the following is a list of those numerical definitions:

1. Unity and Divinity, linked to *Keter* (Crown), the highest Sefirah, symbolizing pure consciousness
2. Duality and Wisdom, linked to *Chokhmah* (Wisdom), the Sefirah of creative insight, representing the first differentiation from unity
3. Harmony and Understanding, linked to *Binah* (Understanding), the Sefirah of intellectual structure and maternal nurturing
4. Structure and Mercy, linked to *Chesed* (Mercy), the Sefirah of expansive love and generosity.
5. Strength and Severity, linked to *Gevurah* (Severity), the Sefirah of restraint and strength
6. Beauty and Balance, linked to *Tiferet* (Beauty), the Sefirah balancing mercy and severity, representing compassion
7. Victory and Spirituality, linked to *Netzach* (Victory), the Sefirah of endurance and eternity
8. Transcendence and Splendor, linked to *Hod* (Splendor), the Sefirah of humility and intellectual beauty
9. Foundation and Truth, linked to *Yesod* (Foundation), the Sefirah channeling divine energy to the physical world

Ancient Egypt & Babylonia

As for the Ancient Egyptians and Babylonians, we have a less systematic numerology. Most of the information is inferred from text through translations. However, using a variety of sources, such as Britannica (2025), *Journal of Egyptian Archaeology* (2023), *Encyclopedia of Ancient History* (2018), *Journal of Near Eastern Studies* (2023), *Encyclopedia of World Religions* (2015), *Times of India*

(2024), and Wikipedia, we can infer the following meanings of numbers for the Ancient Egyptians & Babylonians:

Egyptians:

1. Unity & Creation, linked to *Atum* or *Ra*, the creator gods who emerged from chaos (Nun)
2. Duality & Balance, linked to *Shu* and *Tefnut* (air and moisture), the first divine pair
3. Completeness & Divinity, linked to triads like *Osiris, Isis*, and *Horus* (father, mother, son)
4. Stability & Order, linked to the four sons of Horus, protectors of the canopic jars
5. Life & Multiplicity, linked to Horus as a living god with five aspects
6. Harmony & Perfection, linked to the six sides of a cube or the body's proportions
7. Spirituality & Mystery, linked to seven celestial bodies (known planets) or seven Hathors (fate deities)
8. Infinity & Renewal, linked to the *Ogdoad* (eight primordial deities of chaos)
9. Completion & Plenitude, linked to the *Ennead* (nine major deities)

Babylonians:

1. Unity & Primacy, linked to *Anu*, the sky god, representing supreme authority
2. Duality & Partnership, linked to *Enlil* and *Ninlil*, divine counterparts governing air & fertility
3. Divinity & Completeness, linked to the triad of *Anu*, Enlil, and *Ea*, major gods of sky, air, & water
4. Order & Cosmos, linked to the four winds/quarters of the cosmos
5. Power & Protection, linked to *Marduk*, the chief god associated with Babylon's might
6. Harmony & Creation, linked to the six days of cosmic creation in myths like *Enuma Elish*
7. Spirituality & Divinity, linked to the seven planets (Sun, Moon, Mercury, Venus, Mars, Jupiter, Saturn) & seven heavens
8. Abundance & Renewal, linked to the eight-pointed star of *Ishtar*, goddess of love & war

9. Completion & Wisdom, linked to *Nabu*, god of wisdom & writing

Tarot Numerology

It would be a blatant oversight not to include the Tarot numerical meanings in this section. As any Modern Mystic can attest, working with the Tarot cards is or was a significant aspect of personal growth and spiritual understanding. Certainly, most people have heard of Tarot cards by now, and yet, the depth of their true meaning continues to be misinterpreted by many a new-age practitioner.

This could be an entire course unto itself. The short version of the history is that the first Tarot decks emerged in northern Italy between 1420 and 1440, initially labeled "carte da trionfi" (cards with triumphs). These cards were not created for divination but as a trick-taking card game called *Tarocchi*, similar to Bridge.[13] These decks expanded the standard 52-card playing deck (four suits: cups, swords, batons, coins) by adding a fifth suit of 21 illustrated trump cards and an unnumbered card, The Fool, totaling 78 cards.[14]

In Tarot numerology, numbers 1–9 carry spiritual and archetypal meanings, influencing the interpretation of both the Major Arcana (22 cards/trumps) and the Minor Arcana (56 cards/four suits: Wands, Cups, Swords, Pentacles). Each number reflects a stage in a cyclical journey of personal and cosmic growth. These meanings were formalized in the Rider-Waite-Smith deck (1909), designed by Arthur Waite and Pamela Colman Smith, which standardized divinatory symbolism.[15] It has often been said that the Rider-Waite standard Tarot should be one's first deck in learning the meaning of each card and how to interpret them. There's also an old superstition that says one should be gifted his/her first Tarot deck.

<u>Tarot Numerology Meanings</u>:

1. Initiation & Potential, representing conscious creation and willpower. <u>Meaning</u>: New beginnings, individuality, raw energy; linked to the

---

[13] Britannica (2025)

[14] National Geographic (2025)

[15] *Fabled Collective* (2025)

Magician & Aces. <u>Example</u>: The Ace of Wands signifies a spark of inspiration; the Magician channels divine energy
2. Duality and Choice, representing intuition & polarity. <u>Meaning</u>: Balance, partnerships, decisions; linked to the High Priestess & Twos. <u>Example</u>: Two of Cups signifies love & relationship; the High Priestess, intuition
3. Creativity and Synthesis, representing abundance & creation. <u>Meaning</u>: Expression, growth, collaboration; linked to the Empress & Threes. <u>Example</u>: The Three of Pentacles signifies teamwork; the Empress embodies fertility
4. Stability and Structure represent security and control. <u>Meaning</u>: Order, foundation, discipline; linked to the Emperor & Fours. <u>Example</u>: The Four of Wands signifies celebration within structure; the Emperor rules with authority
5. Change and Conflict, representing growth through struggle. <u>Meaning</u>: Disruption, challenge, adaptability; linked to the Hierophant & Fives. <u>Example</u>: The Five of Swords signifies conflict; the Hierophant questions tradition
6. Harmony & Healing, representing unity and compassion. <u>Meaning</u>: Balance, love, resolution; linked to the Lovers & Sixes. <u>Example</u>: The Six of Cups signifies nostalgia; the Lovers symbolize union
7. Spirituality and Reflection, representing inner victory. <u>Meaning</u>: Introspection, wisdom, spiritual quest; linked to the Chariot & Sevens. <u>Example</u>: The Seven of Wands signifies standing firm; the Chariot denotes control over destiny
8. Power and Renewal, representing resilience & karma. <u>Meaning</u>: Strength, cycles, transformation; linked to Strength (Rider-Waite) or Justice (older decks) & Eights. <u>Example</u>: The Eight of Pentacles signifies mastery; Strength embodies inner courage
9. Completion & Wisdom, representing spiritual attainment. <u>Meaning</u>: Fulfillment, introspection, humanitarianism; linked to the Hermit & Nines. <u>Example</u>: The Nine of Cups signifies wish fulfillment; the Hermit seeks inner truth

* * *

As you can see, many systems of numerology exist worldwide. With some, there are direct historical references. With others, there is more inference. Whichever way you look at it, the basic premise is that ancient civilizations and modern humans alike regard the meaning of numbers as significant. Modern Mystics are attuned to these frequencies, already, with some taking it further into the "Master Numbers," "Angel Numbers," and more. These play a key role in correlating to the energy behind each month. Numerology, along with the chakra number, will be interpreted to give a broad energetic theme for each month.

KEY 3: GREGORIAN CALENDAR

In today's fast-paced world, how would we ever keep track of our commitments or even scheduled "self-care" time without a calendar? Can you imagine a time when you unplugged from our 24-hour day system to not care about what time it was, where you had to be, or what you had to do? It almost seems unfathomable. And yet, what may it have been like to simply live by the sun? To wake with the light and sleep once it waned must have been such a free feeling. How did we ever allow ourselves to get so wrapped up in how we spend our time that we needed to keep track with a calendar of days and months? And yet, here we are. Relentlessly guided by a linear and systematic structure.

The most widely used calendar in the world is named after Pope Gregory XIII, who introduced this new solar dating system in 1582. Before the Gregorian calendar, the world used the Julian calendar, which consisted of 354 ¼ days. But because of a slight inaccuracy, the calendar dates and seasons began to move out of alignment over the centuries. By refining the calendar, the Gregorian solar calendar is accurate to one day for every 20,000 years. So, generally, most of the world accepts this to be pretty good.

It should be noted that the Egyptians are often credited with having the first 365-day solar calendar, tied to the flooding of the Nile and Sirius's rising. Their solar calendar included 12 months with 5 extra days. This structure provided a stable framework for agricultural planning and inspired later calendars, including the Julian and Gregorian systems. However, its lack of a leap year adjustment and misalignment with the true solar year (approximately 365.2422 days) rendered it less effective over time, making it an imperfect foundation compared to the refined Gregorian calendar.

Yet, although the Gregorian calendar is the most widely used one in the world, most of the world's spiritual traditions still use lunar calendars, indicating major holidays in conjunction with moon phases. The Gregorian calendar recognizes moon phases as well, but the synchronicities of particular dates can vary. The Gregorian calendar has months that last 30 or 31 days, respectively. Lunar calendars, spanning approximately 29.5 days, may cause certain holidays to align with specific lunar events in some years, but the actual date will consistently change each year.

If we are to work the Wheel of the Year, it becomes difficult to systematize a wheel that works accurately every year for both the lunar and solar calendars. For this reason, you'll need to find a lunar calendar that will give you the moon phases and the lunar holidays associated with it, if you are to honor the particular lunar holy days with extreme accuracy. There are many of these found free online, as well as apps that you can download to your smartphone or tablet, so do not worry about being confused as to which moon phase falls on which day, as it should be fairly easy to determine this.

This book will also provide information about the monthly moon phases and the spiritual focus. Some work will be required to figure out which specific date they fall on. So it will be quite important to understand the major phases of the moon and which exact days they fall on each month. You'll find more information in Key 6 on the Moon Phases.

For reasons of ease, *The Modern Mystic's Wheel of the Year* will be set up through the lens of a solar calendar, primarily the Gregorian, however, with an emphasis on the lunar energies each month. This feels like a great balance. The sun has often been representative of the male energies, while the moon of the feminine. Balancing the masculine and feminine energies is another way of establishing harmony in our inner and outer worlds—or, our inner spiritual world and the outer worldly realm.

The major holidays from countries and spiritual traditions that are linked to the lunar calendar schedule will be given the closest approximate estimate. This works wonderfully when so many come together to solidify particular energies each month. If you find that a holy day falls on a different month in the year that you're working through this Modern Mystic's Wheel, feel free to honor it differently. This book presents but one option, one road, on the mystic path. And as already mentioned, there is not just one right way.

One final note referring to time: Quantum Physics, the vehicle that drives any calendar, believes that what we refer to as a timeline or events that start to the left and sequentially move through events towards the right, in a straight, linear pattern, is not correct. What physicists have been working on are theories that explain and substantiate the opposite, that time is relative.

Einstein stated in his theory of relativity that time and space are not as constant as we once thought. And Steven Hawking built on this in his Theory of Everything, which then inspired more scientists to continue the work. We now understand that there are many possibilities in time and space, or time-space, and they are not science fiction.

Modern Mystics have a deep connection and understanding of time, space, and relativity. Many have encountered many "out of time" experiences in their awakening, having both lost time and felt time accelerate. Others speak of interesting inter-dimensional experiences such as being in two places at once, feeling connected to alternate or parallel universes, and seeing the breakdown of the time-space continuum. These are all very real and occur during a lucid waking period, often when alone, in a natural setting, completely at peace, and fully present.

If the Modern Mystic is to trust these mystical experiences of time-space relativity, how can they rely on something as linear and limited as a calendar?

Many Modern Mystics and scientists believe that collectively, in addition to moving into a time of increased light and love, humans are shifting into a 5D reality system. If this is true, why should we continue to work within the limited framework of a 3D system? Anything is possible.

The simple truth is that at the time of writing this book, this calendar system is still how much of the world functions. We make room for those who experience time and space differently than this linear system; however, we must align with the reality of the majority to function in today's society and help others, and this is the current structure.

For now, continue working with the seven-day, twelve-month cycle of the Gregorian calendar. And when you feel inspired to move intuitively, please do so.

KEY 4: SOLAR CALENDAR

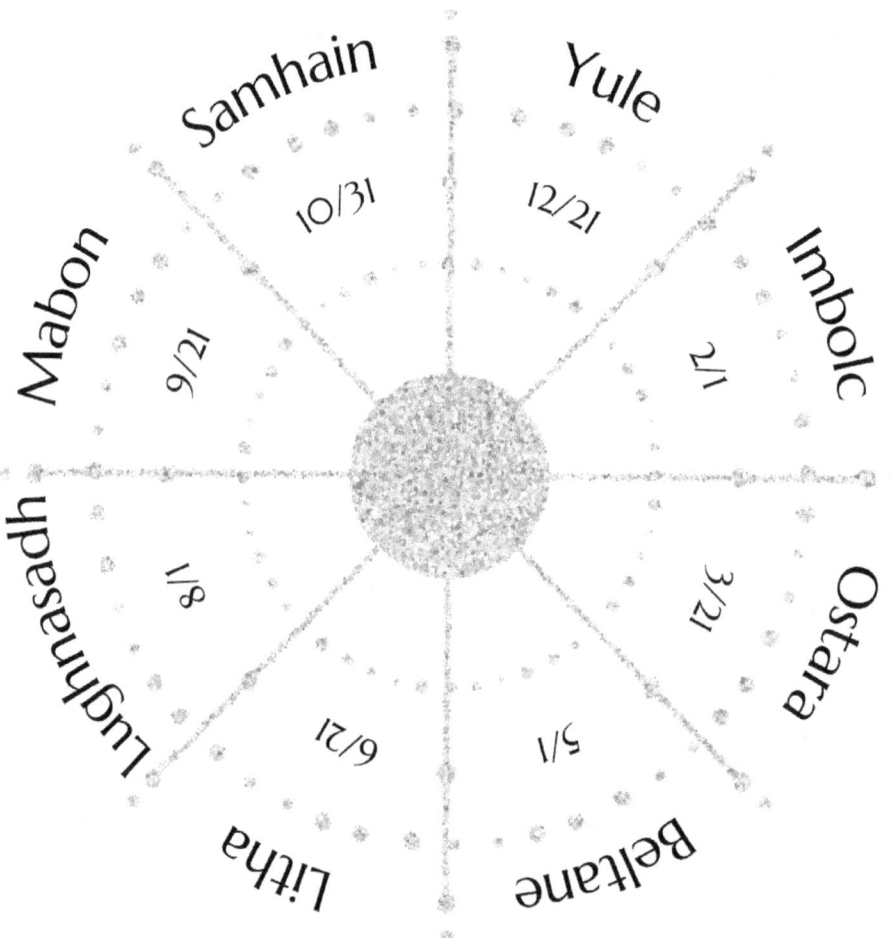

As mentioned, in what seems like a land before time, humans followed the sun. The patterns of the sun throughout the year that created the seasons were important for our ancestors in planting and harvesting crops for food and basic survival. There were no greenhouses or grow lights—there was just the sun. And when it wasn't available for periods, plans had to be made.

Structured around the annual solar events, such as the solstices and equinoxes, the solar calendar marks the changing seasons. Since the majority of people on the planet live in the Northern Hemisphere, this book focuses on those dates. We love our friends in the Southern Hemisphere, who celebrate solar holidays opposite to us, and hope that if you are reading this book, you can accommodate the differences in a way that works for you.

This calendar is often referred to as a Pagan "Wheel of the Year," something that most Modern Mystics are quite familiar with. The roots of the solar calendar can be traced back to ancient traditions, including the Celtic and Germanic peoples. Lacking a single origin, it was formalized as a modern system in the 20th century, largely by Wiccans.

The dates on the Pagan Solar Calendar are sometimes variable because they depend on exact astronomical moments; therefore, the dates range. Again, if the actual solar holiday falls on a different month than the one used in this book, please feel free to honor it accordingly. However, the couple of days' difference does not greatly affect the energy at that time of year much anyway.

This solar Wheel of the Year is reduced into eight Sabbats or spiritual holidays, thereby breaking down the year into even segments.

These Sabbats are:

Samhain
October 31 - November 1

Samhain marks the pagan New Year, a time to honor the dead, associated with the veneration of ancestors. It is also considered to be the end of the harvest. Common themes for Samhain are death, rebirth, and introspection, with traditions ranging from bonfires to feasting, wearing costumes, and creating lavish altars to the ancestors.

Yule - Winter Solstice
December 20 - 23

The Winter Solstice is the shortest day and longest night of the year. It is the promise of the returning light, a time of hope and renewal. Common themes for Yule are rebirth and light, with traditions including lighting candles, exchanging gifts, feasting, and decorating with plants like holly and mistletoe.

Imbolc
February 1 - 2

Imbolc marks the midway point of winter, signaling the first stirrings of spring. This time of year is associated with purification and fertility, with traditions such as spring cleaning and lighting fires in honor of the return of life after the long winter.

Ostara - Spring Equinox
March 20 - 23

Ostara celebrates a day of balance, where the time of night and day is equal. With the arrival of spring, themes include new beginnings, fertility, growth, and balance. For Spring Equinox traditions like coloring eggs, planting seeds, and celebrating nature are common. It is said that one can balance an egg on one end on the day of the Spring Equinox. Give it a try!

Beltane
April 30 - May 1

Often referred to as "May Day," Beltane pays homage to spring in full force with fire festivals and other traditions, like famous Maypole dances, bonfires, Handfasting celebrations, and flower crowns. This is a time of great fertility and love, celebrating life and union.

Litha - Summer Solstice
June 20 - 23

The longest day of the year is celebrated worldwide, from places such as the Druids' famous Stonehenge in the UK to the Mayan ruins of Tikal. This day marks the sun's greatest strength and energy, the fullness of life, and a time of great abundance and vitality. Traditions involving the sun, bonfires, and feasting are often celebrated for Litha.

Lughnasadh - Lammas
August 1 - 2

Lammas celebrates the first harvest, grains, and is a time of gratitude and community. Themes of harvest, abundance, and preparation include traditions like baking bread and making dolls out of corn.

Mabon - Autumn Equinox
September 20 - 23

This second Equinox is another day of balance, but where with Ostara we celebrate new beginnings, for Mabon we honor the descent into winter, and the coming of the death cycle. This is a time of reflection, gratitude, balance, and decline with feasts such as apple picking and giving thanks.

* * *

Our ancestors lived by the sun, and the solar calendar provides us with an invaluable link to the major cycles of the Earth. Humans who work with the solar calendar can utilize the sun's vital energy in the most desirable ways possible throughout the year, avoiding undue burdens and suffering when trying to force energy that goes against nature.

It is said that we live by the sun and love by the moon. Another upcoming section explores the lunar cycles.

KEY 5: SANKALPA

The word "sankalpa" is Sanskrit for an idea or concept formed in the heart. It is a solemn vow made to ourselves, with a specified intention. More than an intention, a sankalpa is a purposeful commitment made with conscious awareness, often to align one's actions, thoughts, and life with a higher truth or spiritual goal. Unlike a fleeting desire or goal, a sankalpa is rooted in the essence of one's being, reflecting the soul's deepest aspirations and connection to the divine or universal consciousness.

Some confuse a sankalpa with *dharma*, but they are two distinct things. Respecting dharma, it is an unwavering life purpose that your soul aspires to. It is the one that you were meant to follow from the beginning, even if you didn't realize it until much later on. Whereas your dharma doesn't change, sankalpas do because our needs evolve as our soul works to elevate our abilities.

Modern Mystics use sankalpas to plant seeds in the subconscious mind at the beginning of spiritual practices. The repetition of this phrase mentally guides the practitioner towards inner transformation.

For Hindus, sankalpas normally accompany rituals or *pujas* to state the purpose, time, place, and spiritual intent, grounding the act in a sacred context. But whether one is performing a ceremony, journaling, praying, or conducting elemental work, sankalpas help us to stay connected to our divine work.

<u>Sankalpas Examples</u>:

- <u>Spiritual</u>:
  "I am one with the Divine, radiating love & compassion"
  "I flow with the wisdom of water and the passion of fire."
- <u>Personal</u>:
  "I embody inner peace and strength in all I do."
  "I am balanced and open in my heart."
- <u>Community-Oriented</u>:
  "I inspire and uplift others through my authentic truth."

There's a way to know your sankalpa. In January, you'll be asked to create this solemn, heartfelt vow. The intention may be to work with this same sankalpa throughout the year. Some people may wish to change it slightly based on the energy of the month, or after reevaluating how things are moving. Others will find it necessary to state a new sankalpa each month. This is entirely up to you and what you feel is most needed. Know that the repetition of your vow will only increase its energy.

Guide to Creating the Appropriate Sankalpa:

- Mediate/reflect deeply, connecting with your true heart's knowingness
- Ask what you want to achieve or become
- Ask what achievement looks and feels like to you
- Express your sankalpa in a measurable way (saving money, stopping a bad habit, etc.) or in a quantifiable way (more passion, more patience, greater sense of self-worth, etc.)
- Be specific, clearly stating what you'll achieve
- Be realistic—you have to be able to achieve it
- Keep it simple so that it's memorable
- State the vow in the positive with conviction
- BELIEVE it!
- Repeat it daily or several times a day.

In Rod Stryker's book *The Four Desires*, he provides strategic outlines for creating successful sankalpas. Rod graciously gave his blessing to use his information in this book, without which, we would be missing some crucial keys in developing a successful sankalpa. A heartfelt bow of gratitude to Rod!

Stryker's Magic Formula:

$$I(s) + I(v) > I(k) = P$$

- S = *Shakti*, the life force behind your initial impulse. The stronger your desire, the more likely you'll achieve your goal
- V = *Vayu*, the force that your Shakti uses to express and fulfill its intention (including physical, mental, emotional, material, social, and spiritual)
- K = *Karma*, the factors (both internal and external) that inhibit you or that make it difficult to achieve your goal
- P = *Prapti*, your desire

Stryker says to combine the total energy of Shakti + Vayu, and if it's greater than your Karma, then you will achieve your goal.[16]

So what happens when your desires do not manifest? This happens when there is a deeper desire driving the energy. *Vikalpa,* the mental constructs or beliefs that separate us from our Highest Self and what we came here to fulfill, are always the culprits of these deeper commitments.

There are many exercises that you can utilize to assist you in correcting any of these constructs. Yoga and meditation are invaluable tools, and one reason that they are included in each month's exercises. When we yoke together body, mind, and spirit, we align with our highest truths and reclaim mastery over the mind stuff.

In January's Moon section, we will create the first sankalpa. Make a note to refer back to these pages and use Stryker's guide when creating this heartfelt and purposeful commitment to yourself for the month. If it's true, it may work for you all year long. However, because numerous influences can change the course of energy at a moment's notice, you will need to review the sankalpa monthly, then, when necessary, update it to something that aligns better.

Remember, it's all a process and a journey.

---

[16] *The Four Desires,* Rod Stryker, page 120

KEY 6: MOON PHASES

Our moon has always captivated us. Since the dawn of humanity, we have looked to the sky as a way of understanding who we are, where we come from, and what our life purpose is. The closest object to our Earth when we view the night sky is the moon. And as everyone is familiar, the moon spins and travels around the Earth, completing one full circle each day. But because the Earth is also rotating around the sun on a different trajectory, how and where we view it in the sky changes throughout the year. And then, there are those phases. Yes, just like in our own lives, the moon goes through changes too.

What does it all mean? And how can we utilize the moon's phases to optimize its energy in creating our monthly rituals and realizing our sankalpa? Let's explore.

Full Moon

If questioned about what they know about the full moon, most people would comment on the energy that it invokes. If you work at a hospital, you know that most babies are born on full moon nights, and that the queues in the emergency room tend to spike as well. If you work for law enforcement, you most likely dread working full moon evenings, because police blotters are also fuller. If you are even slightly observant, you have noted the heightened energy on these evenings and perhaps the eve or two just before or after the full moon.

The key to understanding the full moon is that it is when the lunar energy is at its peak. Lunar, coming from the Latin word "luna," meaning the moon. And do you know what other word comes from luna? Lunatic. That's right. The etymology of the word lunatic comes from the common belief that the moon not only influenced people's behavior but also inspired periods of madness. Hey, if the moon's gravitational pull can drive the tides of the ocean, and people are made up of 70% water, then there's strong evidence to support the moon affecting humanity in some way. And since the moon is the light that guides us through the night, when it is full, its energy is heightened. When considering spiritual work, the full moon is when most of its energy is available to us. So, what is the moon's energy, and what does it symbolize?

As previously stated, the moon is often equated with feminine energy. In yogic philosophy, the moon also links with the element of water, which represents the realm of emotions. In Ancient Mesopotamia (c. 3000 BCE), the moon, personified as the god *Sin* (or *Nanna*), was revered as a source of wisdom and divination. Priests used lunar phases to interpret dreams and omens, linking the moon's rhythmic changes to inner insight and prophetic vision, as recorded in cuneiform tablets like the *Enuma Anu Enlil*.[17]

The common symbolism of the feminine, watery emotions, and intuition can be broadened to cyclical renewal, mysteries and the unknown, guidance, duality, death, and the afterlife. It's easy to see that the energy of the moon is quite powerful. And to the point that the moon is the light that guides us through the darkness, know that during the full moon, we may *feel* things more, but we also have the highest ability to create and manifest during its cycle. Our focus on the passages each month will therefore be on which particular energies to focus on manifesting our sankalpa around the full moon time.

Waning Moon

The phase after the night of the full moon is the waning moon. This is when the moon begins to travel from full to dark. As you can probably already imagine, the waning cycle is a slow process of nearly two weeks of the moon's energy weakening. As we get further away from the full moon and closer to the dark moon, we're slowly losing this light and energy to create. And so, our focus for the waning moon turns to one of letting go and releasing.

To create balance and harmony in our lives, we must look deeply at every piece of our being. This includes the good and the bad, and the ugly places, too. Too much of anything is not a good thing. We need balance to create harmony. Too much manifesting brings in a lot of energy, and that can be overwhelming and depleting, to say the least. People who spend too much time manifesting and creating often don't realize how much overall energy they're bringing into their lives. Often, this creates chaos where one cannot find the time to just relax and be. In a relentless cycle of work and activity, every facet of life can easily fall out of balance.

---

[17] Francesca Rochberg, *The Heavenly Writing: Divination, Horoscopy, and Astronomy in Mesopotamian Culture*, 2004, Cambridge University Press

First, the body gets out of whack, and a few extra pounds start to manifest. Then some aches and pains show up. And then, before you know it, illness and physical issues arise. This often causes mental anguish, with an inability to work or enjoy life's pleasures. And it just continues to break down from there.

Don't wait until your life is out of control to realize the need to balance doing with being and embrace the cycle of releasing and letting go, just as you do the cycle of manifesting.

The waning moon is a perfect time for cleaning and clearing out possessions, habits, and old thought processes. Physical possessions can often be donated to organizations such as Vietnam Vets and local shelters, and come with a receipt that you can give to your accountant at tax time for a deduction. Once you start to clear the physical clutter, it then gets easier to begin to clear the internal clutter in the mind. The more you release and let go, the clearer every aspect of your life becomes. And, the bonus is that you make more space to manifest what you truly need.

In the waning moon phases of the month, we will review what energies we need to look at letting go of in our lives, and how that will support us moving forward.

Dark Moon

The moon cycles to dark for one night when there is no hint of it in the sky. As the waning cycles move towards the dark moon, most people experience low energy and a need for more rest. This is exactly what we should be doing at this time.

As the moon approaches the "Dark Night," as it is sometimes called, we should honor this energy, for this is a perfect time to go within and reflect. Meditation, journaling, long soaks in hot baths, and other such practices are perfect for the dark moon and the period leading up to dark moon night. This will be our focus each month during this stage, and scheduling your self-care and well-deserved downtime around the dark moon night is a perfect strategy. Pencil it in on your calendar now!

New Moon

The day after the dark moon is referred to as the "New" moon. Yes, every month we have a chance to start anew. This new cycle is our rebirth. What seeds we want to focus on planting depend on the energy of each month, and that will be our focus on the night of the new moon. New moon is an exciting time when we can begin to work on what we discovered to be truly important during the waning and dark moon periods.

If you've felt the need to revisit and establish a new or revised sankalpa, the new moon is the night or day to begin.

Waxing Moon

The final phase is the waxing moon. Here, the moon goes from new to full again, and you can feel the energy building with each day that it heads towards full. On the eve or day of the new moon, we will determine what energy to focus on building, and then cultivate it daily during the waxing moon cycle.

* * *

And here is the beauty of it all: every month we get a chance to do it all again. So if life got in the way and we did not manage to get it all done or manifest it all or let it all go, we can try again…

and again…and again.

How perfect is that?

KEY 7: ZODIAC WHEEL

"When the moon is in the seventh house, and Jupiter aligns with Mars, then peace will guide the planets, and love will steer the stars."

This well-known refrain from the song *Aquarius* hints at the symbolism found in the stars. While this song may have been written in 1969, the sentiments of meaning can be traced back to the second millennium BCE, where the earliest evidence of recorded celestial interpretations can be found in cuneiform tablets.

From Mesopotamia, astrology spread to Egypt and Greece. Historians may argue who is ultimately responsible for choosing the final twelve zodiac signs, but for this book's purposes, that is of no consequence. What becomes most relevant here is that this "Wheel of the Year" is an entire metaphor for the human experience and its cycle of life, death, and rebirth, told through the symbolism of the planets and the mythic stories of the stars.

Notably interesting to our Gregorian calendar's twelve months, the zodiac also follows a path of twelve signs and "houses," as we learned in the Numerology key. As with all things, there is a wealth of meaning within each, representative of the human journey.

The most well-known are the twelve astrological signs, which follow the sun's movements through the constellations of the same name:

Sign:	Gregorian Calendar Dates:
Aries	March 21 - April 19
Taurus	April 20 - May 20
Gemini	May 21 - June 20
Cancer	June 21 - July 22
Leo	July 23 - August 22
Virgo	August 23 - September 22
Libra	September 23 - October 22
Scorpio	October 23 - November 21
Sagittarius	November 22 - December 21
Capricorn	December 22 - January 19
Aquarius	January 20 - February 18
Pisces	February 19 - March 20

Most people have come to understand their "Sun Sign" as the astrological sign most prominently featured in the constellation that the sun passes through during the date of their birth. Within each astrological sign are various qualities that often relate to the mythos of the constellation, the guiding planet's energetic properties, and the house representation in which the sign falls.

We will discover more about the mythology in the monthly chapters later in the book. But for introductory purposes, it will be important to understand the basic energies behind the sign, its house, and guiding planet.

Aries
Planet = Mars
1st House = Ego & Personality

The first house is said to represent the ego and personality and corresponds to the fire sign of Aries, the Ram. The ruling planet, Mars, is the planet of energy, action, and desire, bringing with it a heavy dose of courage, assertiveness, and drive. At the magical moment of our birth, our identity and persona are forged. Fire, being the energetic catalyst of birth, it is with a thunderous crack that the fundamental aspects of the self emerge as we present ourselves to the world.

Taurus
Planet = Venus
2nd house = Life Values

The second house is in the earth sign of Taurus, the Bull, whose ruling planet, Venus, governs love, beauty, and pleasure. As Carolyn Myss says in *Sacred Contracts* of the second house, "It represents what you most value and hold dear." Life values represent the things you deem most essential and are where we derive pleasure and power in our lives.

Gemini
Planet = Mercury
3rd house = Self-Expression and Siblings

Gemini, the Twins, along with its ruling planet, Mercury, rule communication and intellect. This first air sign is all about self-expression and presenting the values you assigned from your second house to the greater community. And who do we first begin to communicate these significant aspects to, but our siblings and those closest to us.

Cancer
Planet = Moon
4th house = Home

The water sign Cancer, the Crab, is often associated with our emotional body, and the Moon is also linked to our emotions. At home, we feel safest to be ourselves, to allow those around us to see the real us, all of it. This can represent both our childhood home and our current home; however, it is most representative of our True Home, the place of our deepest love.

Leo
Planet = Sun
5th house = Creativity & Good Fortune

The second section in the zodiac wheel repeats the elementals with new mythos, taking them to a new level in our human development. Thus, we move into the second fire sign, Leo, the Lion, who strolls confidently in on that great ball of fire in the sky, our sun. This "King of the Beasts" certainly has no modesty. Where Aries led the initial fiery blaze of who we are, Leo roars for all to hear. Leo represents the strength needed to seek out opportunities and boldly place oneself in the direct path of fortune, and with the sun's energy, vitality, and drive, they are usually quite successful.

Virgo
Planet = Mercury
6th house = Occupation & Health

Virgo, the Maiden, is our second earth sign. She represents fertility, purity, and the harvest. For her, Mercury represents an emphasis on prevision, analysis, and service. Virgo differs from Taurus as she grounds you in the work that you do in the world, which needs to be in constant balance with your overall health and well-being.

Libra
Planet = Venus
7th house = Marriage & Relationships

The astrological sign of Libra, the "Scales of Justice," is the second air sign aligned with the house of marriage and relationships. It follows suit that the planet Venus falls under Libra's veil as the planet of love. Although marriage is a perfect example of finding balance in a relationship, this house represents all of our relationships: business partnerships, teacher/student, parent/child, etc. It is also important to remember that our relationship to self is just as important to our outer relationships, and yet, it is typically the one that we lose track of the most in life.

Scorpio
Planet = Pluto
8th house = Other People's Resources

Scorpio, our second water sign, the Scorpion, is our eighth house symbol. Although we like to believe that we are our own person, we are always influenced by other people, even when we don't realize it. This house reveals the hidden elements that affect our energy, like ancestral and bloodline patterns, but also financial and legal aspects. It's no wonder that the planet Pluto aligns with this sign, as it governs the subconscious and transformative power.

Sagittarius
Planet = Jupiter
9th house = Spirituality

We move into the third section of the zodiac with the final fire sign of Sagittarius, the Archer, and it reminds us to always aim higher. Jupiter, the planet of expansion, optimism, and wisdom, assists this sun in its mission. Sag is associated with independence and inspiration, which link nicely to the aspects of this house: spirituality, religion, and travel.

Capricorn
Planet = Saturn
10th house = Highest Potential

Capricorn, the Sea-Goat, is our third earth sign, and it is governed by the planet Saturn, which represents discipline, structure, and ambition. In the tenth house of highest potential, this mythical creature allows us to pursue and push ourselves further than we even thought we could go. This is the house where we reveal just how magnificent we truly are.

Aquarius
Planet = Uranus
11th house = Relationship to the World

The air sign of Aquarius, the Water-Bearer, is known for being a forward-thinker, visionary, and sharing enlightenment with the world. Uranus also symbolizes innovation, individuality, and rebellion. As the first air sign, Gemini, shares its values, but Aquarians are often those who contribute to positive change on the planet. We all have this potential, but we must remember that "With great power comes great responsibility" (Spider-Man, 2002).

Pisces
Planet = Neptune
12th house = The Unconscious

The final house corresponds to the third water sign of Pisces, the Fish. This house is about our unconscious mind, our innermost fears, and can be a portal to uncovering intuitive abilities, as well as shadow patterns, similar to the energy of the planet Neptune. This house is all about deciphering and understanding symbols and finding the meaning in it all, without getting stuck in the murkiness of the depths in which our compulsions hide.

* * *

Twelve astrological signs. Twelve houses. Why, then, only ten celestial bodies? Simply put, at the time that the system was developed in ancient times, only seven bodies (five visible planets of Mercury, Venus, Mars, Jupiter, and Saturn, the sun, and the moon) were known. Modern astrology later added Uranus, Pluto, and Neptune to the signs to further expand upon their meaning.

There is some attempt to associate the minor planet, Chiron, with Virgo, who currently shares the planet Mercury with Gemini. Chiron was just discovered in 1977, so modern astrology is still working with the energy of the planet and its association with the zodiac. If it were to eventually embrace this change, that would move the number of planets to eleven. And we just have to wonder if, in time, the twelfth will emerge. Or perhaps it has in the dwarf planet Eris, discovered in 2005, named after the Greek goddess of discord. Most astrologers feel that this is counterintuitive to the energy of Libra's justice. However, perhaps Eris is simply a reflection of Libra's drive and desire to restore balance and harmony.

In time, perhaps the twelve different planets will align with the astrological signs of the zodiac and the twelve houses. In Numerology, twelve (12) represents Cosmic Order, completeness, wholeness, and spiritual completion. We see 12 linked to the Apostles of Jesus, 12 Tribes of Israel, 12 Olympian Gods, and the Egyptian sun god Ra's journey through the underworld, divided into 12 hours of night. We've also already seen 12 linked to the number of calendar months, constellations in the zodiac, and can find it in the hours of the day on a clock. Yes, surely it is only a matter of time before the planets are also 12—even if we discover that they no longer exist in our solar system, or exist in another dimensional realm.

KEY 8: ELEMENTS

One way to work more naturally and harmoniously is to work with the elements. Most people are familiar with the four elements of earth, air, fire, and water. The Greek philosopher Empedocles, in 450 BCE, is often credited as the first to propose the idea that all matter consisted of one of these four elements, and that this was later defined by Plato and his five "Platonic solids" in his dialogue *Timaeus*, written 360-350 BCE. However, other cultures had their elemental theories predating the Greeks.[18]

Chinese philosophy, or *Wuxing*, is known for its five elements: wood, fire, earth, metal, and water. This theory was developed during the late Zhou Dynasty around 475-221 BCE. In the Wuxing theory, the elements are associated with the seasons, directions, colors, organs, and emotions, and so form the base of Traditional Chinese Medicine, Feng Shui, and astrology to explain balance and harmony. A strong emphasis on cyclical change and cycles exists in this Chinese theory.[19]

In Indian philosophy and Ayurveda, *Pancha Mahabhutas* (five elements) differ slightly from the Chinese theory. Indian elemental theory includes the following elements: earth, water, fire, air, and ether/space. The earliest reference to some elemental concepts also appears in the world's oldest text, the *Rig Veda*, written 1500-1200 BCE. While there is a context for creating balance in the Indian methodology, there is more of a spiritual context to the elements.

The Modern Mystic is concerned with all things elemental, from understanding the basic materials of the earth to creating balance and harmony through spiritual experience. For these reasons, you'll find a blend of information throughout our *Wheel of the Year* material. Let's understand the basics here:

Earth

The Earth element relates to the soil, the rocks and stones, plants and vegetation, as well as all life on the planet. Earth also relates to the planet as a whole unit of organic "Oneness," personified in the Greek Goddess, Gaia, the

---

[18] https://www.ebsco.com/research-starters/religion-and-philosophy/classical-elements

[19] *Wu Xing: The Five Elements in Chinese Classical Texts* by Elisabeth Rochat de la Vallée, translated by Sandra Hill, 2008, Monkey Press

ancestral mother of all life.

Earth has a quality of being heavy, dense, and stable. It has an embodied energy of being grounded and foundational. It is the literal rock that we stand and walk on every moment of the day, so it is no surprise that this element is listed in all of the elemental theories we discussed earlier. We will always work with the Earth as it is our home base.

In working with the earth element, we can integrate crystals, flowers, herbs, plants, and metals into our rituals and ceremonies. While Chinese philosophy differentiates between earth and metal into two different elements, our purposes will link metal to earth.

As we already learned, there are three earth signs in the zodiac: Taurus, Virgo, and Capricorn. Taurus is considered a fixed earth sign, so the qualities of earth are most preserved, and they hold firm to the energy. Virgo is mutable, so it adapts and is more flexible. The final, Capricorn, is cardinal and considered an initiator. Capricorns channel earth energy to their highest potential.

In the yogic system, a practice most Modern Mystics gravitate towards, the earth element is heavily utilized. Known by the Sanskrit name *Prithvi*, Earth is the element associated with the 1st chakra at the root or base of the spine. It is considered the starting point of our spiritual development and provides the foundation for all of the other chakras to develop upward towards infinite consciousness.

All postures in yoga are considered to have a seat, a place where you sit down and root. Therefore, all yoga postures have an earth-based grounding point, which is the part of the body that touches the earth. When practicing any yoga posture, it is essential not only to feel grounded but also to press actively into the earth, connecting physically and energetically.

Yoga's sister-method, *Ayurveda*, is the system of health and wellness used in India to create balance. This system has assigned roles to the elements.

Earth Ayurvedic Properties:

Action: Downward, Gravitation
Motor Faculty: Elimination
Wind: Downward (*apana*)
Sensory: Smell
Kosha (layer of human being): Food & Body (*Annamaya*)

In the body, the earth element is associated with the bones, teeth, legs, feet, buttocks, adrenal glands, bowel, large intestine, and overall health.

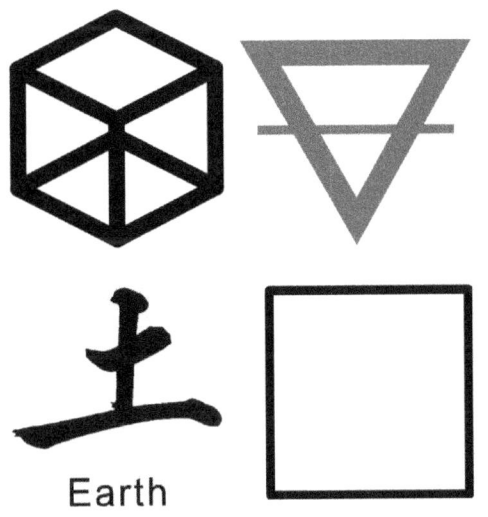

There are many symbols to depict Earth, depending on which system you use. The Platonic solids use a cube, or hexahedron, due to the flat surfaces, which evoke grounding and the unyielding nature of the earth. The alchemical symbol is a downward-pointing triangle with a horizontal line through it. The downward triangle signifies grounding and stability, with the crossbar emphasizing the earth's material qualities. Chinese philosophy (*Wuxing*) utilizes the *Kun* symbol (representing earth as receptive and nurturing) while Indian philosophy depicts earth as a square, the four sides representing the four cardinal directions: north, south, east, and west.

There are many more symbols of the earth, as many as traditions and systems on the planet. For now, know that Earth is the most fundamental of all elements and will be used throughout our manual, as without it, we have no base from which to start.

Water

Water is life. Without it, there would be no human beings. Our bodies are made of approximately 70% water. In utero, we lived in water. People can live for anywhere from 1-2 months without food, depending on a variety of factors, but that timeline diminishes to 3-7 days without water. As the earth gave us the stability in which to anchor, water gives us the ability to move.

Water has the qualities of being liquid, cool, soft, and oily. Working with the water element, we can integrate the use of essential oils, boiling food, drinking from wells & chalices, and performing numerous cleansing and purifying rituals.

Our water zodiacs are Cancer, Scorpio, and Pisces. Scorpio is our fixed sign, maintaining constant emotional intensity, while Pisces adapts and reflects it. Cancer, our cardinal sign, initiates the energy towards creating and fostering relationships, empathy, and emotional nurturing.

In the Yogic system, water is known as *Apas* and relates to the liquid aspects of matter in all of its wondrous forms. It is associated with the 2nd chakra, referred to as the sacral center, known for its association with the emotional realms, creativity, joy, and pleasure.

While working with the earth element in yoga, we find our seat in postures; working with the water element is where we create movement. The various *Namaskars*, especially Sun and Moon Salutations, are perfect examples of linking breath and movement to create fluid expressions of energetic postures. While there are numerous schools of thought about holding postures versus flowing with breath and movement, the *Vinyasa* style of yoga is most suited for working with this and the water element.

<u>Water Ayurvedic Properties</u>:

<u>Action</u>: Downward, Cleansing, and Percolation
<u>Motor Faculty</u>: Procreation
<u>Wind</u>: Outward Moving (*vyana*)
<u>Sensory</u>: Taste
<u>Kosha</u>: Food & Body (*Annamaya*)

In the body, the water element is associated with the blood, urine, lymph, transcellular fluids, spleen, bladder, urethra, reproductive system, hips, and lower back.

[WATER]

Water symbols include the Platonic solid icosahedron, the 20-sided polyhedron with equilateral triangular faces that creates almost a spherical shape to suggest fluidity and flow. The alchemical symbol is a downward triangle, evoking water's tendency to flow downward. The Wuxing represents water with its *Kan* symbolizing water's depths, danger, and adaptability. Indian philosophy's symbol is a crescent, symbolizing the moon and its influence over the tides.

Again, water symbols are everywhere—from seashells to dragons. It is our second, and equally important, element to work with in creating inner and outer harmony. Water's biggest mantra is "Go with the flow," teaching us to adapt and be in perpetual movement.

Fire

The fire element is the last agreed-upon of the five elements in most traditions, and it is another significant one. Fire is the transformative energy of rapid change. Within a human, the containment or release of the fire element is significant to one's well-being. Outside the human person, fire provides light, heat, and allows our food to be cooked for easier digestion. But there is always the ability of fire to get easily uncontrollable, so it must be tempered and managed with constant mindfulness.

Fire has the qualities of being hot, dry, sharp, light, and subtle. Working with the fire element includes embracing the sun and its energy, including receiving valuable vitamins daily from monitored amounts of time outside in the sun's rays. Many ancient cultures used bonfires for sacred rituals of celebration. Dancing, singing, and beating on drums around the bonfire have a long history of significance around the world. More modern uses of fire inside the home include cooking rituals and even warmth around the fireplaces. And, of course, candles represent light and spirit and are used by many spiritual and religious affiliations.

Fire zodiac signs are Aries, Leo, and Sagittarius. Leo is our fixed fire sign, being loyal, confident, and even charismatic. Aries is our cardinal sign, initiating action with courage, sometimes even impulsively. And then there's our Sag, the mutable sign of the free-spirited, philosophical, knowledge-seeking, exploring, and adventurous soul whose spirit can often be restless due to these qualities.

In the yoga system, fire or *Agni* has its origins in the famous *Rig Veda*. For Hindus, Agni is both the fire element and an essential and powerful god known by the same name. Fire is associated with the 3rd chakra, called the solar plexus, which is equated with ego, will, energy, power, and self-esteem.

Working with the fire element in yoga can be found easily in repeated postures or sequences that ignite heat, such as the famous *Surya Namaskar* or Sun Salutation series. We also cultivate this inner heat during yoga postures when we cultivate the famous locks or *bandhas*, especially the belly-lock known as *uddiyana bandha*, which engages the core fire and uplifts *pranic* energy. Yogis also enjoy fire in postures that twist or engage the core.

<u>Fire Ayurvedic Properties</u>:

<u>Action</u>: Brilliance & Luminosity
<u>Motor Faculty</u>: Walking
<u>Wind</u>: Core (*samana*)
<u>Sensory</u>: Sight/Vision
<u>Kosha</u>: Mental Body (*Manomaya*)

In the body, the fire element is in the gastrointestinal tract, specifically in the stomach, pancreas, and gallbladder. The core muscles in the musculoskeletal system also represent the fire element as they are essential for creating and sustaining most movements.

Symbols of fire are the Platonic tetrahedron, a four-sided geometric equilateral triangle, due to its sharp, pointed shape. The alchemical symbol is an upward

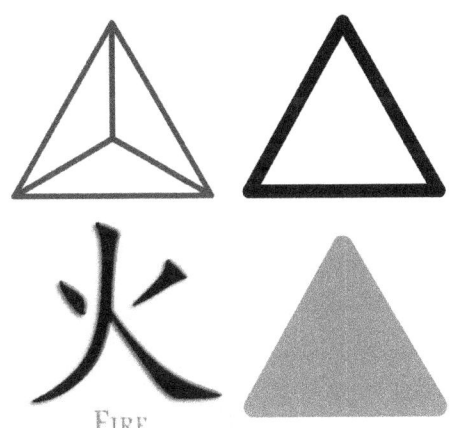

triangle representing heat, energy, and upward movement. The Wuxing Chinese symbol is *Huo,* which visually resembles a flame, with its shape suggesting upward movement and radiance. Indian philosophy's fire symbol is also an upward-pointed triangle, the same as the alchemical symbol. The upward triangle appears over and over as a symbol of flames and fire.

Fire's basic quality is transformation, literally changing matter from one state to another. Its position as "divine spark" and inner energy that creates and transmutes makes this element overwhelmingly significant in ceremonies and ritual. Some might say it is the underlying factor in magic and alchemical practices.

Air

When we are born, we take our first breath. There is an old yogic thought that we come into each life with a fixed number of breaths, and once we reach that number, our time on this earth concludes. For ancient yogis, this drives the philosophy of the various breathing practices whose goals are to increase vital energy in the body and to slow down the breath itself, which has various benefits. Although much material is present in the Hindu philosophy regarding the air element, it doesn't apply to Chinese philosophy. However, due to its significance in various areas, embracing air as our fourth element is important.

The qualities of air are mobile, dry, light, cold, rough, and subtle. When we work with the air element, we consider the wind and the direction in which it blows. For example, an Eastern wind represents new beginnings and impending change, while Western winds cleanse and purify. Southern winds initiate with passion and strength, while Northern winds finish and close out. In some cultures, feathers represent the air element and are used to direct the movement of smoke from fire or herbs, such as ceremonial white sage, used to cleanse and purify energy at the beginning of the ceremony.

Air zodiacs are Gemini, Libra, and Aquarius, all known for their intellect, social qualities, and communication skills. Aquarius is our fixed sign and is often a forward thinker, innovator, and humanitarian. Libra is our cardinal, balancing and seeking harmony and fairness. And then there's our Geminis, our adaptable mutables, excelling at gathering and sharing information.

In the yogic system, air is *Vayu*, which translates to wind. Air has the unique ability to be a formless movement that appears through other forms, such as the wind blowing through the trees, bending branches, and fluttering leaves about. Air is associated with the 4th chakra, the heart-center, and equated with love, balance, and devotion.

As previously mentioned, working yogically with the air element rests much in the breathwork or *pranayama*. According to yoga, there are five qualities of air or wind.

Properties of Air/Wind:

- *Prana*: Forward-moving, inhalation
- *Apana*: Downward-moving, exhalation
- *Samana*: Balancing, circulation
- *Udana*: Upward-moving in the throat, inspiration, & transcendence
- *Vyana*: Pervading, expansion, & integration

We also note the representation of the air element in yoga postures, where we focus on opening the chest area and feel the ribcage expanding and contracting. The case for the practice of Vinyasa yoga's linking breath and movement can also be made for applying it to the air element within the yoga practice. In this form, we inhale for a movement, and exhale to its counter-movement. Each movement should begin on the inhalation and end at the pause or breath retention at the end of that inhale. The counter movement begins on the exhalation and ends at the pause at the end of that exhalation. It is important to recognize when one is moving too fast, as often becomes the case with unlearned students and teachers who come from ego (3rd chakra) rather than love (4th chakra) when teaching.

Air Ayurvedic Properties:

Action: Movement in a particular direction

Motor Faculty: Grasping
Wind: All vayus, but particularly *vyana*
Sensory: Touch
Kosha: Wisdom Body (*Vijnanamaya*)

In the body, the lungs and respiratory system represent air. We also see the air element represented in the heart, thymus, arms, hands, and muscles of the chest.

Symbols of air are the Platonic octahedron, eight equilateral triangular faces resembling two pyramids joined at their square bases, symbolizing symmetry, balance, and mobility. The alchemical symbol is an upward triangle with a line through the top, meaning volatility, lightness, and mind. The Indian symbol is a circle, sometimes with a crescent or wavy line within to associate movement. The spiral is sometimes representative of the air element, too, showing the dynamic, formless nature of air. And while the Chinese philosophy system does not relate to the element of air, the wood element is sometimes replaced by this element. Wood's Wuxing symbol is the *Mu*, resembling a tree that symbolizes growth, wind, and expansion. Also, as mentioned before, to many indigenous cultures, feathers or birds represent the air element, symbolizing air's freedom and connection to the sky.

Air, the movable, invisible element that becomes visible when it connects with another. The basic principle behind the elements of air is that of connection—connection to one another and the connection to the Divine within, that part of us that is unchanging, infinite, Consciousness.

Ether

The final element is ether—that of space and spaciousness. Moving into the most subtle of realms, while the air element may be invisible until it connects with something that makes it visible, ether's qualities are based more on the absence of opposing qualities rather than the aspects of the element itself. It's been said that the origin of ether is primordial, like the vibration that emerges long before it takes the form of sound in the ear. Sound and ether are inseparable.

The qualities of ether are clear, light, subtle, soft, and immeasurable. These qualities of ether lead many paths to envision this element as Spirit itself. The ancient yogis believed that ether was the first element, the one that created all of the others. In its formless self, ether is everywhere, all at once, and in all things, all the time. It is omnipresent, just like Spirit. Spirit goes by many names and many faces throughout the history of the world. One of the things that this book will endeavor to do is explore many of the world's religions and spiritual paths to spotlight each one's unique energy. But the one commonality that they all have is the undeniable faith and belief in that which often cannot be seen or experienced by the other elements.

One way that many different religions and traditions work with the ether element is by chanting or singing songs and *mantras*, as these powerful words or phrases are presented to the world and carried throughout on the vibratory essences.

In typical Western astrology, there are no ether element zodiac signs. There are twelve signs, divided into three of each of the other four elements. A case could be made that an ethereal element exists in all of the signs as the medium of cosmic vibration.

In the yogic system, ether or *Akasha* is the space that all other elements fill. It has often been linked to the 5th chakra in the throat, connected to listening, finding one's voice, and resonance.

Working with the ether element in yoga is a profound experience, for it is the spacious stillness within a posture, the sacred pause in the body, and the breath. That notable absence of breath at the end of the inhalation and exhalation is an expression of ether. Holding postures to marinate and feel how the body relates to time and space is an expression of ether. Meditation is an expression of ether, as the yogi seeks to still the mind and connect to the object of his/her meditation in Oneness.

Working with the ether element in yoga can be difficult for many who aren't used to being in stillness. What the Modern Mystic realizes, however, is that this is where the real magic happens in the practice. It's only when we make space to be in the sacred pause that we learn the secrets to life.

Ether Ayurvedic Properties:

Action: Vibration, expansion, non-resistance, freedom, love, descent of intelligence into the heart of the matter
Motor Faculty: Speech
Wind: Upward and out (*udana*)
Sensory: Hearing
Kosha: Bliss Body (*Anandamaya*)

The areas of the body associated with the ether element are the ears for hearing, throat, and all areas of the throat (pharynx and larynx, epiglottis & trachea) for the vibratory connection to ether, and the thyroid, a butterfly-shaped gland located just below the Adam's apple that produces hormones that influence cellular communication in the body.

Symbols of ether are the Platonic dodecahedron, which has 12 sides symbolically tied to the 12 zodiac signs as a whole. It is the divine substance of the stars and the universe's underlying structure, linking it to cosmic consciousness. There is no universally accepted alchemical symbol for the ether element; however, ether is implied in alchemical texts as the "*Quinta Essentia*" or fifth essence, the Philosopher's Stone, or the unifying spirit.[20] In some texts, a circle represents this alchemical quintessence of pure essence beyond the four elements. Indian philosophy also uses a circle, *bindu* (dot), as the symbol for ether. Again, however, for Chinese philosophy, there is no ether element. Vital energy or *qi* is an expression of ether, which does have a complicated symbol to

---

[20] Pseudo-Lull, *Liber de secretis naturae sive de quinta essentia* (14th century)

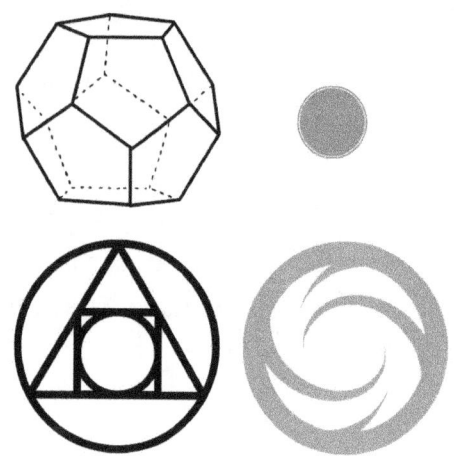

represent this life-force. For *Daoists*, the concept of *Wu* or "the void," mimics the ether element, and is also a circle representing the formless source of all existence.

We could take time to note the many other spiritual and religious symbols that can therefore be equated to the ether element, but that could take up an entire book unto itself. For our purposes here, consider the five-pointed star, the top point of which is often equated to the ether element and the other points to the other four elements, the infinity symbol, or a Buddhist *mandala*.

* * *

The elemental path is the lifeblood of both the Ancient and Modern Mystic, a sacred conduit to the Universal Consciousness, God, or Spirit. Through earth, air, fire, water, and ether, the mystic unveils profound truths, forging an unbreakable bond with the cosmos. Ancient wisdom revered these primal forces, and so must we in our modern age. By embracing the elements, we anchor ourselves to the deepest roots of our being, awakening a vibrant, unshakable connection to the divine essence that pulses through all existence.

KEY 9: ALTARS AND SACRED SPACE

To embark on a spiritual practice, you must first carve out a sacred space where divine energy can flourish. This is especially vital when sharing your home with others. Your sanctuary, whether for meditation, prayer, journaling, or ritual, should be a haven of intention and serenity. Take time to explore your home, apartment, or room, seeking a corner that resonates with your soul. Creativity may be needed to claim this space, but its purpose will anchor your spiritual journey with profound clarity.

Years ago, a friend with several small children was challenged by dealing with this dilemma. She had received as a gift a wooden box with soaps inside, and her crafty husband figured out a way to hang this beautiful box on the wall for her in the bedroom, using it to store her sacred objects and close the doors of the box for safekeeping. It was the perfect solution for a busy household and a reminder that you may have to be very creative in creating your special altar space.

Once the location is figured out, create your altar. What do we put on an altar? These items will be special and unique to you and hold a resonance with you. For this book, we will create a different altar for each month of the year as the energy shifts. Some items may stay consistent on your altar each month, while others will be changeable. This will be for you to determine so that you feel a profound connection to your altar. Even though some items will change monthly, the collective energy created in this same place will build, allowing you to do deeper work as we progress through the year's cycles.

Before we can add any items to the altar, we must be aware of the four cardinal directions of the horizontal plane. Luckily, today most smartphones come with a compass. For those without one, you'll need to go outside pre-dawn and watch for the first signs of the sun to the East. From there, you'll be able to figure out the other directions.

Understand the four directions and how they align with your altar. This is important as each direction is connected to a different element. We discussed this at length in the Elemental chapter, so we will briefly review here. Then, once you know which way each direction aligns to your altar, you can start to gather appropriate items for the altar and place them accordingly on it.

North = Earth

Dirt, Soil, Mud
Stones, Crystals
Pinecones, Nuts, Rice, Fruit
Plants, Leaves, Flowers, Herbs

East = Air

Feathers, Smudging Wands
Incense and holder
Written Mantra

South = Fire

Candle
Cauldron, Pot
Fire-pit, Fireplace, Bonfire

West = Water

Chalice
Seashells, Coral, Starfish
Sea salt, Sea Glass
Water Fountain

Center = Ether

Statue or Picture of Deity
Animal Spirit Totem
Angel, Ancestor

The altar cloth will change each month. This should be placed down on the altar with the other items on top, potentially arranged in the appropriate direction. Scarves work nicely as an altar cloth. Pieces of material, special altar cloths sold at various spiritual and new age stores, or even an article of clothing, can all work as your sacred cloth. Keep in mind that sometimes incense drops off the burner and can make a hole or candles drip, leaving a waxy mess. For these reasons, you want to use something you can wash and clean up instead of that fine silk scarf you purchased from last year's yoga retreat to Thailand (unless you're okay with that).

One item that can remain on your altar, month after month, is the accompanying Oracle Deck created to work with this book. The Modern Mystic's Wheel of the Year Oracle Deck comes with a "Keeper" card: the sankalpa, and 54 other cards, divided into six suits. You can pull a daily card, arrange the appropriate monthly chakra, month, and sabbath cards, or utilize another intuitive method. These cards will help maintain focus on your sankalpa, while also revealing the current energy available to support you and highlighting challenges you face, offering a path to navigate them.

The Oracle Deck can be purchased directly through the website http://www.OneYogaCenter.net

The monthly rituals, prayers, and ceremonies will be in a multi-faith format with a focus on the interconnectedness of all paths. Although each is unique and diverse, they are all a part of the One Consciousness of which we are all a part. Ultimately, if something is not true to you, you won't find the energy to continue working with it. However, you may be blissfully surprised at how easily you connect to the work offered to you here. So, give it a try. But in the end, do what feels best for you.

So, plan your special sacred space and set up an altar area where you can build upon this energy month after month. It will not take long before you feel connected to this space, gravitating towards it as your sanctuary.

KEY 10: THE MULTI-FAITH/INTERFAITH APPROACH

What was the original spiritual tradition of the Earth? We have recorded history dating back thousands of years to Sumerian Polytheism, probably close to 5000 BCE. Was that the first religion? What about the tribal religions that existed before the written word? Some estimates now consider the dating of some of these to be potentially much older than we ever anticipated. Who or what was God to the ancient ones? What aspect of the Divine did they worship? And in the end, is it any different than our modern belief systems?

Christianity may be the world's largest religion, with over 2 billion followers, according to World Atlas and NPR. But Christianity began somewhere around 33 AD, and modern humans have been on the planet for at least 200,000 years. So, although one belief system may be the most popular, it certainly is not the oldest. Does the age of a system even matter to its validity? Or are we splitting apples, grappling for one clear, true path, when there are many commonalities within them?

Scholars often debate the origins of spiritual traditions, as pinpointing their exact dates is a challenging task. Aboriginal Australian Spirituality, rooted in "The Dreaming," a timeless framework, dates to around 65,000–40,000 BCE, making it one of the earliest known practices, with approximately 1 million Indigenous Australians following it today.[21] Prehistoric Shamanism emerged around 40,000–15,000 BCE, evidenced by cave art and burials in France, and persists globally with an estimated 100,000–200,000 practitioners.[22] Indigenous traditions of North American tribes, Pacific Islanders, and African San peoples, who venerate spirits in nature and ancestors, originated between 10,000 and 3,000 BCE, with approximately 1 billion adherents worldwide today.[23]

Kemetic spirituality, the spiritual tradition of Egypt, dates back to 3100-300 BCE and is a modern revival of the ancient Egyptian religion, rooted in the spiritual practices of Kemet (ancient Egypt, 4500–30 BCE). The term "Kemet" (meaning "black land," referring to the fertile Nile soil) reflects its cultural origin. It emphasizes living in harmony with *Ma'at* (cosmic order, truth, balance, justice), venerating the *Neteru* (deities such as Ra, Isis, Osiris, Thoth), and practicing

---

[21] https://aiatsis.gov.au/

[22] Jean Clottes and David Lewis-Williams, *The Shamans of Prehistory*, 1996, Harry N. Abrams

[23] Pew Research Center's 2025 Report (also used for many other world religion numbers)

rituals to connect with the divine, ancestors (*Akhu*), and universal energy. It emerged in the 1970s as a neopagan movement, appealing to those seeking African heritage connections or ancient wisdom, with varied approaches from reconstructionist, which is historically accurate, to eclectic, a blending of modern practices.[24]

After Christianity, which literally shifts our calendar from BCE to CE (formerly BC for Before Christ and AD for Anno Domini, meaning "in the year of the Lord"), we find a blend of newer religions such as Sikhism (1469-1539), Mormonism (1830), Baha'i (1863), and in the 20th Century New Age and Neo Paganism practices like Wicca and Scientology.

One may think that the religion timeline stops there.

But one would be incorrect.

Several intriguing religions emerged in the late 20th and early 21st centuries, likely influenced by L. Ron Hubbard, the science fiction writer who founded Scientology. Raëlism, founded in 1973 in France by Claude Vorilhon (Raël), teaches that humans were created by extraterrestrials called the Elohim and promotes cloning and sensual meditation to achieve immortality. There are 100,000 globally adherent as of 2020.

Falun Gong, founded in 1992 in China by Li Hongzhi, combines qigong exercises, meditation, and Buddhist-Taoist principles to achieve spiritual purification and health and has approximately 10–70 million adherents.[25]

Eckankar, founded in 1965 in the USA by Paul Twitchell, blends Hindu, Sikh, and Western esoteric traditions to emphasize soul travel and spiritual exercises to connect with the divine "ECK" (Holy Spirit). Eckankar has 50,000–100,000 adherents.

Jediism, founded in the 2000s and inspired by the *Star Wars* franchise, Jediism emerged from fans formalizing Jedi philosophy (e.g., balance, inner peace) as a

---

[24] Tamara L. Siuda, *The Ancient Egyptian Prayerbook*, 2007, 2nd Edition, Eschaton Publishing

[25] https://en.wikipedia.org/wiki/Falun_Gong

spiritual path. Gained traction via online communities and the 2001 UK census (390,000 listed "Jedi").

Matrixism, founded in 2004 in the USA, was inspired by *The Matrix* films and was founded by an anonymous group promoting the idea that reality is a simulation, with practices drawn from philosophy and meditation.

Last but not least, we have the Church of the Flying Spaghetti Monster (Pastafarianism), founded in 2005 in the USA by Bobby Henderson. It uses a humorous deity (Flying Spaghetti Monster) to critique organized religion while promoting secular values. It appears that we can always count on the USA for new and cutting-edge science as well as spirituality.

In all seriousness, today, there are thousands of world religions. The most popularly practiced ones are close to 4000 years old, namely Hinduism and Judaism. However, we have more modern traditions that date back less than one hundred years, like Scientology, Wicca, and Rastafarianism. But does the timeline matter when it comes to the significance of religion? What does matter? Should we attempt to define which tradition is more significant than another? How can we determine if Mormonism is less of a religion than, say, Sikhism? Or, here's a better question: why should we even try?

Humans have been looking to a higher power since the dawn of time. Certainly, all of recorded history shows this, so we can assume that what predates recorded history would as well. Divine energy is a constant influence in our lives and goes by many names. Some call it God, Divine Father, Divine Mother, Creator, Creatrix, Supreme Being, Allah, Father Sun, Mother Earth, Yahweh, Elohim, Brahma, Source, Great Spirit, Zeus, Isis, Universe, Jehovah, and many other names constituting this spiritual energy. Different traditions call this transcendent consciousness by different names, but they all agree that some energy is more significant than ourselves.

Whether you were initiated into a particular religion or faith tradition, or found your eclectic blend, this book will explore a Multi-faith or Interfaith approach to modern mysticism, honoring the mystical paths that arose within each faith tradition, unless the faith tradition itself is a mystical tradition. Each path will have equal emphasis with its respective holy days, holidays, and rituals connected to a particular month's energy.

A word on appropriation, which has gotten a lot of press in recent years...

It can be challenging to honor a tradition without changing it and expressing the ritual using the core faith values without being disrespectful. When this is done, those who practice the faith in its original intent feel a gut-wrenching disrespect. On a personal note, I've always felt, and it has been conveyed to me by elders in certain traditions, that when one is open to discovery and practices are done with integrity and respect, we are open to receiving the grace from within any tradition. In this book, any misdirection from those purposes is purely unintentional.

This Multi-faith approach intends to experience different traditions and make room for what their teachings have to offer without expecting anyone to neglect or negate their spiritual path. It is always important to honor personal truth, but how do we know what that is if we do not give ourselves the space to explore all of the options?

The New Seminary for Interfaith Studies (TNS) is a true Interfaith Seminary, and the oldest Interfaith Seminary in the world. In 1969, Yogi Guru Swami Satchidananda and Rabbi Joseph Gelberman met, marking the beginning of the Interfaith movement. Founded in 1981, TNS's mission was "to address the abiding religious intolerance and lack of understanding or unwillingness to understand the faith and cultural traditions of others at that time."[26] This is, unfortunately, something as relevant today as it was then.

TNS strives to allow students to bridge the gap of intolerance in the world by forging an understanding of all cultural and spiritual traditions. There is a strong emphasis on ministering to all equally and on educating the masses of the interwoven similarities in the world's religions and cultural traditions, rather than focusing on the differences. By doing so, we can create a harmonious relationship with each other and with the planet. The tag line at the top of the school's website says, "Celebrating The Gift of Diversity."

---
[26] https://new-seminary.org/aboutus-2/

The Wheel of the Year is traditionally known as a pagan phrase that celebrates the observance of celestial events such as solstices and equinoxes, as well as seasonal festivals. The term "pagan" refers to spiritual practices outside the world's major religions. In other words, paganism is what our ancients practiced, with a focus on nature and the natural movement of energy on the planet. To truly honor the Interfaith Tradition, this book bridges the gap between paganism and the main religions to honor all faiths. For if we are to honor all paths, shouldn't we include, well, *all* faiths? Of course, we cannot include every faith tradition in the world in one Wheel of the Year, so twelve of the most widely used have been chosen.

As the Dalai Lama said, "The purpose of religion is to control yourself, not to criticize others."

So, be open. Be inclusive. Working in the realm of Oneness, considering commonalities within our world religions, faith traditions, esoteric teachings, and all things mystical.

KEY 11: ARCHANGELS & ANCESTORS

We are never alone. In our quest to discover the meaning of life, and through the many harrowing challenges we traverse along the road to Oneness, there are beings right beside us all along the way. Those sensitive to energy, like many Modern Mystics, see or feel these beings. Their presence is sometimes available daily, while at other times it manifests in specific situations. Lay people, with no history of instruction, may never know that these special guides and guardians are always around them, simply awaiting us to call on them to be of service.

Most people are familiar with the term "Guardian Angel," and will usually equate such beings to the dearly departed, watching over them and assisting in averting imminent dangers. These beings are part of the abundant special ones here to help us, existing on another plane, not visible to the norm's naked eye.

So, who are these special beings? And how can we work with them to assist us in the Wheel of the Year?

Archangels transcend faith traditions and cultural systems, availing themselves to anyone who seeks their assistance.

"Archangels are extremely powerful celestial beings. Each has a specialty and represents an aspect of God," says Doreen Virtue. She goes on to say that "archangels are one of God's original creations, and they existed long before humankind of organized religions. They belong to God, not to any specific theology. Therefore, archangels work with people of all different beliefs and paths."[27]

When working with archangels, it's important to remember that, while they are always around us, they cannot interfere in our lives due to our free will. For this reason, we must invite them in when we need them. And be assured, once you do, they'll respond steadfastly.

The Book of Enoch (specifically 1 Enoch, also known as the Ethiopic Enoch), a Jewish apocryphal text dated to around 300–100 BCE, lists numerous angels and provides some categorization or identification of their types based on their roles, ranks, or associations. From Christian Theology, an anonymous author (Pseudo-

---

[27] Archangels 101, xi-xii

Dionysius) wrote the *Areopagite's De Coelesti Hierarchia* (5th Century CE), which systematizes the angelic orders into nine ranks, grouped into three triads: (1) Seraphim, Cherubim, Thrones; (2) Dominions, Virtues, Powers; (3) Principalities, Archangels, Angels (including Guardian Angels). This interesting system of hierarchy, known as "choirs," is broken down as:

- Seraphim: The highest order of angels, closest to God
- Cherubim: Like Cupid, they're usually chubby and full of love
- Thrones: The bridge between the spiritual and material, representing God's justice
- Dominions: The overseers and the managers
- Virtues: Governing the physical universe, watching over the planets, stars, sun, and moon
- Powers: These comprise those who purify the universe from lower energies
- Principalities: These angels watch over the planet to ensure peace on Earth
- Archangels: The overseers of humankind and the guardians, each with a specialty
- Guardian Angels: Those assigned to you throughout your life, always watching over you

For our purposes in this book, we will work with several Archangels, as they are our overseers, and work nicely with specific monthly practices and faith traditions. You will learn more about Archangels Michael, Raphael, Gabriel, and Metatron throughout the year.

In addition to the Archangels, we will also work with numerous ancestors, the wisdom keepers of various traditions that hold knowledge to help us on our individual paths and also in the healing of the planet. The ancestors we will work with in our book are: Shaman, Shaolin Master, High Priest/High Priestess, Medicine Man/Woman, Hermit/Monk/Nun, Sage, Druid, Elder, and Seer.

There are many ways that you can work with the Archangels and Ancestors throughout the year. None is better than the next, so determine each month how you would like to work with these special beings that will provide the most assistance to you. Here are some ways you can consider:

- Invoke at the beginning of monthly rituals
- Daily prayer
- To assist with your sankalpa
- Call in during Moon Phases to assist as needed
- Meditation during yoga practices

Those using the Modern Mystic's Wheel of the Year Oracle Deck have access to invocations/prayers for these sacred beings in the guidebook.

Whichever way you choose to work with your Archangels and Ancestors, remember that daily invocation and practice will create a positive experience. You will be amazed at how accessible these beings are once you create the space for them in your life.

KEY 12: CHAKRAS & YOGA

Everything that exists is energy. From the sun to the plants, from animals to the interplay of energy between living things—it's all a vibratory experience. Scientists and mystics alike agree that our Universe and all that comes with it developed from a vibration. Some call this what physicist Steven Hawking termed the "Big Bang." Others from various mystic traditions refer to this energy as *prana, chi,* or *qi*. No matter the name or the reference, it is all the same. And the only constant thing is that energy is always changing and shifting.

Various Eastern practices have studied and worked with the subtle energy systems for thousands of years. Today, we have technology that can show this energy with special cameras. Science is catching up with what ancient cultures understood for a very long time. In the last one hundred years, the world of Quantum physics has exploded. Physicists and theorists have explored deeply what classical physics and mathematics could not explain. We now find ourselves living at a time when quantum breakthroughs are occurring daily. All of the limiting beliefs that we have had are exploding apart as new realizations are being confirmed by science as to the true nature of all things. It is truly an exciting time to be alive and to witness the yoking together of science and spirit.

And yet, our current systems still do not know how to handle this information. This is why our medical system treats issues on a purely physical level. The physical is the most dense form that energy can manifest. The subtle realms of energy go much deeper and affect the reality of our physical manifestations all the time. Think of a time when you walked into a room and could "cut the tension with a knife." That is the subtle energy. You don't have to be a healer or a shaman to feel that energy because it is so dense that it is nearly physical!

In 1992, a Japanese doctor, Masaru Emoto, performed a now-famous study on the effects of consciousness on water. He put water samples into separate containers and showed how, by speaking and even thinking different words and thoughts to each one, it changed the molecular structure of the water in the container. The ones that were encouraged with loving words rendered beautiful formations, while the ones that were given fearful and disharmonious ones left physically "unpleasant" structures.

Dr. Emoto's study was groundbreaking at the time. This finally proved that energy could affect matter. First, remember that the human body is nearly 70%

water. Now, imagine the effects on the human system after years of experiencing consistent traumatic events versus living in harmonious and encouraging ones.

As mentioned, we have recorded information that for thousands of years, systems were in place to work with this energy. One of the earliest methodologies is yoga. Yoga means "to yoke." It is a system of bringing together body, mind, and spirit through physical and energetic practices. It is, perhaps, the first self-development system to have ever existed. Within the yogic system, there are *koshas*, or layers to the human experience, ranging from the most gross/dense to the most subtle. They are:

- *Annamaya kosha* – physical body
- *Pranamaya kosha* – vital body
- *Manomaya kosha* – mental body
- *Vijnanamaya kosha* –wisdom body
- *Anandamaya kosha* – bliss body/highest shelf

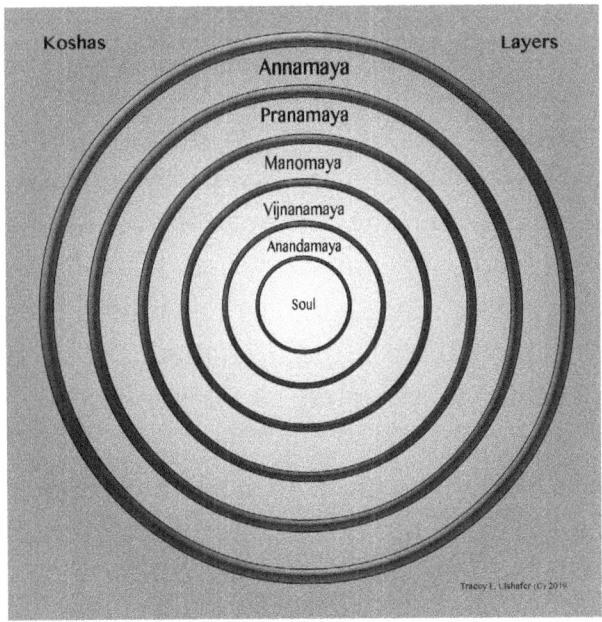

For most people, their awareness ends with the annamaya kosha, and even at that, many people are disconnected from their physical body. It is just what we people do. When challenges arise, today's human beings have been taught to mentally think about them and skip the physical and energetic connections. We have been taught that our mind has all of the answers and that we need to organize things upstairs to understand the world. And it can be quite scary for many to actually "feel" energy on a physical level.

The practice of yoga helps us in a very organized manner and has been extensively written about. What is offered here is a mere glimpse into this ancient practice. For those wishing to understand it more deeply, please seek out a reputable teacher in your area. If you wish to practice at home, check out: www.OneYogaCenter.net/yoga-classes and subscribe to The Vault for unlimited access to 250+ yoga classes for all level practitioners.

For now, let's explore some basics.

Yoga

Ancient mystics had a different perspective from modern doctors. They said one should start with the most recognizable (annamaya kosha) and work towards the subtlest forms (anandamaya kosha). This is one reason why the practice of yoga can be vastly transformational.

We come to the yoga mat and we tune into our body. For many people, this is the first time that this has occurred in their entire lives. The A-HA moments that a new yoga practitioner has within the first year of practice can be astounding. As such, we should all strive to be beginner yoga students. Once we can understand the body and its energy system, we can begin to unlock the true wisdom in the manomaya and vijnanamaya koshas. And from there, it's some work to get to that final bliss sheath. So, where do we start?

This book will show you some typical yoga postures, breathing techniques, and meditation practices to work on these outermost layers of your being, the annamaya kosha.

Yoga is a tradition that originated from the Hindu religion. We know that people practiced yoga for close to 6000 years because of ancient seals that were found in the Indus Valley in caves, indicating people in yogic postures. We have no idea how much older yoga may be, but the first written text that brought this otherwise orally passed down tradition together is named *The Yoga Sutras of Patanjali*.

Patanjali did not write the content of the book, but rather compiled the information in written form for the first time back around 400 CE. In the *sutras*, we learn basic information about the nature of yoga. This system seeks to bring together body, mind, and soul, so that the individual can understand his or her true nature. Through the body, we explore postures that stretch and strengthen the outermost shell of our being. These are the *asanas* with which we are most familiar.

Each month, poses that may assist you in connecting to the energy and theme will be explored. The sections for the yoga practice will offer you three options: a single-posture practice, a classical Hatha Yoga structured class that can last approximately 75 minutes, and a brief 15-minute practice. For the "single posture" practice, sit in the pose for 5 minutes a day, or longer, if you can. Write about what arises when you find that seat in the pose. If you're uncomfortable, use props or adjust to modify the pose. Whatever you do, don't resist being still, finding that seat, and breathing deeply. This is life-changing stuff!

The full-length practices can be conjoined with the videos. Remember that a link to all of the pre-recorded practices was given at the beginning of the book.

* Important note: It is always wise to consult your doctor before beginning any form of physical practice, especially if you have special needs to consider. The yoga practices suggested here can be done by any beginner to intermediate practitioner, as long as you are comfortable performing them or have no contraindications that would supersede the practices. Since yoga was meant to be taught in-person and tailored for each student to ensure that he/she is working at an appropriate level, it is highly suggested to seek a local teacher to assist you with learning proper alignment and modifications for your unique needs.

There are many styles and branches of the yoga tree. This guidebook will utilize the popular Hatha Yoga branch of yoga, aligned roughly with the Iyengar approach, where proper alignment is a focus, and everyone is performing postures appropriately to his or her level. Yoga should never be performed fast-paced or by pushing yourself. Yoga should always be comfortable, albeit sometimes challenging.

There has been a long debate about the yogic system being part of the Hindu religion. Some scholars believe that since yoga is derived from ancient Sanskrit texts on Hinduism that it must therefore be of the Hindu canon. Other scholars argue that this system can be practiced by anyone of any faith or cultural tradition, and that bringing one's belief system to this practice makes yoga something belonging to no particular faith, but rather a system of realization available to anyone, regardless of his or her respective beliefs.

As spirituality is something that must feel right to you, you can decide to embrace the mystical yogic wisdom as another way in which to connect to the energy of each month, or you can find another physical practice that matches the spiritual essence of yoga. Tai Chi, Qi Gong, and other Martial Arts may be of interest. If that feels more appropriate for you, then find reputable teachers and incorporate the energy of the month through other physical practices. This could prove to be more difficult than it seems, as other systems will not align as perfectly as yoga does in this book.

As always, in these pages, you're urged to embrace an interfaith system and honor Hinduism and the value of the yoga practice. In today's age, science has even embraced yoga. Studies by Harvard Medical School and other valued systems can be sought out to show the benefits of yoga practices for many different physical, mental, and emotional issues.

The Chakras

Each month, information about the chakra system is explored. Here we move into the subtle energy layer or pranamaya kosha, utilizing the famous yoga breathing practices, which are the "magic" behind the movement. Without proper yogic breathing, we are merely exercising. Not that there is anything wrong with exercising, but proper yoga breathing enhances your prana, or life energy, oxygenating every cell of your body and bringing in a feeling of vitality, along with peace and contentment. Even after the first practice, you can feel many benefits of proper yoga breathing.

In addition to the physical benefits of yogic breathing, there is the esoteric understanding that the life breath is our connection to embodiment by our spirit. We come into the world with an inhalation, and we will leave this world on an exhalation. It has been said that we come into each life with a predetermined number of breaths, and the yogis believe that by performing proper yogic breathing, we actually slow the breath and thus increase our lifespan. In this manner, we experience Spirit through our breathing. Yoga is, therefore, a mystical practice available to everyone and everybody.

The subtle body chakra system, as known to the ancient yogis, was a seven-level system. If we were to core out the human body from top to bottom, we would find an energy channel through the center, called the *Sushumna Nadi*. We also refer to this channel as the central channel. This is the main network for energy lines. Thousands of other nadis spring from here, in and around, and outside of the body. Some say that the actual number of nadis is endless, and since we understand now that everything is energy, and that each person arises from one vibratory energy source, it makes sense why the energy channels in the body would reach out and away, and connect to energy in all other life forces.

Again, the ancients had a systematic way of understanding energy. But this system was limited to the understanding of that time. In the present era, energy and information are accelerating at an unprecedented pace. Again, the science confirms this. We have now been able to understand many other levels of energy. Many people confirm at least twelve energy centers or chakras, while others insist that there are many more than this number. And since energy is ever-expanding and changing, we may find that by the time this book is available in print, this number will be much greater. However, since the number twelve fits exquisitely for our twelve-month Wheel of the Year calendar, that is our working chakra format. If your experience and expertise bring you to another place, please honor what you know to be true.

Each month, the chakra's details will be shared, along with the energy of the month.

Here is a Chart of Information for Reference:

Chakra	Location	Color	Mission
1st	Coccyx	Red	Security, Survival, Grounding
2nd	Sacral Plexus	Orange	Creativity, Feelings, Joy
3rd	Solar Plexus	Yellow	Personal Power, Inner Strength
4th	Heart Center	Green	Love, Relationships, Healing
5th	Throat	Light Blue	Communication, Creativity, Truth
6th	3rd Eye	Indigo	Intuition, Inner Vision
7th	Crown	Violet	Wisdom, Spirituality, Divinity
8th	Above Crown	Ultra-Violet or Magenta	Life Purpose, Karma
9th	Above 8th Chakra	Gold	Soul Programs, Ascension & Descension
10th	Below body in the Earth	Brown	Nature, Legacy
11th	Hands & Feet	Pink	Energy Conversion
12th	32 points and the Cosmic Energy Egg	Opalescent/ Iridescent	Connection to Source, God essence

The coursework on the chakra system can be hundreds of hours alone. Today's Modern Mystics are generally aware of this system, or at least the seven chakras within the human body. But just like all things, the chakra coursework is a multi-layered one that reveals itself as we dig in and peel back the layers, one at a time.

Don't be surprised if you unearth new information with this work, even if you are a seasoned practitioner with an already large body of knowledge of the chakras.

* * *

The Modern Mystic's Wheel of the Year - a Multi-Faith Path to Living in Harmony is a themed monthly guidebook that includes several "keys," including the "Chakras and Yoga" key. Since this is a significant amount of information each month, carefully curated yoga practices are provided. And since it is always recommended to practice yoga with a teacher, in person, who can instruct you how to negotiate each posture and breath to the best of your ability and for your specific body, that is, first and foremost, the best method to practice.

Due to their years of somatic integration, many Modern Mystics have cultivated home yoga practices. Those choosing to walk the solo path can utilize the suggested single posture, Hatha Yoga practice (approximately 75 minutes), or mini-class (approximately 15 minutes) to cultivate the appropriate energy each month.

Those who need more guidance in the home practice have pre-recorded classes available to them. For your convenience, they are all together on the website. To access this special page, you'll need to access the secret page with your cipher.

So, if you haven't already done so:

1. Open to the "Treasure Map Cipher" on page 4
2. Decipher the cipher!
3. Head to the website and put in the code

Now that the 12 keys have been explained in detail, we are ready to get on the road to our destination. Hopefully, you packed lightly because we need to make space to bring in anything new.

Part 2 of the book takes us on our monthly journey throughout 12 months—and beyond! Just be open.

Here we go...

[Cipher Code: 12MysticWheel12]

Part 2

January

New Beginnings

The Wheel of the Year turns again at midnight, and a new year clicks into position. Everything about January symbolizes new beginnings: from the meaning of the number "one" being new beginnings and change, to the Roman god, Janus, whom the month is named after, meaning opening a new door to a new year. January offers an opportunity to begin with a new slate, wiping fresh the previous year's energy. For this reason, we must take a small step backward in time and reflect upon last year for a moment.

New Year's Eve

As we will detail for December, on the final day of the year, December 31st, we consider what your biggest accomplishments were for the year. Reflecting on what we manifested and created for ourselves is paramount. With a positive focus, we reflect on how we feel about completing those items. Upon that initial reflection, we shift our focus to any unfinished business that needs to be attended to. This could be some things that were thought about but not started, initiated but never completed, or long-term challenges for which the best course of action is still being determined.

Carving out time for inner work and reflection is necessary, even though many people celebrate New Year's Eve with lavish parties and social events. It's imperative to be clear about the energy brought into the New Year. This can be done through meditation, journaling, or community sharing circles. One thing is certain: rushing this aspect can lead to confusion about deep personal truths, motives, and goals.

Once you are clear, certainly celebrate! Celebrate all of your accomplishments and the blessings that the year brought you. Some may celebrate with others and share stories of the year, while others may decide that a quiet evening alone, celebrating in your own way, is the best method. Neither way is more right or advantageous than the other. And there is nothing wrong with choosing yourself and private time over collective partying if that feels right for you. To be successful in navigating the Wheel of the Year, it's important to tune inward for heightened awareness and trust that you are following your true self in the journey.

January Energies

The first month of the year provides an obvious alignment with the number one (1). One represents new beginnings and change. It is the beginning of everything and anything—the Alpha to the Omega. There's always an excitement to any new venture, and the New Year certainly holds much anticipation. As all is cyclical, it is understood that the journey through life is one with many ups and downs. January offers a renewed hope for releasing all the energy associated with the "downs," while improving on the "ups."

January kicks off the coldest part of the year in the Northern Hemisphere. After the winter holidays and the New Year, people tend to hunker down inside more, both hibernating and contemplating. We are supposed to be eating warmer foods and nurturing ourselves during this inward time.

The Winter Solstice marked the longest night of the year, which just passed approximately ten days ago. We are now in the deep throes of darkness. It is a common daily circumstance to find oneself less energized than normal. It is not unusual to stick close to home, heading out mostly for needed supplies and little else. This is not to be looked at as a bad thing. This is what winter is all about, and honoring the darkness and the inward movement of natural energy is important in creating the balance we need. A byproduct of attempting to hustle about and do too much, or "burning the candle at both ends," is being a recipient of a weakened immune system. Therefore, it is of an urgency that we resolve ourselves to embrace the inward pull and use our remaining stamina wisely.

The energy this month is Earth. The Earth is a solid mass with vibration and movement, but not a lot of flow. The stability that the earth element provides is the basis for everything. It's specifically tailored to provide a solid foundation to work upon. Using this time of year to appreciate this by moving slowly and methodically, establishing your own foundational support for the upcoming year is a significant connection to be made.

With this emphasis on inward movement and darkness, January makes a fabulous time of year for meditation, contemplation, and planning. These are the types of things we should be spending our time doing, rather than moving from one social event to another. These are the events that support us in winter. And a major key to manifesting what the Highest Self truly wants is to be clear exactly what that is. How can we do this if we are too busy? January provides the needed energy for this to occur. When we slow down and tap into these tools, we will be pleasantly surprised to find an inward current of energy supporting us and for our highest good.

January begins in the astrological sign of Capricorn, and halfway through the month, it changes to Aquarius. The reason that astrological signs do not fall neatly in line each month is that the ancient Babylonians, who are given credit for realizing that the sun seems to pass through twelve different constellations each year, before returning to its original starting point, chose to begin their New Year on the Spring Equinox in March. As we know, our calendar is a more recent advent, one that the ancients who watched the sky did not use. When everything was changed to the new calendar, astrologers kept the original one and began the year with Aries, instead of moving it to Capricorn, because it made the most sense to do so. This is why the signs do not line up so neatly each month, as we might like them to. Nonetheless, we can understand that the energy of January is aligned with that of the Goatfish and the Water Bearer.

If your sun sign is that of Capricorn or Aquarius, then even though this time of year has a strong inward pull, you may feel the most energized and vibrant now. Capricorn begins with the Winter Solstice, the day that the sun begins its movement out of the darkness, and somewhere around December 22nd. As January arrives on the tail of the Goatfish, this renewed energy fits, since it's a more appropriate symbol for Capricorn.

The Goatfish is a representation of Babylon's god, Ea, who ruled over the power of the life-giving waters beneath the earth. If life begins in the water, then, again, we have a beautiful connection to Capricorn and new beginnings, the major theme for January. This practical astrological sign is also an earth sign, the element associated with January.

From Capricorn comes Aquarius, the second sign of January. The water bearer arrives at a time when the Nile River traditionally floods, a symbol of fertility. With Capricorn connected to new beginnings and Aquarius to that of fertility, we have a perfect link to setting intentions and preparing to create new beginnings. As we begin January with Capricorn and focus on the New Beginnings, we end with the flowing waters that renew and fertilize all things.

The gemstone for January is the deep red Garnet stone, known for its grounding properties, also linked to the first chakra's color and foundational quality. Snowdrops are the flower for the month, meaning New Beginnings.

Holidays and Holy Days

Throughout the world, many traditions honor the energy of renewal and new beginnings in January. The Shinto tradition in Japan also honors January 1st as New Year's Day. It is called *Gantan-sai*. Shinto is an ancient religion that means the "ways of the Gods" and is associated with the spirits that reside in nature. The Shintos strive to always strengthen their connection to nature. On *Gantan-sai*, Shintos visit their sacred temple and pray for purification and renewal. Mahayana Buddhists celebrate the New Year on the first full moon in January. They also go to their temple and light candles to bring happiness and good luck for the coming year.

Makar Sankranti is the Hindu Sun festival, and it is held on or around January 14th each year. This is an unusual change for the Hindu spiritual holidays, as most fall on a lunar calendar. However, because this particular festival honors the sun, the solar calendar is followed. It marks the first day that the sun moves into Makar (Capricorn), and the days begin to get longer. It is common in India for people to go to the sacred river Ganges during Makar Sankranti and bathe with reverence for the sun.

World Religion Day, a Baha'i idea to commemorate the fact that most of the world's religions hold common threads and that there are harmonious principles that connect them all, perfectly captures the essence of this book, making it a welcome holiday in setting the tone of honoring diversity all year round. This special day falls on the third Sunday of the month.

A Spanish tradition, St. Anthony's Blessing of Animals Day, on January 17, is a day when domestic animals are blessed to bring fertility and abundance. What wonderful energy to also introduce for the New Year! We are reminded that all living beings are to be honored and respected. Both World Religion Day and St. Anthony's Blessing of Animals Day are reminders to keep our intentions heart-centered and of an uplifting vibration.

January ends with a Zoroastrian winter festival called *Sadeh* on the 30th. It marks the warming of the Earth. Although we may not feel so, we can be assured that there is a slow movement towards the light and warmth that began even with the Winter Solstice. The Earth is constantly changing as the cycles rotate, and although more Holidays and Holy Days occur within the month, these all honor the essence of the theme of New Beginnings.

Chakra Connection

1st Chakra

Sanskrit: *Muladhara*
Meaning: *mula* = root, origin or essence, *adhara* = basis or foundation
Location: Base of the Spine

This is the starting point of our spiritual development, where the spiritual energy (*Kundalini Shakti*) is slumbering, awaiting activation as we begin our journey towards enlightenment.

The number "one" is also associated with the first chakra. The connection of the first chakra, or Muladhara, is a reminder that this grounding energy requires looking at our root, our foundation, and all of the components of our life that connect to our feeling safe and secure and that nourish us.

Think of the three major areas of foundational energy: home, health, and work/finances. While the companion Workbook to this book will identify additional areas of self-inquiry, here are a few journaling prompts for the first chakra:

Home: Does my home still feel like the place where I am safe and secure?

Health: Do I have any outstanding physical or mental health issues to attend to?

Work/Finances: Do I enjoy my work, and does it support me?

The first Chakra, Muladhara, connects to the Earth element. The *Yantra* (mystical diagram) of the first chakra is a four-petaled lotus flower, each petal representing one of the four functions of the psyche: *manas* (mind), *buddhi* (intellect), *chitta* (consciousness) & *ahamkara* (ego). It contains a four-sided square, representing the four directions: East, South, West & North. Within the square is an upside-down triangle representing the archetypal feminine energy of the womb of Mother Earth.

Moon Phases

Dark Moon:

During the Dark Moon in January, meditate and go inward to create the energy that you need this year for the highest good of all. If you do not dive deep enough, your intentions may be too superficial and only serve yourself. When this occurs, often our manifestation is met with mixed energies. When we align for the highest good of all, we ensure energy will manifest appropriately. But be careful not to set intentions for specific outcomes, as this can limit our ability to create and manifest. Instead, leave some room open for the Universe to bring in the energy in fun and exciting new ways.

New Moon:

Since this is the first month of the year, it is quite important to know the new moon date. This is the first new moon of a new year–major new beginnings are afoot, and another clicking of the wheel and setting it deep into place. What are our intentions for this New Year? Establish them with the new moon, and integrate them through the Waxing to the Full Moon.

If the 1st of the year and the new moon do not synchronize close together in a year, then decide if it is more important to focus on the new beginnings on January 1st, at the new moon date, or both—nothing is wrong. This is a starting point, so the choice is yours to make. Some years, this may leave you with more than one new beginning for the first month of the New Year. When this occurs, it is evident that *major energy* needs to shift, so hopefully you have reflected much on the waning and dark moon phase of December to be clear what that is. However, if you did not, you can use January's waning period and dark moon to break it down further.

It is important to start the New Year with a sankalpa or right intention. This is a Sanskrit word from *sam-klrip*, "to be brought into existence, wish, or produce." On the night of the new moon (unless you performed it on January 1st), take a moment to write down your New Year sankalpa (refer to Part 1 of the book for examples and workbook for guidance).

Once you develop a sankalpa that speaks to you and honors your true intentions for the year, you will be able to consistently drive energy towards this desire. Remember that while January may be a perfect time to start a new intention, it does not mean that if you miss the target and realize in March or July that you need to course-correct that you can't. The moon cycles will guide you with restructuring or realigning as you go through the year.

Waxing Moon:

The Waxing cycle is the beginning of the manifestation of the New Beginning energy. Like with the new moon, every moon cycle for January is ultra-significant. This is the first time energy is being driven to the New Year sankalpa. Use the waxing moon cycle to consistently honor these wise intentions.

Waning Moon:

During the waning moon, let go of any obstacles that arise in your path. While working harmoniously with natural energy will always render positive results, remember that other energies could be affecting the timeline of the outcome. *Karma* is one of these forces. So you may not understand why things are not coming to fruition as quickly as you had hoped, but that is never any reason to give up if your intention is of the best vibration and for the greatest good of all. Be patient and stick with it.

January can feel like an overwhelming month if we pack it in with too much change. Remember to use the dark moon times to meditate and formulate, and then slowly begin to integrate things at a pace that you feel comfortable with. The first month of the year is ripe with New Beginnings and setting the right goals and intentions so that the energy continues to flow and manifest throughout the year.

Faith Tradition: Shamanism

"The new caretakers of the Earth will come from the West, and those that have made the greatest impact on Mother Earth now have the moral responsibility to remake their relationship with Her, after remaking themselves."

– Don Antonio Morales, Q'ero Shaman

Shamans, of many different traditions, work with nature to create harmonizing energies and strengthen their connection to the natural world. All of the ancestors of the Earth's spiritual traditions once practiced a form of shamanism. It is known to be the oldest form of spiritualism in the world, 40,000 years old or more. The word Shaman means "one who sees in the dark" and refers to the Shaman's ability to journey and enter into different worlds to create healing.

From ancient rock art in Siberia to archeological finds in South America, the traces of ancient civilizations give us merely a glimpse into the roots of our first spiritual tradition on the planet. It is believed that the Australian Aboriginals are the oldest known Shamanic peoples, with some evidence suggesting that they roamed the outback around 40,000 to 50,000 BCE. Regrettably, the predominantly oral nature of this tradition provides scant evidence, also compounded by the reluctance of contemporary Aboriginal communities to share their profound spiritual world with outsiders. And when they do, it's for mere peeks into the actual framework.

The Trois Frères Shaman, often called "The Dancing Shaman", is a famous cave painting from the Cave of the Trois Frères in Ariège, France, dated to the Upper Paleolithic period, approximately 13,000–15,000 BCE. Although there are no words or symbols, he speaks volumes about the history of Shamanism. The Andean Q'ero Shamans, while a more recent Shamanic tradition, are steeped in ceremony and offer more accessible resources for Modern Mystics.

As most likely the first spiritual tradition, it seems fitting to work with this worldwide and vast faith tradition for January, with a focus on the Andean legacies.

Symbol: Sacred Spiral

The symbol for January is the Sacred Spiral. This is a universal symbol found across cultures and time periods, representing concepts such as growth, cyclical time, and the interconnectedness of life. Its origins are ancient and not tied to a single culture.

Perhaps the most profound observation of the Sacred Spiral is that it can be found everywhere in nature, from shells and sunflowers to whirlpools and galaxies. It's a fundamental DNA throughout the natural world and therefore a foundational element, aligning with our first month of the year.

But the Sacred Spiral can also be found in prehistoric art as early as the Paleolithic and Neolithic eras, dating back tens of thousands of years. Carvings at Ireland's Newgrange and France's Gavrinis depict these spirals, often triple or double, etched into passage tombs.

The Andean culture linked to the Inca and pre-Inca cultures in Peru shows the spiral in textiles, pottery, and architecture, representing the *Amaru*, a symbol of wisdom and transformation, or the spiraling path of spiritual growth. In the Americas, the Hopi in the American Southwest depict spirals in their pottery and rock art, and the Mesoamerican feathered serpent Quetzalcoatl is depicted with spiral motifs. The spiral can also be found in Hindu and Buddhist art, Taoism, African cultures, and Polynesian cultures, among many others.

The Sacred Spiral is everywhere, from the most minute fiber of our natural world, and woven into almost all ancient spiritual traditions on the planet.

Smudging

As January is the year's first month, we must appropriately set the tone and clear away the past. Smudging is a perfect remedy for releasing the old and transmuting the lower vibrations. It's a Shamanic tradition using the smoke of certain ceremonial herbs or sacred wood.

In North America, Native American Indian tribes use Ceremonial White Sage for this ritual, while the South American Shamans use Palo Santo. Both are high vibrational natural gifts for renewal and cleansing, but with different properties.

Studies by the University of San Diego have shown that White Sage has anti-bacterial properties that can reduce the growth and survival of multiple bacterial species.[28] Science has confirmed something that tribal elders and healers have known for centuries: negative or lower vibrational energy cannot exist in the presence of White Sage. Palo Santo is a sacred wood with a lighter, more cedar-type smell than sage, which is pungent and earthy. While no research studies have been conducted to date on the nature of Palo Santo, it translates from Spanish to mean "Wood of the Saints" or "Sacred Wood." Shamans trust that using it in ceremonies and healings promotes positive and uplifting effects, such as raising one's spiritual vibrations, offering protection, and clearing all unwanted energy.

Always have White Sage and Palo Santo readily available. Allow yourself to be intuitively guided as to when to use each. And certainly, if you are cleansing, now for the New Year, you may want to make a blend of both. There is no right or wrong, only what is. So, use whatever you feel resonates with you the most.

Items Needed:

- White Sage and/or Palo Santo
- Shell or Clay Bowl
- Feather or Smudging Wand
- Lighting Torch/Matches

Preparation:

Bathe or wash your hands, at the very least. Call in ancestors, angels, and guides. Take time to breathe deeply, focusing on being fully present.

---

[28] https://www.sandiego.edu/kumeyaay-garden/plant.php?ID=2

Procedure:

1. Begin at the main entrance or front door of your space.

2. Invoke the Sacred Spiral by drawing with your right, symbolizing forward movement.

3. Light the sage, blow out the flame, and use the smoke.

4. Push the smoke around the door with your feather or wand in a clockwise spiral movement, three times.

5. From the front door, move throughout the house, through every room, pushing the smoke throughout.

6. Invoke the spiral in corners or areas where you feel that energy may have stagnated.

7. Pay particular attention to doorways and windows where energy can enter the home, and smudge in spirals around those entryways.

8. Smudge new things that came into the home, as well as your older items

9. Do not forget to smudge basements, crawl spaces, attics, closets, and under furniture.

10. When you return to the front door where you began, open the door, and push the smoke out.

11. Leave any remaining White Sage or Palo Santo on the front stoop to burn out.

12. Once the cinders have cooled, release the remains to the earth.

Smudging can be done anytime energy needs to shift. Feel when this needs to happen and utilize this Shamanic practice as often as you need, but most certainly at least at the beginning of each new month of the year.

January Altar

- **Altar cloth:** Red, the color of the first chakra, or an Andean textile/cloth

- **Flowers:** Snowdrops or Carnations. If you cannot find snowdrops, Carnations can be of any color, offering the appropriate energy that you are looking to connect with for this year: white for good luck, red for love or admiration, pink symbolizing friendship.

- **Candle:** A white or red candle at the center of the altar

- **Crystal/Stone:** Garnet stone, several garnet stones in spiral shape, or a prayer bead bracelet or necklace with Garnet beads. Red Jasper can be used in place of Garnet.

- **Symbol:** Sacred Spiral symbol created with crystals, in a picture, or any object with this symbol carved or painted on it

- **Essential Oil/Incense:** Palo Santo, used by South American Shamans for cleansing & renewal

- **Herbs:** Ceremonial White Sage, bundled or loose (if loose, you will need a shell or bowl for burning and a feather for moving the smoke)

- **Other items (optional):**
  - *The Modern Mystic's Wheel of the Year* Book, Workbook, and Oracle Deck
  - Natural items that work for your sankalpa. Example: if you are starting or going back to school, you may want to put a picture or statue of an owl, symbolizing wisdom
  - Picture of Lord Ganesha, a Hindu deity who represents new beginnings, or a picture of another spiritual being that holds special meaning to assist in working through these new beginnings
  - Shamanic items on the altar, such as rattles, smudging supplies, animal bones or feathers, and even snake skins

Angel/Ancestor: The Shaman

Each culture has an original tradition based in Shamanism. These indigenous cultures all had a person thought of as a healer, diviner, or meditator, able to achieve altered states of consciousness to interact with spirits for healing and guidance. Each Shamanic tradition is unique, with the Shaman known by many different names.

In Mongolia and Siberia, the Shaman is named Böö (male) or Udgan (female). In North America's Arctic area, they're known as Angakok. Navajo healers in the Southwest are Hatałii, with Cherokee in the Southeast as Didanvwisgi. The Q'ero Shaman from the Andes goes by the name Paqo, and the Shipibo of the Amazon, Curandero.

The Asian Shamans of Central China are called Txiv Neeb. Korean Shamans, Mudang, are most commonly female. The Nepalese call their Shamans Jhakri or Dhaamee. And in the Philippines, they're Babaylan. Nigerian, South African Shamans are Babalawo. Scandinavians: Völva. And Australians: Wulla-mullung.[29]

No matter the indigenous people, there is a name for the holy person who conducts rituals, passes down wisdom, heals, and stays aligned with the natural energy on the planet, ancestors, and star-beings.

This month, you may wish to research who the Shaman of your native culture is. Although you may live in the USA now, to which land can you trace your family's origin?

For example, if your family is of Irish descent, you can trace your Shamanic roots back to Ireland and the seers there. Druids will be invoked in October; however, Druids or Drui are one form of Irish Shaman. Another Old Irish female seer is called Banfháith or fáith for general practitioners. Since Druids will be worked with in another month, perhaps one of the latter would be more useful. This is for you to decide.

Another avenue for this month is to work with the Paqo of the Andes, especially since our ritual is a Q'ero Despacho Ceremony.

---

[29] Wikipedia

Spiritual Teacher and Angel Communicator Kyle Gray provides a beautiful invocation in his medicine oracle deck, *Angels and Ancestors*.

Gray's Invocation:

> "Guardians of the four corners, Mother in the Earth, Father in the Sky, Angels, Ancestors, Sacred Ones, I call on you and welcome you here now!"

With a focus on Shamans, you may want to use a more specific invocation, such as:

> "Ancient Ancestor, _____, I call on you and welcome you to provide wisdom and healing as I enter this (meditation, ritual, practice, etc.). Guide and protect me on my journey until I return safely. So be it!"

Use your intuition on who to invoke this month, and how, and know that the Shamans will be with you.

January Ritual: *Despacho* Ceremony

The Q'ero Shamans of Peru, a Quechua-speaking indigenous people from the high Andes and descendants of the Inca, are considered one of the most respected wisdom keepers in the Andean region for preserving ancient Inca ceremony. They perform the *Despacho* ceremony to harmonize, heal, and protect after each earth cycle. This ceremony offers an opportunity to renew, give gratitude, and release any lower energies, which assists the Shaman when seeking to align with the three worlds: upper, middle, and lower.

The lower world is represented by the serpent and is a place to connect with the inner world and our past. The middle world, represented by the puma, is considered our Human World in the here and now, where we observe our physical world. And the upper world, represented by the condor, is a place of the future, where we can contact ancestors and spirit guides to see the bigger picture.

Shamans continually work to create harmony and healing, and this seems a perfect ritual to perform at the beginning of the year as we set new intentions. My friend and keeper of Andean wisdom, Jorge Luis Delgado, wrote a wonderful book titled *Inka Wisdom: Return to Joy*.[30] In his book, Jorge gives us a succinct vision of the *Ayni Despacho* ceremony that he describes as a "prayer bundle." Instead of recreating, we bow to Jorge's wisdom and experience with Despacho and provide a succinct version here:

Preparation:

Begin with a large piece of white paper. Fold into thirds one way and then the other, leaving nine squares. This will house the offerings. The offerings each receive a prayer before being placed on the paper. The offerings are added in layers, in a mandala pattern, until all are together. Then, the white paper is folded into a square and tied as a gift, which is then burned in a ceremonial fire, buried in the earth, or released into water.

The offerings can be many different objects, but should be well thought out, each symbolizing something significant. Here are some ideas of what to add as offerings, all to give to *Pachamama*, the feminine life-sustaining energy of Mother Earth:

---

[30] *Inka Wisdom: Return to Joy*, Jorge Luis Delgado, Self-published and printed in Peru 2018

- <u>Sugar</u>: represents sweetness and love
- <u>Red or white carnations</u>: red for the earth, white for the heavens
- <u>Rice & grains</u>: fertility, abundance, and bring prayers to fruition
- <u>Raisins</u>: for our ancestors
- <u>Alphabet noodles</u>: to step beyond language
- <u>Animal crackers</u>: for animal spirits and health
- <u>Candies</u>: represent everything we are in a relationship with
- <u>Loose sage or incense</u>: to feed the elements of the earth
- <u>"Play" money</u>: ensuring the success of the Despacho
- <u>Honey</u>: for honoring the sweetness in life
- <u>Confetti or sprinkles</u>: celebrating life
- <u>Black licorice</u>: protection
- <u>Flower petals</u>: healing
- <u>Corn</u>: reciprocity to Mother Earth for all she has provided us in the past
- <u>Chocolate</u>: a gift for Pachamama
- <u>Other</u>: bring in any other burnable objects to symbolize the worlds or spirit energies that you wish to create harmony with, such as crystals, feathers, shells.

<u>Steps for Despacho</u>:

1. Create Sacred Space by lighting White Sage or burning Palo Santo, lighting candles, saying prayers, calling in spirits, directions, winds, grandfathers, or whatever feels right to you to create a sacred space.

2. Lay out the folded paper and begin to layer the objects by placing one at a time down, noting aloud what they represent. Make sure to state your intentions clearly as you invite all the energies together in harmony, as you make this offering to Pachamama.

3. Create a *K'intu* using three Coca Leaves (or bay leaves or flower petals). Arrange the leaves in a bouquet with stems pointing down. Focus and blow your heavy energies into the leaves with your breath. Raise the K'intu to the sky, offering the energies to Father Sun and then to Mother Earth, adding it to the Despacho.

4. Once you have filled it with your words, prayers, and visions, thanking Pachamama for all that she has provided you, fold the bundle like a gift from left to right, right to left, then bottom up and top down. Tie a cord around this previous gift.

5. The Despacho can be gifted in various ways:
   a. Create a ritual fire and burn it for transformation
   b. Give it to a natural water source to release it
   c. Bury it in the earth for transmutation

6. Spend time quietly contemplating the harmonizing gift.

As with any ritual, the spiritual component needs to feel right and authentic to you. Shamanism is quite inclusive and open to all people. The Andean culture is a nature-based spiritual practice. Delgado explains the Andean theology as follows:

The Inka understood that all life comes from light, and all light is love. They held a strong connection to nature, knowing that the expression of love on Earth can easily be found in the expressions of life found in nature. There is no love that is not in service. For instance, rain brings life to the Earth. In that way, it is in service to Mother Earth and the children of Mother Earth. All nature is in service to life. We humans are also part of nature, and because of that, we are also in service to life. We are the Children of the Sun.[31]

What Delgado so eloquently explains is that we are all a part of this Andean shamanic culture, because as human beings, we are each a part of nature. How much more inclusive can we be than with this way of thought?

---

[31] Delgado, J. *Inka Wisdom*, page 15

Tracey's Personal Reflection

When arriving in Peru on retreat, Jorge greets me with a hug and a simple phrase, "Welcome home." Undeniably, this is true. Each time I return to Peru, I feel a homecoming and a connection to the land and the people greater than before. The Incan culture and Shamanic practices do speak volumes through the land, and I've found that those who travel with me also feel this connection quite early on in our travels.

To date, I have led three spiritual retreats in Peru, and each time I've experienced profound awakenings through the land. In 2019, while at the Moon Temple in Sacred Valley with a group of women, the temple revealed this message to me to share with the group:

> *The time for being small is over. We are the healers of the world, and our time to activate and step up is now.*

If we are to speak of interfaith spiritual practices, I cannot think of a better one in which to start a new cycle and a new year than that of Andean Shamanism and how it creates space for all to duly be "Children of the Sun."

Despacho from ceremony in Sacred Valley, Peru, 2016

Tracey with Jorge Luis Delgado in Saqsaywaman, Sacred Valley, Peru, 2023

January Yoga Practice:
For Grounding & Providing Foundation for New Beginnings:

This practice is for all levels, and no yoga experience is required. However, it is always recommended to consult a doctor before beginning any new physical program. Remember to modify anything for particular conditions that you may be experiencing, and to always follow your breath for the truth about a feeling that arises.

Yoga Posture Sequence for Grounding and Support:

Any new structure needs a solid foundation. As we are starting anew, we must begin with the grounding energies of the first chakra and those of the earth element. The practice should be slow and steady, with long holds. If you become uncomfortable, look at possible modifications. Your natural breathing will be the key to the practice. If you can maintain a steady breath, then you can stay in the posture. If your breathing becomes strained or erratic, you may want to come out of the pose or rest.

Remember that this practice must suit you, and that this is merely a suggestion. There is no exact right time in which to practice, although many yoga teachers believe that practicing at the same time every day both builds up the energy of the practice as well as provides one with the ability to learn more about his or her entire being. Decide when you wish to practice, and don't worry if that changes day by day. January gets dark early and stays dark longer, so do what you can when you can do it. If the practice changes day by day, that is also fine.

Energetically focus on the earth element and the feet and legs. The rhythm is slow and steady like the earth, and you are always feeling what is touching the ground and pressing into the earth through those areas.

Single Posture Practice: Lotus (*Padmasana*)

Come to a comfortable seated position. Using a folded blanket, yoga block, or cushion under your seat is suggested. Place each foot on the opposite thigh. Press your knees towards the earth, grounding down through both of your sitting bones and the knees, creating a stable triangular base for your body to root downward into the Earth. As you press downward, lengthen the spine upwards towards the sky. Release the shoulders down and back, lifting the chest and sternum gently upwards. Place your hands, palms down, on your thighs. Close your eyes, if you are comfortable doing so, look towards the tip of your nose, and take several long, deep breaths through your nostrils.

* This posture can be used to begin any yoga class or meditation practice. Using a mudra, breathing technique, or other yoga tool appropriate for any of the chakras can align with that particular energy.
* Modification: leave the feet on the floor, aligning the ankles to the pubic bone. Or, allow the legs to be straight. Find a seat that is comfortable for you.

Mudra & Meditation:

Come to the easy-seated pose or Lotus seated pose. Place hands on lap, palms up. Touch thumb to ring finger for the *Prithivi* mudra or Earth hand position. Spend time in meditation and reflection on your sankalpa. Then close the practice by bringing your hands to your heart, bowing your head, and repeating the intention or prayer.

Breathing Practice: Natural Breath

There is something so perfect, so unique, and so simply satisfying in honoring one's breath. How often have you thought about your breath, or the fact that, without your conscious understanding that it keeps happening every moment of your life?

Tune into the natural flow of your organic breath. Follow the flow of inhalation to exhalation. Notice any pauses in between them. Maybe count the inhalation and the exhalation to find if they are in sync or out of rhythm. Make an intention to get those numbers close together or the same, but do not worry if that does not happen. Instead of using that as a goal, simply allow yourself to experience all that is your breath.

You will feel the sensation of the breath coming into the nostrils as a cooler sensation than the exhalation that moves out of the nostrils. You may notice parts of the body naturally expand outward, like the belly, ribcage, and chest, as you take in breath. Likewise, the exhalations may provide you with the knowledge that those same areas naturally contract inward. Or, you may find that your breath is something altogether different than this. It is all good. Simply observe the breath, and when your mind wanders, bring it back on point.

If you are performing this breath daily, see if it changes if you do it in the morning versus the evening, or what changes day by day. Log this information in your journal.

Hatha Yoga Sequence:

Supine on Back – Breath Work	Lotus/Easy Seated	Lateral Bends	Seated Twists	Staff	Forward Fold
Half Forward Fold	Cobbler	Table	Cat/Cow	Child	Downward Dog
Runner's Lunge	Plank	Low Cobra	Locust	Child or Downward Dog	Standing Forward Fold
Mountain	Warrior I	Tree	Squat	Bridge	Supine Pigeon
Supine Twist	Happy Baby	Corpse - Final Relaxation	Easy Seated or Lotus	Meditation	Closing

* Note that the pre-recorded practice may differ from the sequence above.

Short 15-minute Practice:

- Easy Seated with Breathing & Sanklapa
- Forward Fold
- Child
- Downward Dog
- Low Cobra
- Mountain with sankalpa
- Happy Baby
- Corpse

January Recap

We have started a New Year. It is said that the energy you work with on these first days, the people you surround yourself with, and the intentions that you set go a long way to creating the type of year you manifest. The Earth-based energies of this month, including the Shamanic ritual and smudging of your personal space, will help to release and remove lower vibrational energy as we move forward positively and in gratitude.

Use the yoga practice to support the grounding energies that assist you in providing clarity on what is truly important and for the highest good of all. Remember to work with the moon phases to establish the best times to work with the releasing energy and the new energy accordingly.

By the end of January, you have hopefully created a solid foundation on which to move forward with your *sankalpa*. For February, energy shifts, and you will need the support of January's practices to effectively work with those energies to support your sankalpa and intentionally live in harmony with the planet.

February

Harmony

February Energies

With all of the new energy surrounding January, there is a deeper plunge into the inward journey for February. In the Northeast hemisphere, we are deeply consumed by winter, and although the light is getting stronger and longer each day now, we still feel a pull to stay inside with warm foods and the comforts of home. Being the second month of the year, February is associated with the number two (2), which in numerology signifies happiness and cooperation, and also connects to the second chakra, which is associated with happiness, joy, and creativity.

February's actual name is *Februum*, which is Latin for purification. It is also connected to the Roman goddess Februa, who was an overseer and purifier of things. The month of February presents numerous opportunities for purification, aimed at fostering both inner and outer harmony.

You may have moved furniture and other items around in your home or office in January. With the Smudging ritual and cleansing of the previous year to focus on the new beginnings for this year, there should now be a flowing energy, connected to the second chakra's water element. With the foundations set in January, February offers the opportunity to move energy into the right positions for creating lasting harmony.

The water bearer sign of Aquarius ushers in February—how appropriate. The image of Aquarius is the human Water-Bearer, pouring out the water of life from two vases. In the Babylonian astrological stories of Gilgamesh, we find a familiar story by another name, that of Utnapishtim. Utnapishtim, an immortal figure, was once the human embodiment of Aquarius. By listening to the Divine Word, he built a boat and saved himself from the great flood. In Mythic Astrology, Ariel Guttman and Kenneth Johnson reveal that this Babylonian story is the prototype for the flood story in Genesis.[32]

Halfway through the month, Pisces, the fish, comes flowing in. It is interesting to note that the number two plays a pivotal role in both of this month's water signs: in the vases of Aquarius (although not all representations show two vases) and as the two fishes in Pisces. Water, water, and more water are in the charts for February, energetically speaking. Again, those within these signs may feel quite vital in February. And since the element water is known to be cleansing and

---

[32] Mythic Astrology, Ariel Guttman and Kenneth Johnson, Llewelyn Publications, 1998

purifying, we continue to move unwanted energy out to create a more harmonizing energy.

While the weather may preclude one from running in the raindrops or splashing around in a waterfall, encouraging a connection to the element water in whatever way available is important this month. Drink plenty of fluids, as this time of the year can be quite cold and dry. If you do live in colder climate areas, think of drinking warm or hot water and teas to keep in balance.

You also want to encourage long, hot soaks in a tub, perhaps with Epsom or sea salts. If you belong to a gym or facility that offers steam baths, partake. If not, you may want to put your own steam tent together. This can be done as easily as putting hot water and appropriate herbs like eucalyptus or lemongrass in a crockpot, bringing it to a boil, wrapping a towel around your head, and leaning towards the steam, carefully. If you have the means to purchase stronger material to hang, you can get an umbrella and hang it from the ceiling, wrap the material around it, put a chair and the crockpot inside, sit in, enclose yourself, and voila—full steam tent!

The stone of February is Amethyst, known for its calming properties. It is a stone of tranquility and spiritual harmony. Violets, the hardy flowers of February, thrive in cold climates, reflecting their qualities of resilience and balance.

Holidays and Holy Days

February 1st marks the beginning of World Interfaith Harmony Week, an annual United Nations observance. This week marks a platform where all faiths can come together in harmony as a unified show of goodwill.

The pagan sabbat Imbolc is on February 1st or 2nd and marks the halfway point between the Winter Solstice and Spring Equinox. This holiday celebrates fire, light, and the return of life, and is associated with the goddess Brigid or Brid, celebrated as the goddess of healing by the ancient Celts.

A newer holiday grounded in folklore, Groundhog Day, is celebrated on February 2nd. It is another nod at the eventual coming of spring, depending on whether that little guy sees his shadow or not. If he is not in harmony with the outer world, he retreats, signaling six more weeks of winter. Although Groundhog Day was first documented in 1887, its roots in Germanic traditions show animals like badgers and bears being observed for similar weather predictions. These influences laid the groundwork for Candlemas Day, the Christian Festival on February 2nd, marking the presentation of Jesus at the temple and the purification of Mary. In medieval Europe, Candlemas was associated with weather divination: clear weather meant prolonged winter, while cloudy weather predicted an early spring.

Many cultures celebrate the coming of Spring in February. The Hindu and Sikh holiday *Vasant Panchami* highlights the coming of spring and is honored on the fifth day of the new moon in February. The Japanese Shinto holiday *Setsebun* marks the night before Spring. On *Setsebun*, *Mamemake* is a Bean-Throwing ritual, whereby roasted soybeans are thrown out the front door at a family member wearing a devil or demon mask and yelling "Devil's Out—Fortune In!" This is thought to purify the home of misfortune and ill health, creating greater harmony for the family.

Daoists, Buddhists, and Confucianists all celebrate the Chinese New Year, which can often occur in February. Again, due to the lunar calendar association with this holiday, it is difficult to predict with accuracy if this holiday arrives in late January or February; however, there are more potential days in the second month of the year, so for our purposes, we will discuss it here. On the first new moon in February, a new animal totem is projected for the year. Although this book does not examine Chinese Astrology, it would be an appropriate time to determine your guiding animal totem and how it plays into your personality and your life challenges and strengths. Understanding these aspects of yourself may be another layer to creating harmony within.

Two holy days that cannot be assigned to February, but are likely to occur here, are Nirvana Day, the day that the Buddha achieved enlightenment, and *Lailat al Miraj,* commemorating the Prophet Muhammad's journey to Mecca and his ascent into heaven. Buddhists and Jains both celebrate Nirvana Day, some on February 15th, and others with the lunar calendar Full Moon of the 4th or 5th month. For Muslims, the holy day Lailat al Miraj is celebrated on the 27th day of Rajab, the seventh month of the Islamic lunar calendar. On these two significant days, the founders of two major faith traditions are honored not only for their mystical aspirations but for their tangible achievements in establishing spiritual paths that have guided countless others.

Christians usually honor Ash Wednesday in February, although it could fall in another month, depending on the lunar calendar. It is celebrated six weeks before Easter, and is a period of prayer and fasting known as Lent. The purpose of Lent is to prepare oneself to be closer to God and lasts the same forty days that Christ is said to have spent fasting in the desert, during which he endured many temptations by Satan.

The overly commercialized holiday, Valentine's Day, celebrates love and affection with the Feast of St. Valentine. Although recognized as a saint, little is known about St. Valentine. However legends say that during one of his arrests in 269 AD that he secretly married couples, so that the husbands would not have to go off to war, and that on the day of his execution, he left a girl who's eyesight he had healed a note signed, "Your Valentine." Recognized today as a patron saint of love, happy relationships, and all couples, this holiday encapsulates a vital aspect of February's energy of harmony: uniting individuals to foster joyful and balanced relationships.

Chakra Connection

2nd Chakra

Sanskrit: *Swadhisthana*
Meaning: *swa* = one's own, *adhisthana* = dwelling place or residence
Location: Sacral Plexus

This Chakra represents the unconscious mind and its storehouse of mental impressions (*samskaras*). These desires make it difficult to raise the *Kundalini* above this energy center.

Swadisthana, the name of the second chakra, means sweetness and refers to the nectar or juiciness of life. Life should be sweet and enjoyable, which this chakra reminds us of. When life is sweet, we are happy. And being happy is a direct result of being in harmony with all facets of life.

While the first chakra gave us a solid foundation, the second chakra, through its connection to the water element, permits us to move about, explore, and create a life that is chock-full of joy. See the companion Workbook for more questions, but here are a few considerations to reflect upon with the second chakra:

<u>Joy</u>: When you reflect on your life, do you smile?

<u>Creativity</u>: What is your creative outlet?

<u>Fluidity</u>: Is there an area of your life that no longer flows?

The Yantra (mystical diagram) is a six-petaled lotus representing the modes of consciousness. These *Vrittis* are affection or indulgence, pitilessness, destructiveness, delusion, disdain, and suspicion. Within the center at the bottom is a white crescent moon called *"Ambhoja Mandala,"* representing the water element, which is said to be flowing, cleansing, and adaptable.

Moon Phases

Dark Moon:

The dark moon of February is the time to meditate and reflect on what parts of your life need more harmony: your body, your mind, your energy, your spirit, or another aspect? Perhaps you have noticed that with the new changes you implemented in January, some people in your life are causing chaos because they disagree with the "new" you. You have to determine if those people are no longer in alignment with your Highest Self. Maybe since you began a regular spiritual practice, you have determined that something within this work no longer supports you appropriately. Or, with a regular yoga practice, you may notice parts of your physical being that are not in harmony. Use the Dark Moon night to be extremely clear about anything you're not in vibration with.

New Moon:

On the new moon, set wheels in motion to move in the type of energy you want that will promote a more harmonious inner world. Consider your sankalpa and where you can shift energy to assist with that commitment.

Waxing to Full Moon:

The waxing to full moon period is the time to dive into creating harmonizing energy throughout your life. If you do this daily for two weeks, you will establish a good energy moving forward and will feel the benefits of being lighter and clearer. The full moon for February is when you should pull out all the stops for harmonizing. The ritual for this month will vastly assist with this.

Waning Moon:

Once you arrive at the waning moon period, shift to releasing the chaos and incongruent energies in your life. Remember your sankalpa, and decide what needs to be cleared to assist you in moving in the right direction towards this clear and heartfelt intention.

For January, we started a new year, and now in February, we work on harmonizing our lives to find lasting sweetness.

Faith Tradition: Taoism

"There was something formless and perfect before the universe was born. It is serene. Empty. Solitary. Unchanging. Infinite. Eternally present. It is the mother of the universe. For lack of a better name, I call it the Tao."

– Lao Tzu, Tao Te Ching, Chapter 25

Nothing speaks harmony like Taoism. Taoism began with a Chinese Master named Lao Tzu, who wrote the *Tao Te Ching*. Lao Tzu's teachings in this famous book discuss "The Way," or The Tao. This philosophy views all aspects of life as energy, guiding one to live in harmony with the elements, chi, or life energy, and nature. Many readers of this book may find that upon deeper investigation, they already resonate with many Taoists' views of the world, such as living simply and with moderation, compassion, and humility, where other Taoists' ideas, such as *Wu-wei*, or engaging passively, yielding, and working naturally, may feel more like a foreign idea.

The World Religion Database (2023) estimates that 8.7 million people practice Taoism, primarily in China and Taiwan. A search reveals that there are no precise numbers, and the actual number of adherents varies from 10 to 170 million people. However, it is an accessible tradition for many due to its focus on living life in harmony and balance.

As an important note, Taoism is sometimes written as "Daoism." These are interchangeable due to the same Chinese character. Both Tao and Dao represent "The Way," and are the same core principles used. Therefore, it is possible to run into this confusion when digging deeper into Taoism. Just know that it is virtually the same thing.

Symbol: Yin-Yang

The Taoist Yin-Yang symbol explains this harmony well. One side of the yin-yang is white, and the other is black, spotlighting the two extremes of energy: one aligned with the moon, feminine, cold, and passive, and the other with the sun, masculine, hot, and active. These identical shapes fit perfectly together inside a circle.

However, the beauty of the symbol is in the third aspect: the *bindhus*. The small white dot inside the black side and the small black dot within the white side reveal a true harmony: that within the darkness, there is light and, likewise, within the light, there is darkness. In a world based on duality, it is particularly poignant to understand that everything is not just black or white.

The Yin-Yang's two parts, again, align with February as the second month of the year.

February Altar

- **Altar cloth:** Orange, the color of the second chakra, or an altar cloth with the Yin-Yang symbol

- **Flowers:** A bouquet of Violets or Irises

- **Candle:** Orange or a white candle, as white includes a balance of all colors

- **Crystal/Stone:** Amethyst crystal, prayer bead or bracelet, or necklace, as this is the birthstone of February. However, many people prefer to work with orange crystals, such as Carnelian, due to the connection with the chakra color—either will work nicely.

- **Symbol:** Yin-Yang picture or form

- **Essential Oil/Incense:** Jasmine, Taoist flower offering of balance, serenity, unity

- **Herb:** Ceremonial White Sage and any other herbs that bring in a property that helps you to create better harmony within

- **Other items (optional):**
  - *The Modern Mystic's Wheel of the Year* Book, Workbook, and Oracle Deck
  - A shell filled with sea salts to represent the water element of the second chakra
  - Chalice filled with water, wine, or juice
  - Any other item you would like to bring in from January's altar that represents a harmonious energy that you want to build upon or that holds meaning to your sankalpa or highest intentions.

Angel/Ancestor: Shaolin Master

Throughout Asia, Shaolin Masters are the highly trained practitioners of various martial art forms, attached to vigorous spiritual traditions. These Masters are not simply strong fighters, as one may think. They are dedicated to their faith and the pursuit of enlightenment practices, and work with energy to harmonize and cultivate vital life-force through a body-mind-spirit practice.

Although Shaolin practitioners are known to be disciples of Buddhism, they grew to encompass all of China's spiritual traditions. Shaolin Masters of the Dao (Taoism) practice *Qigong*. Qigong combines slow, flowing movements and breath techniques for a style of moving meditation. This practice harmonizes the *qi*, or vital life-force of the body.

You can easily find some Qigong classes online if you're not familiar with these exercises. Similar to Tai Chi, Qigong takes years, some say a lifetime, to perfect a sequence or flow of movements.

An interview with Qigong practitioner Albert Dumapit, from my show *The Quantum Healer*, which can be found on my YouTube channel. Dumapit instructs some simple Qigong techniques for most level practitioners, without any need for prior experience. Here is a link to that interview: https://youtu.be/-tqloVTQj4A.

As we align with Taoism this month, we work to harmonize with the natural energy available. We will not be Shaolin Masters by the end of the month, that's for sure. However, we can invoke the Shaolin Masters of the past to be with us as we practice all methods of harmonizing this month.

An Invocation for Shaolin Master:

> "Qigong Master, Shaolin, be my guide and show me The Way. Assist me in finding fluid movements and adaptability as I work to cultivate and release energy appropriately this month. May your faithful discipline be a guiding force throughout the month as I work to harmonize my inner and outer worlds."

Finishing, place hands together, and bow in respect to the Master.

February Ritual: Taoist/China/*Feng Shui*

Many people read from *The Tao Te Ching* their entire lives to understand its deeper esoteric meanings. Taoism is a full branch of study. *Feng Shui* is a Taoist method of harmonizing natural energy in our environment, beginning with the exterior of our home, the way it faces, what is around it, the neighborhood, and then inward to each room, creating energy flow.

A popular method is called *bagua*, which divides the home into nine equal sections. Each room can also be divided into nine equal sections. The entire process can be quite overwhelming, so begin by applying the bagua to the home as a whole to establish balance and harmony. Once the entire home has been addressed, deeper exploration of individual rooms can follow. Then go outside the house to aspects of your life that you can harmonize, such as your workplace.

Preparation:

- Blueprint or interior design of the home on a flat piece of paper
- Printed bagua with the map of the nine sections. Search the internet, but here is a brief diagram:

WEALTH & PROSPERITY Wood/Purple Crystals, Plants, Aquariums, Dream catchers, Chimes – keep uncluttered and energized	FAME & REPUTATION Fire/Red Awards, Diplomas, Certificates, Trophies – all records of achievements	LOVE & MARRIAGE Earth/Pink Heart shapes, Rose Quartz – keep it clean and full of love
HEALTH & FAMILY Wood/Green Pictures of family & friends, work-out equipment, Yoga room, Bowl of fruit	- CENTER - Earth/Yellow Balance – Culmination of all areas of your life	CREATIVITY & CHILDREN Metal/White Creative endeavors, Photographs of children, Paintings and Artwork, Piano or instruments
WISDOM & KNOWLEDGE Earth/Blue Bookshelf, knick-knacks showcasing something you've learned, Meditation nook, Reading area	CAREER Water/Black Affirmations, Life Purpose reminders	HELPFUL PEOPLE & MENTORS Metal/Gray Teachers, Spiritual Guides, Ascended Masters, Angels, Gifts from departed, books or articles about those who influenced you

Steps for Feng Shui:

1. Bagua: Set the interior design blueprint and the bagua papers side by side and review the areas/rooms individually.

2. Main Entrance: Begin by looking at the Main Entrance of your home, which should sit directly in front of the bottom section of the bagua. See where the front door sits?
   - Is it in the Wisdom, Career, or Helpful People section?
   - Is your door painted the appropriate color to go with the section it's in? Or does that color feature prominently in the area of the door?
   - Do you have the front door adorned appropriately with an item that represents the section?
   - This is where most energy enters your home, so review that it is pleasing and accommodating, with nothing in the way. Normally, we cannot change the location of the front door unless we are doing major renovations. So if you don't like something about it, what else can you change around it?
   - A black or blue rug at the front door attracts opportunities.
   - A fountain near the front entryway keeps positive energy flowing in. These work especially well when the front door is at the center of the Career section. However, if the front door is not in that spot, review other ideas or plans that go with the area it is located in. Remember to harmonize each area according to the bagua.

3. Colors: Move through your home room by room, looking for if you've used the appropriate harmonizing colors, elements, and items. Remove items that do not belong in a particular area to one that is best suited for them.

4. Clutter: Find areas in each room that are cluttered. Notice where clutter is piled up, and if that area of your life is also not flowing with energy. Move the clutter through reorganization or total removal. Consider moving furniture around, or removing it entirely from the house if it does not have a purpose or is creating an issue with being able to move around freely. Look at the corners of rooms where energy can sit as well. Also, never have dark corners in a room. Hanging crystals, placing mirrors, or another talisman can help change the energy in an area.

5. Bedroom: The hope is that this room is in the love and marriage area of your home. This is for sleeping and romance, so remove any television or

electronics from this room. Do not block energy to your bed, and try to have it at the center of the room with nightstands on each end, evenly balanced. Whenever feasible, avoid positioning the bed under a window or facing a bathroom. Ensure that the bed is solid-framed and store nothing underneath it. Do not keep any other stimulating items such as books, sharp objects, exercise equipment, or some houseplants in the bedroom.

6. Bathrooms: Bathrooms should be relaxing and peaceful colors with a minimum of clutter. Always keep the toilet seat down when not using it, or it represents the energy of that area of the home going down the drain. Dripping faucets are a symbol of wealth dripping away, so maintain your plumbing. Keep bathroom doors closed when possible.

7. Home Office: Ensure that you face the door to your office, with your back against a wall for an ultimate power position. Make sure the desk chair has a back with arms. Keep the garbage can emptied, do not leave leftover food, and always keep the desk free from clutter. Put small flowers or a dragon on the left-hand side of your desk for good luck.

You will notice that the more energy you put into creating balance in your home that the more energy starts to flow. Cleaning and organization are always significant rituals. Cleaning out clutter and removing unnecessary items always creates more space for other energy to move in. This is our balance: to receive something, we need to give something. This is the reciprocal energy of nature.

If we are too greedy, hoard, or become overly attached to things, this creates stagnant or stuck energy in life. This is a great ritual to do before you move into a new home or when you want to create new energy in an office or other personal location.

Interior decorators are incorporating Feng Shui as a normal part of their business nowadays. The term is widely recognized, and one does not need to adhere to the Taoist faith to practice it.

As Rev. Dr. Jessica Sommar, faculty member of The New Seminary for Daoism and Crisis Management, said, Taoism is Shamanic in nature, with indigenous roots. According to Sommar, the magical elements of Taoism practiced today, including Feng Shui, may be practiced by anyone; however, the Priests govern the ceremonial aspects of the tradition.

Have fun in February with Feng Shui!

Tracey's Personal Reflection

When my husband and I built our first home, I utilized the bagua and Feng Shui to create a harmonious living space. Everyone who came to our home noticed a calming and inviting presence within. Even our neighbors who had built their homes at the same time—some of whom had the same model home as us—reflected on how differently it felt inside our home.

Our powder room was located in the Health & Family section of the home, and a little into the Wealth & Prosperity area. I placed a note on the toilet seat asking people to close the lid, as leaving it open symbolizes "money going down the drain." Everyone loved it, and there was a noticeable difference when the seat was left open versus closed.

I even created harmonizing rituals within the walls, under the floors, and around the property, working to manifest positive energy everywhere.

In front of our home, at the center where the Career section is located, my husband installed two waterfalls that cascaded down into a koi pond. It was beautiful. We loved hearing the falls, the fish drew kids from the neighborhood, and as small business owners, our businesses thrived for many years. When we decided to sell the home, a realtor suggested we remove the water feature because she felt it might appear as a hazard to people with small children. From the moment we removed the pond, energy shifted in both of our businesses, resulting in challenging times.

Everything is energy. The Taoists created a methodology we can follow to create a harmonious flow in our lives. I have seen it at work, and I have witnessed when I stray from it how energy stagnates, stops, and even retreats. If we are to spend a lengthy period somewhere, then shouldn't we love it, and shouldn't it support us in every way possible?

If you want to shift energy, bring Feng Shui into your life. Use it at home, at work, and anywhere else to create a harmonious flow. It really works!

February Daily Yoga Practice:
To Unlock the Sweetness of Life

This practice is for all levels, and no yoga experience is required. However, it is always recommended to consult a doctor before beginning any new physical program. Remember to modify anything for particular conditions that you may be experiencing, and to always follow your breath for the truth about a feeling that arises.

<u>Yoga Posture Sequence to Allow the Sweetness Flow</u>:

Energetically focus on the water element, going with the flow with ease and grace. Try to allow movements to move stuck energy in your body. Focus on the hips and opening the lower back and pelvic areas to allow this energy to move more freely through you. Note any emotions that arise, and always breathe deeply when in the postures, using *ujjayi* breath.

The water element is quite eclectic. It can be still, like a pond, slow, like a lazy river, or fast, like a waterfall. With this in mind, start any movements slowly, warming up by feeling into your body. Allow the breath to synchronize the movements, like a moving meditation. If you find yourself in the groove, you may naturally move a little faster through repeated postures; however, stay committed to being mindful and careful without pushing yourself— this applies to all postures.

<u>Single Posture Practice</u>: One-Legged Pigeon (*Adho Mukha Eda Pada Rajakapotasana*)

On your hands and knees or from downward-facing dog, step the right foot forward and across behind the left wrist, sliding the foot in towards the body. Carefully bring the right knee down to the floor behind the right wrist. Check that your right knee is to the right side of the mat and that the leg is diagonal on the yoga mat from right to left. Keep the hips squared towards the floor, not leaning to the right side. If this occurs, pull the foot closer to your body. Lengthen the left leg backwards, pointing the toes towards the back wall and spiraling the left inner thigh upwards towards the sky. Come onto the tips of your fingers and walk them up to your body, lengthening your spine. Look back over each shoulder and ensure that the left leg and foot are straight, making any adjustments that you may need. Look forward and slowly exhale, walk the arms out, coming down onto the forearms, and with the option of bringing the forehead to the floor. Close your eyes, if you are comfortable with that, and gaze towards the center of your forehead. Repeat with the left leg forward.

> * Modification/Variation: Supine posture, crossing the right foot to the left thigh, flexing the right foot, and allowing the right knee to drift away from the body without shifting the hips and pelvis. Some people may stay here, or you can lift the left leg and hold it with your hands, drawing it into your chest. You can also use a yoga strap or belt to wrap under the left knee and pull it towards you. Or you can place the left foot against the wall. Keep your head down flat on the floor, lengthening your spine. Use a pillow under the head if needed. Continue to energetically push the right knee forward and simultaneously pull the left thigh inward. Eyes can be open or closed, focusing on one spot. Take several deep breaths. Repeat with left leg crossing over right thigh.

Mudra & Meditation:

Come to easy-seated pose or Lotus pose. Place your hands on your lap, palms up. Touch thumb to pinkie finger for the *Varuna mudra* or water hand position. Spend time in meditation/reflection. Then close the practice by bringing your hands to your heart, bowing your head, and closing with an intention, prayer, or reciting your sankalpa. Notice any areas within you that now seem to have more flow and energy.

Breathing Practice: *Ujjayi* or "Ocean Sounding"

Begin seated in a comfortable position with the spine straight. Draw the throat backwards as you inhale through the nostrils, making a soft sound like the ocean. On exhale, keep the throat slightly closed, creating the same soft noise—we call this the Ujjayi breath. Some people refer to it as the Ocean Sounding Breath since it mimics the sound of the ocean's waves crashing upon the shore. Other people refer to it as the "Darth Vader" breath because the sound is similar to the famous Star Wars character. Another nice explanation is to pretend that you are fogging up a mirror, but with your mouth closed. Use the same muscles for the exhalations.

Ujjayi breathing should be soft, not forced, and audible, but not so powerful as to take over all the sound in the room. It is important to relax the other muscles of the face and instill a relaxed, peaceful demeanor while practicing Ujjayi.

Repeat this breathing for several minutes. There is no time frame. Repeat until you feel calm and relaxed. You can bring it into the entire practice. The sound will help keep the mind focused and serene, so that the energy that is brought up will give you more power within the postures. Try using Ujjayi breathing while performing chores that need a little more force, like using a screwdriver, scrubbing the tub, or lifting something heavy. It helps to use this breathing whenever you need to. Try it anytime!

Hatha Yoga Sequence:

Easy Seated – Ujjayi Breathing	Body Rolls	Head/ Neck Rolls	Shoulder Rolls	Cobbler	Animal Stretch with Cat/ Cow
Seated Straddle	Table	Body Circles	Barrel Rolls	Cat/Cow	Child
Downward Dog - Walking	Lizard	Squat	Mountain	Warrior II	Goddess
Standing Starddle Fold	Other Side Repeat: Warrior II, Goddess, Stand FF	Dancer	Extended Leg	Seated Pigeon	Rock on Back
Rolls Back/ Circle Knees	Happy Baby	Corpse - Final Relaxation	Easy Seated or Lotus	Meditation	Closing

* Note that the pre-recorded practice may differ from the sequence above.

Short 15-minute Practice:

- Easy Seated with Breathing & Sankalpa
- Seated body, neck, and shoulder rolls
- Table pose for body and barrel rolls
- Lizard
- Mountain to notice energy flow
- Goddess
- Squat
- Supine Pigeon
- Happy Baby & Corpse

February Recap

The water element is essential to our health and well-being. Without water, there is no life. We begin our life in our mother's womb, feeling safe to grow and manifest into our full being. The dramatic impact of the birthing process can leave individuals uncertain about navigating life and embracing a life filled with joy and happiness. Where January gave us a solid foundation, February provides us with the energy to move, create, and flow.

By the end of February, you should feel more in harmony in your body and your home, thanks to the Feng Shui ritual and yoga practice. But use these practices throughout the month, putting continued emphasis on your sankalpa, so that you can find a true harmony, one that prepares you for the rebirth to come in March.

March

Rebirth

March Energies

The year's third month is known for its common phrase, "March comes in like a lion, and out like a lamb." In the Northern Hemisphere, March can be a tricky month—thus the lion and lamb analogy. Often, March begins with freezing temperatures, bringing the most difficult winter storms. Conditions are mixed throughout the month with both temperate and frigid days. Then, usually near the end of the month, Spring arrives, the first glimpse of new life appears, and the sun shines brightly. Mother Earth has her cycles. There's no rhyme or reason to March regarding year-to-year comparisons, so we must honor its prerogative to be mutable. This also teaches us to trust the Universe's flow and know that everything sorts itself out in its own timing.

Three (3) represents growth, expansion, and spiritual synthesis, often associated with dynamic energy and transformation. Whether it is uniting duality by reconciling two extremes into a third "side" or the significance of the mystical energy of the triadic nature of the cycle of life-death-rebirth, the fiery energy of March provides the transformative qualities desired in any spiritual endeavor, and yet it does so quite naturally.

March flows in off the Piscean waters of Neptune, an angry, vengeful god whose violent tendencies are associated with the raging waters of the Ocean—a powerful force to be respected. Pisces is represented by two fish, seeming to be swimming in opposite directions. While the Pisces of February tend to be more visionaries and dreamers, those falling deeper into March are more concerned with the material aspects of life. Thus, all are on full alert by the time fiery Aries energy charges in. Aries is ruled by the god of war, Mars, and represented by the ram, the four-legged beast known for beating its head against the hardest surfaces, over and over and over again. As the baby of the zodiac, Aries makes up for its immaturity with its strength and determination.

The flower of the month, Daffodils, represents rebirth, our theme for the month. Our gemstone for March is Aquamarine, often equated with serenity and calming energy; however, it is also a stone of renewal and courage—qualities that ignite personal transformation.

Growth and expansion wouldn't happen without fire, the element associated with Aries and the third chakra. Between that, the powerful weather patterns, and the spiritual synthesis of the triad, March is a robust month full of life and energy.

This is a perfect month to drive vast amounts of energy towards your sankalpa. And the practices for March will assist you in doing so.

Holidays and Holy Days

March was originally the first month of the year in the Roman calendar due to the Spring Equinox, and many spiritual traditions still adhere to this timeframe, celebrating their New Year. The Spring Equinox occurs when the night and day are at equal length and begins the time of the year in the Northern hemisphere where our first buds of Spring sprout. This occurs on or around the 20th-21st of March, and was originally known as *Ostara* or *Eostre*, which later became known as Easter. Although Easter can fall in March, because it follows a lunar calendar, it sometimes arrives in April; therefore, we must consider more pagan roots for the essential meanings. Eggs have always represented new life and growth, and are a common symbol for Ostara, Easter, and other respective Spring Equinox holidays.

Vikram Samvat, the Hindu New Year, is celebrated on the full moon day of March or April. *Nyepi* is the Balinese New Year, which occurs the day after the new moon in March or April. And *Losar*, the Tibetan New Year, is also celebrated in March on the first day of the lunisolar calendar. We have already talked about the many New Year holidays in January, but there is a significance in the energy of new beginnings, combined with March's energy of rebirth and transformation, having these holidays pop up again now with an emphasis on witnessing the actual progress through the first blooms of Spring in March.

For Christians, Lent and the holidays leading up to Easter are paramount to their faith. Easter can fall in March, and even when it doesn't, Lent and Ash Wednesdays can. Lent, the six weeks of penitence before Easter, is a time of prayer and fasting. Fasting, a practice employed by mystics globally, offers numerous transformative benefits for the body, mind, and spirit. Hindus can also fast during this time for *Maha Shivaratri*, honoring the birthday of Lord Shiva and the overcoming of ignorance/darkness. And then there are the holy days of Islam that often fall in March.

Ramadan is a month of fasting (*sawm*) from dawn to sunset, prayer, charity (*zakat*), and self-purification, observed by Muslims worldwide. It occurs in the 9th month, and often in March, as it falls in 2025. It's a period of intensified spiritual practice culminating in *Laylat al-Qadr*, the "Night of Power," commemorating the Qur'an's revelation to Prophet Muhammad and *Eid al-Fitr*, the festival of breaking the fast, with prayers, feasting, and charity, signifying the end of Ramadan.

St. Patrick's Day, when the patron saint of Ireland is honored for bringing Christianity to Ireland, occurs on March 17th every year. Finally, a holiday with a fixed date for March! And what is the symbol for this day? The shamrock, a three-leafed clover!

Of course, there are many more holidays and holy days from vast spiritual traditions that can fall in March each year. The thread of commonality in many of them is the focus on overcoming challenges through faith and alignment with God, in the triadic cycle that culminates in rebirth.

Chakra Connection

3rd Chakra

Sanskrit: *Manipura*
Meaning: *mani* = jewels or brilliance, *pura* = city or house
Location: Solar Plexus

This is the *Hara* center, a power center that provides balance, stability, strength, and activity. In martial arts, it is considered the center of Chi (life force). It is the center of the lower mind, objective, and material, influenced by the emotions.

Manipura is the name of the third chakra, and means "lustrous gem." The color yellow and the connection to the sun, and personal power, spotlight March's energetic quality of being the impetus driving energy upward towards manifestation. January gave us our foundation, and with that solid base, February allowed us to flow and create. Now, for March, it is time to kick it into high gear!

Plants do not grow without the sun's energy. How will your sankalpa manifest without popping it with shots of energy? See the companion Workbook for more questions, but consider these few journal prompts on your third chakra:

Energy: Do you feel vital and alive?

Autonomy/Individualization: Do you have a strong sense of self?

Fire: Fire transforms; are you comfortable with using fire energy when needed?

The Yantra (mystical diagram) is a ten-petaled lotus flower whose Vrittis (whirlpool) are spiritual ignorance, thirst, jealousy, treachery, shame, fear, disgust, delusion, foolishness, and sadness..

The inverted fiery triangle with a blazing sun at its center, the downward-pointed tip indicating the origin, the upward widening indicating growth & development.

Moon Phases

New Moon:

Consider if other things are coming into play that trump your original sankalpa and change your focus. The energy you began to create this year may have opened you up to some other unexpected things. Your Highest Self will be guiding you towards following what is best for it. Do not allow your ego to grab hold of a goal and keep pushing if it is no longer needed. The new moon is a perfect time for shifting course or planting more seeds into your current one, but use the dark moon night to reflect on this.

Full & Waxing Moon:

This cycle of the moon is when its energy is most heightened, which aligns with the energy of the third chakra. Full moon represents manifestation, so if by this time of the year some of your energy towards your sankalpa has dwindled, decide how you can drive energy towards your highest intention in the biggest way possible, and plan to do something huge on the night of the full moon. The energy of the waxing moon is perfect timing to strategize how to best use your energy this month.

Remember February's lessons of creating harmony and going with the flow. You may need to take some reflection time this month to assess if things are not flowing in the right direction for you, but something else has come up that feels right on a deep level. One of the pitfalls of the third chakra is that a little will and fire go a long way. Too much, and we create brushfires and devastation. So temper the fire a little bit by grounding to the Earth and honoring the flow of water energy as well. Never forget the lessons you learned as you grow, and how to use them cumulatively as you continue on your path.

Dark to Waning Moon:

After the full moon and up to the dark moon night, you will want to lay off pushing energy, or else you may burn out. This represents the balancing aspect of March. You need to cultivate some restoration after that full moon, when the moon is waning and going dark. This will keep you in balance and not allow your energy to diminish, losing out on manifesting what you were truly meant to do because you feel depleted. And since spring is just beginning, you are not going to want to miss the growing sunlight's energy the next few months and its ability to help you ignite more towards your goals.

Don't forget to use the night of the dark moon to reflect on the sankalpa and if it still serves your energy appropriately.

Faith Tradition: Islam

"Beyond the ideas of wrongdoing and right-doing, there is a field. I'll meet you there. When the soul lies down in that grass, the world is too full to talk about."

– Jalaluddin Rumi

Islam is the second-largest and fastest-growing religion in the world. NPR finds that by 2050, it will have equal numbers to Christianity and then surpass it to be the largest faith tradition in the world.[33] And even though Islam is one of the three Abrahamic religions and shares the Old Testament of the Bible with both Christianity and Judaism, it is perhaps the most misunderstood religion to Westerners.

The five pillars of Islam refer to the creed of confession of faith that "There is no god but God," and "Muhammad is God's prophet," consistently praying five times a day, giving at least 2 1/2 percent of one's wealth to charity, making a pilgrimage to Mecca at least once in one's life, and observing Ramadan.

The Persian Sufi poet and mystic, Jalaluddin Rumi (1207–1273), frequently explored themes of spiritual rebirth in his poetry, particularly the transformation of the soul through divine love. His quote, "Die before you die, and rise in the Beloved," shows us this.[34]

With such significance in its practices that fall during Ramadan, and the transformative energy of spiritual renewal, Islam feels like a perfect faith tradition for March.

---

[33] https://www.npr.org/sections/thetwo-way/2015/04/02/397042004/muslim-population-will-surpass-christians-this-century-pew-says

[34] https://www.kosmosjournal.org/kj_article/die-before-you-die/

Symbol: Phoenix

The Winged Heart is the Sufi symbol of universal spirituality, embracing all paths to the Divine, reflecting Sufism's inclusiveness. However, there is another winged symbol also associated with the Sufis, that of the Phoenix. The Phoenix is a mythical bird that, near the end of its life, sets its nest ablaze and then returns, rejuvenated from the ashes.

Although the first symbol of the Phoenix can be found in Egypt as a sacred bird associated with the sun god, Ra, Sufis adapted it from Persian mythology, as the bird of wisdom and renewal named Simurgh. Found in Christian, Buddhist, Hindu, Chinese, and other cultures and belief systems, the Phoenix has many symbolic meanings and can often signify a purification or catharsis through death.

The Phoenix's fiery connection feels most appropriate for our March energies.

March Altar

- **Altar cloth:** Yellow, the color of the third chakra, is associated with solar energy, represented in the increase of the sun every day after the spring equinox and up to the summer solstice

- **Flowers:** Daffodils, representing the rebirth of spring

- **Candles:** Three candles, representing the Trinity: one white for purity, one red for devotion, and one gold for divinity and the Trinity

- **Crystal/Stone:** Aquamarine stone, prayer bead or bracelet, or necklace. Some people prefer to work with Citrine as a yellow stone for March, while others like Tiger's Eye, which is a brownish-gold color. Any of these stones will work nicely on your altar or worn in March.

- **Symbol:** Picture of the Phoenix, representing rebirth from the fiery flames of transformation

- **Essential Oil/Incense:** Myrrh, Middle East resin for cleansing and rebirth

- **Herbs:** Ceremonial White Sage and Ginger, as mentioned in the Qur'an as one of the beverages of Paradise.

- **Other items (optional):**
  - *The Modern Mystic's Wheel of the Year* Book, Workbook, and Oracle Deck
  - Fire-pot or cauldron
  - Symbol of the sun
  - Let's light a fire under your sankalpa by bringing items that inspire your Sacred Heartfelt Vow.

Angel/Ancestor: Archangel Gabriel

Archangel Gabriel's name means "The Strength of God." He's one of the two archangels specifically named in the Bible, with strong ties to several traditions. He's the angel who appeared to Daniel in the Old Testament to help him understand his visions.

Daniel 8:15-26:
A voice commands, "Gabriel, make this man understand the vision" (Daniel 8:16). Gabriel appears "like the appearance of a man" and explains the vision, revealing it concerns "the time of the end" (8:17). He details the rise and fall of kings.

Daniel 9:21-27:
"The man Gabriel, whom I had seen in the vision at the first, came to me in swift flight" (9:21). He delivers the prophecy of the "Seventy Weeks," predicting Jerusalem's rebuilding, the coming of an "anointed one" (messiah), and further trials.

In Islamic texts, Gabriel (Jibril or Jibra'il) is the chief messenger angel, delivering revelations to Adam and Muhammad, ultimately providing him with the Qur'an.

Hadith of Gabriel (Sahih al-Bukhari, Book 2, Hadith 43):
Context: Jibril appears as a man in white with black hair to Muhammad and his companions. He teaches the core of Islam, confirming his role as a divine educator. Muhammad later identifies him as Jibril, saying, "That was Gabriel who came to teach the people their religion."

Jibril's Revelations to Prophets (Sahih Bukhari, Book 55, Hadith 605):
He is described as the angel who brought revelations to all prophets, including figures in the Old Testament, such as Adam, Noah, Abraham, Moses, and Daniel. He consoled Adam after the Fall (Genesis 3), taught Noah to build the ark (Genesis 6), and delivered messages to Moses and Daniel.[35]

Tafsir on Surah 16:102 and 26:192–193:

---

[35] *New World Encyclopedia* (web:6)

Surah 16:102 says, "The Holy Spirit has brought it [Qur'an] down from your Lord."

Archangel Gabriel is known as the Messenger or Dreamer. He brings us messages, guides, and supports us in our spiritual endeavors and life. He is often referred to as having a white ray or halo, and is also supposed to be the Archangel of the Western direction.

<u>Invoking Archangel Gabriel to be Your Messenger</u>:

"Dear Archangel Gabriel, thank you for giving me clear messages and for guiding and supporting me to be a clear messenger to help others, as you do."[36]

To close the prayer, turn your head to the right, saying, "*As-salamu alaykum wa rahmatullah*" (Peace and the mercy of God be upon you). This is addressed to the angels on your right side who record good deeds. Then turn your head to the left and repeat, "*As-salamu alaykum wa rahmatullah.*" This is addressed to the angels on your left side who record wrongdoings

---

[36] *Archangels 101*, page 41

March Ritual: Sufi Whirling Dervish Meditation/*Sema*

Recall a time when you were younger, a time when you felt free and alive. Maybe you threw open your arms, in love with all of the world, and spun yourself around and around and around with pleasure. That is the idea behind the Sufi Whirling Dervish moving meditation.

The Whirling Dervish practice, known as sema, is a central ritual of the Mevlevi Sufi order, inspired by the 13th-century poet and mystic Jalaluddin Rumi. This meditative dance is a profound expression of the Sufi mystical path, where dervishes whirl to mystical music and poetry, symbolizing the soul's journey to God, embodying spiritual rebirth.

The whirling is a deep, moving meditation whereby the constant turning keeps the inward focus reaching ecstatic states of oneness with God. Whirling can take years or a lifetime to master. While the Sufis wear distinct robes and dress with deep symbolism, for our purposes, you may wish to wear flowing robes of your own—white like the Sufis or another color if you prefer. It is said that the skirt evokes the Phoenix's radiant plumage, preparing for fiery transformation, while the circular space reflects the cosmic orbit of rebirth. Since it is March, you can also wear the colors associated with the Phoenix and fire: orange and yellow.

Music drives the movement of whirling. Artist Omar Faruk Tekbilek offers a free 10-minute piece on his YouTube channel that you can access here to start: https://www.youtube.com/watch?v=BkxkJwW5tNY. Begin slowly and follow the music's pace as you move. You can always download another track and play it on a loop for longer dances.

<u>Three Parts of the Dance</u>:

- <u>*Na'at* or Praise to the Prophet</u> - Recite this: "Love is the path of my Prophet. I was born through love, Love is my mother," from the poetry of Rumi.
- <u>Flute and/or Drum Solo</u>
- <u>The Whirling</u> - To begin whirling, spin clockwise with one hand raised (to receive divine grace), one lowered (to share with earth), and eyes tilted upward. The ritual includes four *salams* (cycles), each with a focus:
    1. Recognizing God's truth, beginning the soul's ascent
    2. Surrendering the ego
    3. Experiencing divine love
    4. Returning transformed

Dervishes gradually slow their spinning, returning to stillness with arms crossed, symbolizing unity with God. They bow to the *Sheikh*, acknowledging the journey's completion.

Upon completion of the whirling dance, many read prayers or the Qur'an, but you can also read and reflect on Rumi's poetry.

<u>Whirling Tips:</u>

- Best done on an empty stomach
- Wear loose clothing
- Keep your eyes open but soft and unfocused
- If nausea arises, discontinue the meditation

The Indian Mystic, Osho, offers this advice: "Become a whirlpool, an energy whirlpool, lost completely in it: no witnessing, no effort to observe. Don't try to see; be the whirlpool, be the whirling.

In the beginning, you may not be able to stand so long, but remember one thing: don't stop by yourself, don't stop the whirling. If you feel it is impossible, the body will fall automatically, but don't stop. If you fall, there is no problem; the process is complete. But don't play tricks with yourself, don't deceive. Don't think that now you are tired, so it is better to stop. No, don't make a decision on your part. If you are tired, how can you go on? You will fall automatically. So don't stop yourself; let the whirling itself come to a point where you fall down."[37]

For those who wish to dive deeper into the Whirling Dervish practice, a wealth of knowledge about this practice can be found at: <u>https://memorycherish.com/whirling-dervishes</u>.

---

[37] https://www.osho.com/meditation/osho-active-meditations/osho-whirling-meditation

Tracey's Personal Reflection

Spinning for a child is effortless. Children naturally trust, have robust enthusiasm, and a plethora of energy. They're also a lot closer to the floor, so when they fall tend not to get very banged up. On the other hand, twirling for adults can be riskier. Assuredly, you need the space for this month's ritual, and if being inside doesn't work, you may need to move it outside to a clear place, free of tripping hazards, and perhaps even a soft ground for a more pleasurable landing, should you require one.

I always loved to spin. I recall many times in my younger years, holding onto a friend's hands and whirling each other around and around, both of us laughing and eventually crashing to the ground.

The picture below was taken in my late 40s, at one of my last yoga studios. It was a moment when I felt full of life, exuding joy, and overtaken by Spirit. Someone had done a Whirling Dervish Meditation at the yoga studio years before, but I couldn't get into it then. I was probably more worried about someone getting hurt. But on this day, I put on some of my favorite yoga music, full of mantras and soulful melody, I threw open my arms, and I spun and spun and spun. Yes, I set up my camera. Social media days were upon us, and even though I didn't know what I might use the photo for. I hope you can see the joy and free abandon through the picture.

I'm not sure how long it lasted, but I can say that time felt irrelevant once I was in this space with Spirit. And no, I didn't fall. I simply slowed down and then rested on the floor for some time, basking in the glory I felt.

While I do not consider myself a master of Whirling Dervish, I can admit to loving to spin and twirl, even in the second half of my 50s. While other friends and family members suggest that they "get sick" in this movement, I still find it exhilarating!

March Daily Yoga Practice:
For Energy of Rebirth

This practice is for all levels, and no yoga experience is required. However, it is always recommended to consult a doctor before beginning any new physical program. Remember to modify anything for particular conditions that you may be experiencing, and to always follow your breath for the truth about a feeling that arises.

Yoga Posture Sequence to Energize the 3rd Chakra:

Energetically focus on the fire element and building fire for transformation. Heat will build quickly, so work at a comfortable pace, not allowing the fire to get out of hand. Focus on the abdominal area and mid-back, or "core," also known as the solar plexus. Breathe deeply when in the postures, using *ujjayi* breath unless it is an appropriate time to use the *Kapalabhati* breathing.

Do not equate fire with fast. Feel for a slow burn in your practice. This will allow you to continually be mindful of your posture and work in a comfortable place that's available to you. For some, energy can rise too quickly, causing dizziness and symptoms of overheating. If this occurs, come to the floor and work on grounding and slow, deep breaths, perhaps breathing in through the nose and out through the mouth.

Single Posture Practice: Seated Spinal Twist (*Ardha Matsyendrasana*)

From a seated position, stretch the legs forward, flexing the feet and pulling the flesh from under the seat out. Bring the right leg in towards the hip with the foot flat on the floor. If possible, cross the right foot over the left leg, placing it flat on the floor. Flex the left foot and engage the left leg. Draw the belly in and lift the spine towards the sky, feeling each of your spinal vertebrae creating space. Use the left hand to pull the right knee in towards your chest as you gently twist the body to the right side and into the bent knee. Place your right hand behind your body, like a kickstand. Now bend the left elbow and place it above the right knee, pressing against it to twist your upper chest and neck to the right. Gaze over the right shoulder, just past your nose, taking several deep breaths into the belly. Twist from the upper chest and neck, but keep the lower back and hips grounded and stable. Repeat pose, bending the left knee and twisting to the left side.

Modifications/Variations: Supine Spinal Twist *(Supta Matsyendrasana)*

Lie on your back, lengthening the spine. Pull the right knee to the chest, taking several deep breaths. Option to stay here, breathing into the belly. To twist, bring the right knee to the left side of the body, and scoot the left hip underneath the right, bringing both hips to the center of the mat, stacked on top of each other. The left leg should be straight while placing the bent right knee across the body. If the right knee does not touch the floor, place pillows or yoga blocks under it. Open the arms, working the right shoulder as flat to the mat as possible. You can try to lift the left shoulder and nudge the right down. Turn your head to the right, gazing passed your right hand and fingers. Repeat bending the left knee into the chest with the option to twist.

Mudra & Meditation:

Come to easy-seated pose or Lotus seated pose. Place hands on lap, palms up. Touch thumb to ring finger for the *Agni mudra* or fire hand position. Spend time in meditation/reflection. Then close the practice by bringing your hands to your heart, bowing your head, and closing with an intention or prayer, perhaps restating your sankalpa.

Breathing Practice: Kapalabhati

"Breath of Fire" or Kapalabhati breathing is rapid pumping of the abdominal muscles that creates intense heat, fast. Take a few deep breaths through the nose, in and out. When ready, inhale deeply, then on the exhalation, sharply draw the abdominal muscles back (some people say in and upward). On the exhale, release the abdominal muscles. Repeat. The pace can start slowly and build to be quite rapid. This pumping should continue for twenty to forty rounds. If you get dizzy, stop or slow down.

Kapalabhati is a very important cleansing yogic breathing that also initiates the fire energy in the belly, which helps to transform and cleanse. There are some contraindications, however, for this dynamic breathing exercise. Do not perform this breath if you have had recent surgery, unmedicated high blood pressure, are pregnant, hernia, colitis, or woman during menstruation.

Hatha Yoga Sequence:

Easy Seated – Kapalabhati Breathing	Lateral Body Stretches	Seated Spinal Twists	Seated Forward Fold	Table-Top	Upward Boat
Table	Cat/Cow	Downward Dog	Core Stabilization	Downward Dog	Plank
Child	Side Planks	Low Cobra	Locust	Downward Boat	Child or Downward Dog
Standing Forward Fold	Mountain	Chair	Warrior I	Warrior III	Bridge
Supine Spinal Twists	Fish	Corpse - Final Relaxation	Easy Seated or Lotus	Meditation	Closing

* Note that the pre-recorded practice may differ from the sequence above.

Short 15-minute Practice:

- Kapalabhati breathing
- Seated Lateral Bends & Twists
- Upward Boat
- Downward Dog
- Core Stabilization
- Plank
- Supine Twists
- Corpse Pose

March Recap

Sometimes it feels like we have lived lifetimes once we get to the third month of the year, and sometimes we have! Once the fires begin, we have the energy behind us to catapult our wishes and deepest desires to fruition. The rituals and practices for March will help you when you feel stuck or just in the continuation of moving energy forward. But if you start to feel burnt out, take a break. March begins the gradual building of energy towards the Summer Solstice in June, so we are only beginning to feel it coming, but, oh, what a month!

Remember to work with the moon phases for optimum support from the energy in the sky—as above, so below. While we began the year with an intimate sankalpa, by March, we will see some of the fruition of the seeds that we planted for the New Year, and we must make adjustments accordingly. By the end of March and with blooms sprouting, April moves us upward into the heart and a space of love. It will help us to calm the fires when the ego can get out of control.

April

Love & Devotion

April Energies

If there ever was a theme that had been spoken of, written about, or art created in the name of, it is that of love. Love transcends time. Love has no borders or boundaries. Love can heal even the most rotten—ask the Grinch. Love is the whole reason that we are here in this life. We incarnate to learn lessons and be better people. This implies that we may have done some unloving things in another lifetime, or that we experienced love and it was so moving and so meaningful that we wanted to experience it again in an even bigger way. Let's explore why love is the theme for April, our fourth month of the year.

The meaning of April comes from the Latin *Aprilis*, which has a link to the Greek goddess Aphrodite, the goddess of love and beauty. In Numerology, the number four (4) means love and compassion. And the fourth chakra's energy is love and balance. April's birthstone is the diamond, a symbol of love when given as a gift to one's betrothed. As Shakespeare shared, "Love begets love." When we focus on the energy of love, we bring more loving energy towards us.

The popular saying, "April showers bring May flowers," holds true for many places in the North. The Spring Equinox passed, the days are getting longer, and the sun's energy is warming up the area. Combine this energy with a little water, and soon things are blooming everywhere. Certain plants begin blooming as early as February or March, ensuring that by April, all flowers and trees are starting to bud and blossom. Many people begin to experience "spring fever" and feel the need to run away for the day or take time off work or school. This is happening because we are feeling the growing light, and we are feeling more expansive than the former confines of winter.

Interestingly, the two zodiac signs in the fourth month are those of Aries, the Ram, and Taurus, the Bull. Both are very strong energies—one of fire and the other of earth. Isn't love the strongest energy? You will probably note that those born at this time have strength of character that can appear abrupt or challenging, but comes from a deep sense of love and purpose. These are the sorts of people that you can count on when the going gets tough because they will always be there for the people that they love.

As mentioned, April's gemstone is the Diamond, known for its strength, but also the symbol of love and marriage in an engagement ring. Daisies are the flower for April, representing youth. But in Norse mythology, the daisy is the sacred flower of Freyja, goddess of love and beauty.

It is easy to see the connectivity to the energy of love for April, rather than for February, as some might consider, with its contrived Valentine's Day. With love comes devotion, the energy of Divine love, something we learned about in March's Sufism tradition.

And so, we move into this high-vibrational month with an open heart. And do remember that April's element is air, so use your words lovingly and kindly, and tell those close to you how much they mean to you daily. Allow your loving words to flow through the air, elevating everyone around you.

Holidays and Holy Days

April 1st is known as "April Fool's Day," which, at first glance, may not seem very loving. The origins of this holiday stem back to ancient cultures that celebrated New Year's Day on or around April 1st, as it was closest to the original New Year of the equinox. There are many other stories about how April Fool's Day spread across other countries, but what is most interesting is the connection to The Fool in the Tarot cards. Of the seventy-eight cards in the deck, the Fool is the first one: the number zero (0), considered to be the highest card in the deck.

Typically depicted as a beggar or vagabond, the Fool looks upward towards the heavens, with his heart wide open, as he appears to be about to step off a cliff. There is no care in his world because he has faith and love on his side. He fully trusts that the Universe is with him every step of the way. Interestingly, in regular playing cards, the Fool is used as a trump card that can fill in for any other card that the player needs to finish a play. The Fool is versatile and the most valued card to have when playing cards. In Tarot, the Fool represents believing in the universe and having faith in the future. This childlike quality of trust comes from a very special, loving place that you find when you are at peace with Great Spirit and your place in the Universe. He epitomizes the energy of love and devotion!

The Fool reminds me of another guy who took a giant leap, the Hindu god Hanuman. Hanuman is the monkey god and a loyal devotee of Rama. The famous story disclosed in the epic tale, the *Ramayana,* says that Rama's wife and soul lover, Sita, was captured by the Demon Ravana and taken to what is now Sri Lanka. Sita and Rama's love story is legendary, but so is the love and devotion of Hanuman for his king, Rama. Hanuman, upon coming to the Cliffside in India facing Sri Lanka, is forced to take drastic measures, leaps effortlessly across the divide, saves Sita, and returns her to Rama. In yoga, this is where the posture resembling a full split receives its name, "*Hanumanasana.*" Both Hanuman and Rama share a birthday celebration in April, celebrated by Hindus with many festivals and reminders of how love transcends all.

Earth Day, appropriately placed on the twenty-second day of the month as the number 22 is considered the highest "Master Number" in numerology, symbolizing spiritual purpose, life path, and inspiration to take right action. Currently, we have one planet, and it is in a cycle of depletion, superstorms, and misuse. It is safe to say that every person has a responsibility, of the highest level, to do his/her part in increasing our planet's health and vitality, thus ensuring the longevity of our species. If we are to speak of the energy of love, how can we not discuss the loving action we must take for the very ground that we walk upon? How can we not pour love into attending to Mother Earth? We can no longer turn away, expecting someone else to do the work. We must all work together. This is a call for all of us, and it is of the utmost urgency.

I would be amiss not to mention that if Easter were to fall in April, we would have an opportunity to expand to what we refer to as "Christ-Consciousness." In other words, it is our divine nature to expand to the essence held by Jesus Christ. This was exemplified in his teaching:

Chakra Connection

4th Chakra

Sanskrit: *Anahata*
Meaning: Unstuck, unbeaten, or unhurt
Location: Cardiac Plexus, Heart-Center

The Anahata Chakra is the inner temple where the divine *atma* (the flame of life) resides. Self-realization, also known as God-Realization, involves the recognition of our own Self, the *atma*.

April's energy of the fourth month aligns with the fourth chakra, Anahata, which means, "unstruck," "unhurt" or "unbeaten," for it is true that in the end, only love will prevail.

The color of this energy center is green, like the color of most plants on Earth. This is the chakra in the middle of the three lower and three upper chakras in the human body, and, as a bridge, can heal all of the others. Coming off the fiery energy of Manipura, Anahata tempers the flames with a cool breeze as it represents the air element. In fact, without the element of air, we would have nothing in which to stoke the fire to begin with, would we?

We are reminded again to always move from a place of love in all of our thoughts and actions, to ensure that we are projecting the right energy into the world. How do we determine if we are working appropriately? See the companion Workbook for more questions, but consider these few journal prompts on your fourth chakra:

Love: Do you allow yourself to receive love just as easily as you give it?

Relationships: Who are the most significant relationships in your life?

Devotion: Do you feel a deep devotion to any person, place, or thing?

The Anahata Chakra is the inner temple where the divine atma resides. Self-realization, also known as God-Realization, involves the recognition of atma, the part of us that is pure, unchanging, Infinite Consciousness, and love is the key energy.

The Yantra (mystical diagram) of the fourth chakra is a 12-petalled lotus representing the qualities of joy, peace, love, harmony, bliss, charity, purity, compassion, understanding, forgiveness, patience, and kindness. The 6-pointed star, or hexagram, at the middle of the symbol consists of two interlaced triangles, one pointed up and one down, symbolizing the power of Spirit and matter merging, and the feminine & masculine harmonizing.

Moon Phases

<u>New Moon</u>:

On this month's new moon, do something that deepens or rekindles the energy of love in your primary relationship—whether with yourself, another person, or with Spirit. Spending a quiet night at home, unplugging from electronics and external stimuli, can be all that you need to create a romantic and/or deeply loving environment to connect. If you are by yourself, make your favorite dinner. Take a hot bath or soak in the tub with rose petals, and afterwards rub rose oil on your skin. Go to bed early and allow yourself to do anything else that feels loving and kind.

<u>Waxing Moon</u>:

As you work through the waxing moon stage, focus on the energy of love in all things: your relationships, work, and all other aspects of your life. Notice where there is a lack of loving feelings, and try to work on creating more of it by focusing on what you appreciate in each aspect.

Concerning your sankalpa, infuse it with love and continued devotion, as well. This will ensure that you are truly aligned with your commitment.

<u>Full Moon</u>:

When the full moon hits again, do something wonderful with someone you are particularly close to. Plan a special evening, and avoid any hot buttons that may lead to challenging subjects. Of course, if that special someone is yourself, you should not find it too difficult to have an enjoyable evening, as long as you are not engaging in negative self-talk. It may be good to write yourself a love letter you can read on the night of the full moon. This is a great evening to spend with your best friend. Loving relationships with friends also need energy and connection.

<u>Waning Moon</u>:

After the full moon, when the energy starts to wane, know that love is still all around you. Keep feeling the love, sending the love, and moving from a place of love. Push as much love into every day that you can. Be a love pusher! Send love to strangers. Send love to the dearly departed. Then, when you get good at sending out love to those you love, start sending love to those who have previously wronged you. Send love to those you currently have difficulties with. Just keep sending the love. You can send love by visualizing the person, and sending a green beam of light to them, or it could be writing a kind note that you burn instead of sending, or by reaching out to them lovingly.

But that's not the end. When you have worked through those with whom you have had challenges, it is time to send love to those who may wish to harm you. That's right. To truly be a loving soul, we must continue to send love to even the darkest parts of the planet. When we do this, we allow the light to shine. This is our true goal this month—to awaken the light in all living beings, through love.

As for that sacred sankalpa, nothing brings more emphasis to what lights your heart on fire than loving energy. If you spend time focusing on improving love in every facet of your life and being, this heartfelt goal will naturally flourish.

Faith Tradition: Christianity

"Lord, make me an instrument of your peace: where there is hatred, let me sow love; where there is injury, pardon; where there is doubt, faith; where there is despair, hope; where there is darkness, light; where there is sadness, joy."

– St. Francis of Assisi, Prayer of St. Francis

While all faith traditions profess to hold dearest to their tenets the covenant of love, alas, we must choose one for the month. Christianity may have the largest membership of any religion in the world, but that doesn't provide the best reason for it to grace the space of the theme of love. What provides a good reason, however, is its unassuming founder's sincere intention to pass along the ministry of love to all. One of his most famous quotes is, *Love one another, as I have loved you, so you must love one another.* – John 13:34-35

Jesus Christ was born of humble origins. We know about his famous birth, eventual ministry, and even more famous death and subsequent resurrection, but much of his life remains shrouded in mystery. Some speculate that during the "lost" years, Christ was learning about healing, meditation, and other pathways, possibly through the Indian sages, the *Rishis*. Certainly, Christianity shares many components of compassion, forgiveness, and love with Hinduism and Buddhism. However, this theory is speculation, as there is no written or historical evidence to support these claims.

With Easter often falling in April, celebrating Christ's resurrection seems quite fitting as a tradition for April.

Throughout Christian history, numerous mystics have emerged, with Mary Magdalene, the original Christian mystic, serving as a central figure in this tradition. With love as the primary theme, we lean into this faith tradition for April's aspect of love and devotion as perhaps the most written-about system of faith in the world.

Symbol: Rose

The cross is the central Christian symbol, representing Christ's selfless love, redemption, and resurrection. It would be fitting to use the cross as the symbol for April. However, the rose is a potent symbol of love, beauty, and divine devotion, often associated with the Virgin Mary and linked to Mary Magdalene in mystical traditions.

The rose is a symbol of purity, due to its perfection and beauty, and is also a universal symbol of love, two qualities quite significant in Christianity. In the *Encyclopedia of Secret Signs and Symbols*, it is noted that the rose is also a symbol of secrecy, which is intriguing when considering the Magdalene energies we work with this month, and the methods in which the Divine Feminine has been severely relegated from the interworking of Christianity and the mystery schools in which Christ and Mary Magdalene may have been initiated.

April blooms illuminate this beautiful flower. And in our ritual, we will learn that the oil Spikenard's floral fragrance also aligns with the rose.

April Altar:

- **Altar cloth:** Green, the color of the fourth chakra, and much life on planet Earth

- **Flower:** A bouquet of Daisies, Sweet Peas, or Roses with ample greenery

- **Candle:** Green or pink candles

- **Crystal/Stone:** Diamonds may be difficult to find or purchase. Consider a Herkimer Diamond, which is a powerful type of quartz that comes from Herkimer, NY. If you cannot find one, use a Rose Quartz or Green Calcite to emit the energy of love.

- **Symbol:** Anything with a heart or in the shape of a heart, along with more roses, particularly if you don't have them on the altar as flowers

- **Essential Oil/Incense:** Rose, a Christian symbol of both Mother Mary & Mary Magdalene, representing love, devotion, and tenderness, plus Spikenard, Olive (or Rose) for the ritual

- **Herbs:** Ceremonial White Sage and Mint, as April's official birth month herb, reflecting the fresh, revitalizing energy of spring

- **Other items (optional):**
    - *The Modern Mystic's Wheel of the Year* Book, Workbook, and Oracle Deck
    - Statue or picture of Christ, Mary Magdalene, or both
    - Pictures of loved ones or any other devotional deity should grace your altar this month—anything that reminds you of unconditional love.
    - Your sankalpa, the Sacred Heartfelt Vow, needs deep reverence this month, so ensure that something that reminds you of it is on the altar.

Angel/Ancestor: Archangel Raphael

His name means "God Heals," and he is the Green Ray of healing light. Although not specifically mentioned in the Bible, Archangel Raphael has come to be known as one of the most iconic archangels in the brethren.

In Catholicism, he is St. Raphael, patron saint of physicians, travelers, and matchmakers. His symbol is the caduceus, a winged staff with two intertwined serpents, representing peace, diplomacy, and negotiation, linked to the Greek god Hermes, also a messenger. It is often mistaken for the medical symbol, and they are closely related. However, that is the Rod of Asclepius, which features a single snake wrapped around the staff. Either way, both symbols fit nicely for our Archangel.

Raphael is named in several of the Dead Sea Scrolls, always in the capacity of healing.

> 1 Enoch 40:9:
> Here, Raphael is named as one of the four principal archangels, and it is revealed that he "presides over every suffering and every affliction" of the people

> 1 Enoch 10:7:
> God assigns Rachael to "Heal the earth which the angels have corrupted, and proclaim the healing of the Earth."

Angelic Reiki practitioners and other healers and light workers invoke Raphael and other archangels before facilitating any healing work. Starseed entrepreneur, Steve Nobel, guides his clients to work with Raphael as the gatekeeper of the Eastern Direction, that of the rising sun. Initiating Raphael for any healing endeavor ensures swift and speedy action.

Although there is no canonical evidence linking Christ, known for healing miracles in the New Testament, to Archangel Raphael, they do share the healer archetype. In the *Book of Enoch*, Raphael binds the demon Azazel and heals the Earth.[38] The *Book of Enoch* predates Christianity.

---

[38] *Enoch* 10:4–8, 2nd century BCE

In her book *The Archangel Guide*, Doreen Virtue speculates that Archangel Raphael guided Christ's healing ministry; however, that also lacks historical evidence. It's a good thing that Modern Mystics lean into other facets of wisdom, because there's a strong belief that Christ and the Magdalene are so aligned with Raphael.

Archangel Raphael Healing Invocations:

"Dear Archangel Raphael, angel of healing, bring your green ray of light into my field, and heal my body, mind, and soul in all ways. With your light, may I be a perfect specimen of health and well-being. Amen."

"Archangel Raphael, guide my hands to heal as I work in my healing practice. Align my healing with the Highest Light and for the greatest good of all. Amen."

April Ritual: Anointing of the Feet

Many believe Christ spent time in India, learning from the Rishis and Ascetics about yoga, meditation, and healing. Many theories exist concerning his relationship with Mary Magdalene, backed by The Gospel of Mary, a part of the Gnostic Gospels found in Nag Hammadi, Egypt, in 1945. The proof of Christ's history comes mainly from the Bible's New Testament Gospels, of which the Gospel of Mary didn't make the cut. Rather than speculate on these reasons, suffice it to say that she was a pivotal figure in his work.

In Christian mysticism, Mary Magdalene is often seen as a mystic and disciple who exemplifies selfless love and spiritual longing. Her anointing of Christ is a ritual act of love, symbolizing devotion, sacrifice, and spiritual intimacy. She embodies the essence of the true mystic in every sense. The anointing, described in the Gospels (John 12:1-8 and Mark 14:3-9), is a pivotal moment where Mary Magdalene anoints Jesus' feet with costly spikenard oil, using her hair as a towel, preparing him for his death and resurrection. This occurs six days before Passover, as the event is tied to the Jewish lunar calendar.

The ritual is described as Mary pouring the spikenard from an alabaster jar onto Jesus's feet, and letting the oil flow generously, filling the room with fragrance (John 12:3). In Mark 14:3 and Matthew 26:6, the anointing is on Jesus's head, suggesting a dual act. Anointing of the feet symbolizes humility and service, while anointing of the head signifies consecration.

Mary Magdalene's anointing of Christ with spikenard from an alabaster jar embodies the mystical love of April, its fragrant sacrifice and intimate devotion, thus preparing Jesus for resurrection, reflecting Easter's redemptive love.

The devotional act of washing the feet of a spiritual teacher or elder is also found in Hinduism, Sikhism, Buddhism, Jainism, and Islamic Sufism, and as such transcends one faith tradition, just like the essence of love.

Preparation:

Consider who you would like to honor with this anointing tradition for April's ritual. This should be someone who has guided your spiritual journey in some way. It may be a parent, grandparent, or other elder in your family or community, and possibly someone who served as a healer or spiritual teacher for others. It should be someone that you have a profound respect and love for. Once you determine who you will honor with this ritual, schedule a special time to perform it with him/her, uninterrupted.

Items Needed:

- Chair
- Large Towels (2-3)
- Spikenard, Rose Oil, or Olive Oil (perhaps more than one option)
- Foot Bath (optional)
- Tea and/or refreshments

Steps:

1. Guide your loved one, teacher, or elder to the chair, asking him/her to have a seat. Make sure that any telephones are silenced and doors are closed. You will want uninterrupted time for the ritual.

2. Kneel at his/her feet, placing your hands at your heart in prayer. Take several deep breaths here, connecting.

3. When you are ready, thank your special person for being in your life. Detail what they have meant to you, and how much they truly mean to you. Do not rush through this. Take your time. Ask them to receive this loving gesture. If they wish to engage in conversation, honor that.

4. When you're ready, raise their left foot, placing a towel underneath, and allow it to rest on your thighs. Using the appropriate oil, generously rub it into the bottom of the foot. Apply the oil to the top of the foot and massage it in. After lovingly anointing the foot, place it on the towel. Repeat on their right foot.

5. If previously agreed upon, once both feet are anointed, you can proceed to the head. If you are not anointing the head, wrap the feet in the towel, one at a time, wiping off any extra oil, and offering to place their sandals on their feet.

6. Anointing of the head can be done in several ways. At the very least, place a towel on the person's shoulders to catch the extra oil. Using a wash basin or sink may also be a nice way to catch the oils. Ask them to lean their head backward so the oil doesn't run into their eyes. Begin to generously

allow the oil to flow from the forehead backwards and down the hair. Use your hands to pull the oil down the hair, lovingly. Squeeze the end of the hair, allowing the extra oil to run off and down into the towel or basin.

7. When you complete anointing the hair, bring your special person hot tea or their favorite beverage. Then, sit near them on the floor, allowing for the ritual to continue naturally, through conversation, silence, prayer, or however it feels best.

Spend this special time for as long as you can.

You may decide to share this ritual with another person, or many people, in April. It is a lovely ritual that inspires love, deep respect, and complete devotion.

My friend Bógar Argon Carrillo of Blue Dragon Alchemy says of the anointing, "Through scent and sacred touch, Love remembers Itself." To learn more about the alchemy of anointing, contact him at: www.bluedragonalchemy.com

Tracey's Personal Reflection

I am a Thai Bodywork practitioner. This ancient practice, steeped in Thai Buddhism, is a beautiful modality of massage and bodywork that has miraculous healing benefits. I've seen many people get up from a Thai Massage completely refreshed and renewed. I, myself, have received countless sessions in Thailand throughout the years. It is, by far, my favorite type of bodywork to both give and receive.

Before anything else is done, we wash our client's feet. Of course, there are sanitary reasons for this, but the main purpose of washing the feet comes from Buddhism. This is a symbolic act of respect and humility, often practiced before rituals, meditation, or entering sacred spaces. This humble gesture is sincerely missed when I visit Western spas, which profess that they offer Thai Massage. For me, without this gesture, it is not an authentic treatment. When I cannot offer a true washing of the feet, I will at least wash with a basic home-made sanitizer made from water infused with Thyme oil, which is a natural antiseptic.

I have also had the privilege of anointing the feet of both of my Grandmothers, near their death. This act of honoring the person is sometimes also a purification ritual in preparing the physical body for its journey to the afterlife. In both cases, I used Frankincense oil to anoint their feet and the head. In Christian tradition, the forehead is typically anointed; however, certain regional practices also include anointing the feet. This very loving and devotional ritual was a personal experience for me that I did not share with my family.

My beautiful friend, Elina, has her feet washed by Buddhist practitioner, David, before her Thai Massage

Washing and anointing the feet may be different practices, but with the same purpose. I always say that with any ritual, it is about intention. Besides, after working with March's intense month of fire and rebirthing, a big dose of love and humility in April goes a long way.

April Daily Yoga Practice:
To Open to Love

This practice is for all levels, and no yoga experience is required. However, it is always recommended to consult a doctor before beginning any new physical program. Remember to modify anything for particular conditions that you may be experiencing, and to always follow your breath for the truth about a feeling that arises.

<u>Yoga Posture Sequence for Opening to Love</u>:

Energetically focus on breathing in each pose. While holding, feel the breath moving in and out, and send it into the area of the body that you are focusing on. Allow the breath to help you create a deep connection with the body, and imagine that with each breath you are sending the very cells love and healing. If you focus your breathing on the areas of the front and back of the heart center, you will feel a big expansion in this area. As air is the element, we expand upon that through breathing.

Allow the body to move in and out of poses like a light breeze, flowing. We don't need any gusts or hurricane-force winds, so keep it slow and mindful as you move. Emphasizing the movement of breath and body, as we did with the second chakra's water element, is also quite useful as we focus this month on air or wind (vayu).

<u>Single Posture Practice</u>: Heart Openers (Yoga Mudra on left & Eagle Arms on right)

From either a seated or standing position, reach the arms behind the back, interlacing the fingers. Squeeze the shoulder blades together and back, opening the chest. Lift the chest and sternum upward. Gaze is slightly up, towards the ceiling. Hold for several deep breaths. Then release the hands and bring the arms forward in front of the chest.

Next, wrap the right arm under the left, place the hands on opposite shoulders, and hug yourself. Keep arms wrapped, but raise elbows off chest, pulling shoulders forward. Release the hands and bring them up, touching the palms together. Either close your eyes or gaze softly forward through the arms, taking several deep breaths. Repeat this final sequence with the left arm under the right. Release hands to the sides of the body.

Modifications/Variations:

If you cannot clasp your hands behind your back, use a yoga strap and hold it behind you, taught. Squeeze the shoulder blades together into the back, lifting the chest and sternum. Hands do not need to touch or even be close together. When you cross your arms forward in front of you, you can remain in the hugging position, or your hands do not need to touch when you lift the elbows.

Breathing Practice: *Anahata Pranayama* – Heart Chakra Breathing

Most people forget that many chakra centers have front and back openings. The back of the heart center is an important area to find breath for, as it opens up to the energy of Divine Love.

You will want to sit with your spine straight, preferably not with your back against a chair or wall. Try to align your spine equally front to back so that you can feel the openings in both areas of the heart chakra. When you are ready, take an inhalation, breathe, and visualize the breath moving into the back of the heart chakra. This would be right between the shoulder blades. Breathe in here, and then breathe out through the front of the heart chakra. Continue to circulate the pranic energy through your heart chakra.

Be aware of your emotions as well as physical sensations. If you experience any pain in the chest or the back, this could be stuck energy. Be aware if you need to stop pranayama, but try to stick with it if possible, and continue to move the energy through from back to front until the discomfort eases.

In our culture, where we tend to slump forward and arch our backs, this breathing will help to physically adjust your posture, keep the front of the heart-center and chest open, and allow the loving energies to flow effortlessly throughout your body.

Do the breathing for up to five minutes or more a day, either in with your regular yoga practice or separately as its own practice.

Focus on yogic breathing when performing daily tasks, watching television, or reading. Notice your breathing all the time.

Mudra & Meditation:

Come to the easy-seated pose or Lotus seated pose. Place hands on lap, palms up. Touch thumb to index finger for the *Vayu mudra* or air hand position. For this mudra, the index finger is bent to touch the base of the thumb, rather than the tip. Spend time in meditation/reflection.

Hatha Yoga Sequence:

Supported Reclining Fish with Breathing	Seated Easy Pose 4,4,8 Breathing	Cobbler	Seated Straddle with Lateral Stretches	Child's with Prayer Hands	Table
Thread the Needle	Cat/Cow	Hero with Yoga Mudra	Downward Dog	Table with Opposite hand to Foot	Cobra
Locust with Yoga Mudra	Camel	Child or Downward Dog	Gorilla	Mountain	Warrior II
Proud Warrior	Extended Side Angle	Standing Straddle Bend	*Hanum-anasana* – Full Splits or Runner's Lunge	Bridge	Wheel or 2nd Bridge
Supine Spinal Twists	Fish	Corpse - Final Relaxation	Easy Seated or Lotus	Meditation	Closing

* Note that the pre-recorded practice may differ from the sequence above.

Short 15-minute Practice:

- Supported Reclining Fish Pose with the *Anahata* breathing
- Thread-the-Needle
- Hero with Yoga Mudra
- Locust with Yoga Mudra
- Bridge
- Corpse
- Easy Seated with sankalpa

April Recap

April is all about love. For some, embracing love if we have been unloving to others or ourselves is very difficult to begin with. Start by focusing on something you already love, and work on the sensations and feelings that arise when you feel that love. Then, try to bring that forth into the rest of your life.

Once you get good at feeling the energy of love, you will begin to automatically invite in the light, the divine love, the highest form of love. Some of this energy moves into another upper chakra, but we can pave the way here at the heart center, which prepares us for the next month's energy.

May

Fertility

May Energies

Many cultures celebrate the concept of fertility. In ancient times, honoring fertility was as common a devotional practice as worshipping the sun. Travel the world, and walk into a tourist or metaphysical shop and see phallic symbols carved out of local wood—some on deities and others simply in their ecstatic state. In Bali, such statues share a shelf with Buddha statues, happily together.

Because humans needed to find meaning in the world, they observed their surroundings and designed goddess symbols. These full-figured women, with enlarged bellies, pregnant with the world, explained creation. The oldest stone goddess is referred to as the Acheulian Goddess. She is known to be much older than the previously known carved statue named Willendorf, dated approximately 30,000 years ago. Another ancient goddess resembling these large, fertile images is Inanna. Inanna, a Sumerian goddess, was worshipped around 7000 BCE. Another famous fertility goddess is the Egyptian goddess Ma'at, whose symbol, the ankh, is notably the most famous hieroglyph and appears as a combined male and female symbol. It is known as the symbol of life.

The meaning behind "May" is Maia, the Greek and Roman goddess of fertility herself. This is a rare occasion where Greek and Roman mythology keep the same name for a god, so she must be quite special! In Greek, Maia can mean midwife, female doctor, good mother, foster mother, or aunt. She is also said to be the oldest and most beautiful of the seven sisters who formed the constellation of Pleiades, which, when visible, marks the beginning of summer. Her festival is celebrated on the Ides of May on the 15th.

Again, we are reminded of the popular saying, "April showers bring May flowers." May is the peak of spring in the Northern Hemisphere, marked by blooming flowers, agricultural growth, and festivals. While Memorial Day isn't celebrated until the last Monday in May, it has become known as the "unofficial start of summer," something that those who celebrate Memorial Day for its original meaning have become gently disturbed by. But, more on that story later. For now, let us relish May as the month where it is evident that the planting of seeds, in whatever way they were planted, is beginning to take form in the manifest reality of life.

The number of the month is five (5), and five represents curiosity, freedom, and change, because it sits in the middle of the numbers 1-9, and as such, represents a pivotal point of decision-making. Five also has a link to the human body, for certainly we have five fingers on each hand, five toes on each foot, and five physical senses. In the earth plane, we have five elements: earth, air, fire, water, and ether. There's a link on the spiritual plane between the number five and the stigmata. Christ's wounds were five: two on his palms, two on his feet, and one on his side. Eerily, there are also five Catholic saints, said to have received the stigmata: St. Francis of Assisi, St. Padre Pio, St. Catherine of Siena, St. Faustina Kowalska, and St. Rita of Cascia.[39] With the connection to human life and the number five, we can see how the energy of union, an important factor in fertility, aligns with May.

Our gemstone for May is the Emerald, known for the qualities of hope, love, connection to nature, and wisdom. The rich green color beckons the energy of fertility! Lily of the Valley is the flower for May, and it represents purity, virtue, sweetness, and a return to happiness. But it blooms in late spring (May in the Northern Hemisphere), a time of peak fertility when the earth bursts with new life after winter.

Astrologically, we come into May on the sturdy horns of Taurus, the bull. This dependable energy reminds us that the rewards of our sprouting seeds came from hard work and determination earlier in the year. If we are to receive such gifts, it is only from putting constant energy into their manifestation.

Gemini rolls in at the second half of the month, around the 21st. The mythology of Gemini begins with a boy meeting a girl. Well, that's not exactly the whole truth. It began with a God and a mortal: Zeus and Leda, wife of King Tyndareus of Sparta.

Zeus seduced Leda, and from that "union," she produced two sets of twins: one set male and one set female. Castor and Pollux were the male twins, and Helen and Clytaemnestra were the females. It is said that two of the children were actually the children of King Tyndareus, and thus mortal, while the other two were the offspring of Zeus, and therefore demigods. Thus, Gemini is described as "a part of a 'quaternity,' a fourfold symbol of wholeness which includes male and female, human and divine elements."[40]

Either way, the ushering in of Gemini, with the male/female twins, is another way of anchoring the union. The union of male and female relates to fertility

---

[39] https://medium.com/@CatholicTV/5-saints-who-bore-the-stigmata-72c90079c1fe

[40] Graves, Robert, *The Greek Myths*, ibid., Vol. 1, pp. 206-7

through its role in creation, balance, and cyclical renewal, manifesting in physical procreation, symbolic complementarity, and spiritual wholeness.

Holidays and Holy Days

May is a beautiful transition month, where we can focus on the energy of union and fertility. April's theme of love opened us up to the energy of union in a nice way. Without love, there won't be a union. And without union, well, what is fertility? People only come together when feeling the energy of love, our theme for April. See how everything starts to flow together to tell a beautiful story of us?

May 1st, or "May Day," is a pagan holiday called Beltane. Beltane marks the actual beginning of summer and is often celebrated by creating another phallic symbol, the Maypole. Usually made of birch wood, the Maypole is inserted into the earth, decorated with a ring of flowers on top to represent the fertile goddess, and brightly colored ribbons are then tied to the top of the Maypole. Men and women create a dance around it, weaving the ribbons around the pole while singing and dancing. The festivals on Beltane honor the sacred marriage and union of the god and goddess, which is also a celebration of fertility and fruitfulness. The symbol of the Maypole is that of the sexual union of male with female. If the ribbons do not break, this is said to be good luck for a fertile and fruitful year. Some other rituals performed on Beltane include building a bonfire with apple, birch, fir, hazel, oak, willow, and vine, and, of course, eating, drinking, and being merry!

Buddha's Birthday is celebrated on the first full moon of the 6th month of the lunar calendar, which quite often corresponds with May. It may feel at odds that Beltane and Buddha's birthday may share the same timeframe, as one is a celebration of sexual union and fertility, and the other is a practice where monks take vows of celibacy. This reminds us that fertility is not just about the ability to create life, but the power to create anything that we focus on: from art to our sankalpa.

Another holy day that corresponds to this time of year and could fall in May is Ascension Day in both Christianity and Baha'i (although these correspond to May 30th at the end of the month). For Christians, this holy day commemorates the bodily ascension of Jesus Christ into Heaven, forty days after his resurrection. For Baha'i, it commemorates the death of Bahá'u'lláh, the founder of the Bahá'í Faith, in 1892. Although Ascension Day has two different meanings, there is a shared essence of energy transmutation to a higher realm of being. This speaks to the fifth chakra connection of purification for this month.

Mother's Day falls on the second Sunday in May. Although this is a modern holiday, it has many ancient roots. The Roman festival of Cybele, held in March or April and later extended to May, celebrated Cybele, the Great Mother, through processions, offerings, and dances honoring fertility and motherhood. The mother of Olympian gods, Rhea, was celebrated in spring festivals like the Kronia (April/May), with feasts and offerings for agricultural fertility. The Greek goddess of harvest and motherhood, Demeter, has a female-only fertility ritual in May called the Thesmophoria, a three-day festival celebrating the cycles of life. The primordial Earth Mother, Gaia, was revered in spring rites in April/May, symbolizing universal fertility. Mothers worldwide deserve at least one day a year for all they do. For without them, none of us would be here.

Memorial Day, observed on the last Monday in May, honors those who sacrificed their lives for our nation. Intended as a solemn occasion, it often features decorations, fireworks, picnics, parties, alcohol, music, and merriment in the United States. As May celebrates the union and fertility of life, Memorial Day deepens our gratitude, reminding us to temper festivity with reverence, drawing from the biblical story of Sodom and Gomorrah—a cautionary tale shared by Muslims, Christians, and Jews about the consequences of hedonism.

Chakra Connection

5th Chakra

Sanskrit: *Vishudda*
Meaning: *suddhi* = purification, *vi* = enhances this quality
Location: Throat Center

The divine nectar called *amrita* is a kind of sweet secretion at the *bindu* center (located at the back of the head, between the ajna and Sahasrara chakras) and flows down to Vishudda for purification. The pure nectar is a mystical elixir of immortality that nourishes the body, ensuring excellent health and longevity.

May's chakra is the 5th, or Vishudda, meaning purification. The location of this chakra is the throat, and it is the smallest energy center thus far. For this reason, we often see a bottleneck of energy occurring and blocks arising. As the throat center is linked to our mouth, we see its connection to communication in a big way. And so, we need to keep this pathway clear and purified to communicate truthfully and appropriately. This is an essential component of any relationship.

The fifth chakra is linked to the last of the five elements, ether, although it is said that the pure energy of ether is from which all other elements are created. This explains a symbolic meaning to the chakra's name, which means purification, and the pathway towards truth. This is also our second creative center. In the second chakra, creativity is born, while in the fifth, that creation is expressed and shared with the world.

We are reminded again to always move from a place of love in all our words and actions, to ensure we are projecting the right energy into the world. How do we determine if we are expressing ourselves appropriately? See the companion Workbook for more questions, but consider these few journal prompts on your fifth chakra:

Communication: How do I communicate best?

Purification: Do I have any toxicity in my life that needs to be cleared?

Ether: What do I consider ethereal?

The fifth chakra, Vishudda, is said to be a gateway to liberation. The 16 petals of the lotus in the yantra represent trust, loyalty, wisdom, confidence, intelligence, faith, truth, and heaven. In the center of the symbol is a downward-facing triangle with a circle inside it, representing the element ether. The origin of ether is primordial. It is the vibration that exists before it takes the form of sound in the ear. Sound and ether are inseparable, showing us the connection to this communication center.

Moon Phases

<u>New Moon</u>:

The two weeks leading up to the New Moon can help you to remove unwanted energy perfectly. However, one could make a case for starting a new detox program on the night of the new moon and focusing on manifesting detoxification through the full moon. They don't call it "Spring Cleaning" for nothing.

<u>Beltane and the Full Moon</u>:

Find out what the moon cycles are and how they correspond to Beltane. This will be an important month to work with the waxing and full moon, and if it auspiciously falls around the time of Beltane, then there will be a lot of abundant, fertile energy to draw upon when manifesting. Indeed, celebrate the full moon energy around Beltane with festivities, because in years when it falls around the waning and dark moon, look to honor fertility and union with the utmost reverence.

<u>Waning Moon</u>:

Remembering that the throat chakra's meaning is purification, this is also a great month to consider a detox or a cleansing ritual, especially during the waning moon. Remember that it is always recommended to consult a doctor or nutritionist. There are many detoxification programs, and you want to use the one best for you. You'll want to ensure that you use a good method, with only the best and most wholesome ingredients.

The "Lemonade Cleanse" is a popular springtime liver cleanse. Elson M. Hass, MD's *Staying Healthy With the Seasons* offers brilliant details on this cleanse. His book is a perfect accompaniment for this Wheel of the Year, for those who wish to do this with the expert guidance of an integrative medical doctor. For those who are not ready to tackle that aspect of physical cleansing, you can review your life as it pertains to toxicity. Refer to the workbook for more guidelines.

<u>Dark Moon</u>:

Since May has many energies: union and fertility, purification, communication, and creativity, on either May 1st or the night of the dark moon, depending on how it falls this month, you may wish to meditate or create a ritual to clarify what specific work needs to be done this month, and nail that down. You can use various divination tools, such as a pendulum, or try muscle testing or meditation.

Remember that whichever focus you use for May, you will want to work with it consistently throughout. Don't focus on purification for a week and then move on to creativity for another week. Keep the focus throughout the month and work through a full moon phase from new moon to full for manifesting, and day after full to dark for releasing.

In addition to these methods, let's see how to work with the energies of fertility and union for May.

Faith Tradition: Kemetic

"The divine is in all things, from the Nile's flow to the heart's beat, for Ma'at weaves truth and order through every breath of creation."

– Anonymous Kemetic Wisdom, *Book of the Dead*

May's association with springtime growth, abundance, and renewal aligns naturally with fertility, and the Kemetic tradition, rooted in ancient Egyptian spirituality, emphasizes life, creation, and cyclical regeneration. Kemetic spirituality is based on ancient Egyptian religion and centers on Ma'at (cosmic order), life, and cyclical renewal, with fertility as a key aspect of creation, agriculture through the Nile's flooding, and divine procreation, as in the story of Isis and Osiris's union.

While the number of actual Kemetic practitioners in the world is difficult to determine, Kemetic Orthodoxy, founded in the 1980's estimates approximately 500-2000 globally. However, the Ancient Egyptian population grew to 80,000+ in the Ptolemaic period, in temples like Karnak and Memphis numbered 80,000+, and the fact that millions of people (15.7 million in 2024 alone) travel to Egypt as tourists, yearly, proves that the fascination with its history, mysticism, and spirituality continues to impact the world views of numerous people.

How many of these people practice any Kemetic spirituality is anyone's guess. It may be another mystery, wrapped in a riddle, such as the great Sphinx itself. But one thing is for certain: the world has always been fascinated with ancient Egypt. Understanding this faith tradition in more detail seems fitting for a month's theme of fertility, fitting in with the people's focus on the Nile's cycles, and the fifth chakra's quality of communication, linking to the prolific writing system that these ancient ones left carved on temple walls and in scrolls.

Symbol: Ankh

May's symbol is the famous Egyptian hieroglyph, the ankh. The ankh represents life and immortality, often held by deities in tomb art, and symbolizes the vital force of creation, central to fertility. The ankh is also said to represent both the male and female genitals, the sun coming over the horizon, and the union of heaven and earth.[41]

Its cross shape with a looped top has made its way from the ancient Egyptians to Christianity, where the idea of immortality and life after death became a message of Christ's. Modern Wiccans now wear the ankh as a symbol of protection, and even the actor and musician Elvis Presley was known to wear one amongst his many other crosses. When this was scrutinized, he said, simply, "I don't want to miss out on Heaven because of a technicality."[42]

---

[41] *Encyclopedia of Secret Signs and Symbols,* page 14

[42] *Encyclopedia of Secret Signs and Symbols,* page 14

May Altar:

- **Altar cloth:** Blue, the color of the fifth chakra

- **Flower:** A fresh bouquet of Lily of the Valley flowers

- **Candle:** Blue

- **Crystal/Stone:** like Diamonds, Emeralds may be difficult to come by or extremely expensive. You can use any blue stone for the energy this month. Lapis Lazuli, known as the "Stone of Truth" or Turquoise, a good luck stone heavily used by the Egyptians, work as a great alternatives for this month.

- **Symbol:** Ankh jewelry, image, or statue

- **Essential Oil/Incense:** Blue Lotus Absolute, used in Egyptian Fertility rituals

- **Herbs:** Ceremonial White Sage and Lemon Balm, associated with calming and restorative effects, are considered a "heart's delight" and "elixir of life."

- **Other items (optional):**
  - *The Modern Mystic's Wheel of the Year* Book, Workbook, and Oracle Deck
  - New journal, drawing or music paper, and a writing instrument
  - Anything that you created: pottery, artwork, writing, etc.
  - Instrument, to play music on
  - Music you enjoy singing or dancing to
  - Egyptian statues or artwork
  - Items that remind you of your sankalpa

Angel/Ancestor: High Priest/High Priestess

All Mystery Schools embody the divine principle, whether it be masculine or feminine, in the archetypes of the High Priest and High Priestess. These individuals serve as a bridge between worlds, assisting in the creation process. Their acts are highly ritualistic, steeped in magic and alchemy, that transform the physical world.

Their iconic stories are made for the big screen, with movies spotlighting their craft in the most captivating ways. Most Modern Mystics align with these archetypes in a past life that cry out in the present to be heard, and claiming our right in these roles is an act of remembrance like no other.

The most notable Egyptian High Priest is Imhotep, who was mentioned in Part 1. Imhotep lived in the 3rd Dynasty, 2650 BCE, whose name is inscribed on statues and papyri. Another well-known Priest is Anen, High Priest of Amun, who managed the famous Temple of Amun at Karnak.

As for High Priestess, look no further than Hatshepsut, known as "God's Wife of Amun," who lived in the 18th Dynasty, 1479–1458 BCE. As God's Wife, Hatshepsut performed rituals in Amun's temple, embodying the goddess Mut and ensuring divine fertility.[43]

Because the gods are considered divine beings, they would not be known as High Priests or Priestesses; however, their cults had many High Priests/Priestesses who served them. The cult of Isis is perhaps one of the most well-known, with many women (and men) today recalling their time as a Priestess of Isis in Egypt.

If you consider yourself a Modern Mystic, you are in this fine lineage. Whether it's as a Priestess of Isis or a reincarnation of Imhotep himself, align yourself with the energy of this archetype as you work the rituals and practices throughout the month.

<u>Activating the High Priest/High Priestess Within</u>:

1. Bathe, cleanse, and put on fresh clothes of a high frequency (white linen is best)

---

[43] *Women in Ancient Egypt*

2. Meditate, pray, and attune to the energy within and without

3. Utilize a breathing practice that links your body, mind, and spirit to the One Consciousness that bridges time and space.

4. Say, "I claim my right as a High Priest/High Priestess. From this moment forward, I embody the divine, serving as a bridge in creating magic for the Highest Good. Kheperu (may it become)."

5. Bring in any other mystical aspects that may assist you in this connection

May Ritual: Fertility Festival

The fertility festival *Wepet-Renpet* ("Opening of the Year") was historically celebrated in ancient Egypt around July and August, marking the Nile's flooding and agricultural fertility. Modern Kemetic practitioners adapt it to early May 1–5, to align with spring's peak growth in the Northern Hemisphere, resonating with spring festivals like Beltane. It celebrates the renewal of life, fertility of the land, and divine creation, often honoring the god of agriculture and regeneration and Isis, goddess of motherhood and fertility.

The ritual for Wepet-Renpet invokes the Nile's fertile inundation, symbolizing life's abundance with offerings given to Osiris and Isis, mirroring the union of male and female. The Ankh, symbolizing eternal life and the masculine-feminine union, is central, raised, or worn to bless fields, wombs, or creative endeavors. As this is a festival, it's a ritual performed with a group, just as with Beltane. So gather your besties, close family, and others in your community who will love to share in the joyous feasting and merriment.

Preparation:

- Set a date in May, send invitations, and plan the location. The location should be near the water. If you have a natural waterway near you, like a river, that is optimal. A small stream, the ocean, or another natural body of water will also work. If being near the water for this festival is not an option, you can go to the water later to give offerings.
- Prepare the feast, or ask others to contribute to the communal meal. Specifically, have items consisting of bread, dates, and wine (or grape juice as a substitute) to celebrate fertility's fruits
- Wear your ankh with white or your favorite color flowing robes
- Prepare offerings of water, seeds, or barley
- Prepare chants/hymns, printed out for participants—it could be a simple hymn like "Osiris, bring life; Isis, nurture it," or something else

Festival Practices:

Assemble the group near a stream or body of water, adorned with or holding gleaming ankhs. Everyone pours water to bless the earth, and shares food in gratitude to the deities for nurturing crop growth. It should feel like a springtime party for life.

Another strong ritual is creating a procession to the water, carrying ankh amulets or banners, and chanting the hymns you prepared. The offerings should then be poured into the earth with the intention of prayers for an abundant harvest. Take time to pause as a group and hold these intentions before returning to the other parts of the festival.

Although not a Kemetic tradition, creating a Maypole would honor the element of fertility, as it does for Beltane, and meet the communal aspects of the festival ritual. Of course, this added step is at your discretion, if you feel aligned to include it.

Maypole Steps:

- Items needed: Maypole, ribbons, and a garland of flowers
- Erect the Maypole by digging a deep hole in the ground, planting the pole, and packing the dirt around it. If this is too arduous a task, look for a tree that can serve as your Maypole. Then, fasten the flowers and ribbons to the top
- Each person holds a different color ribbon and begins to dance around the maypole, chanting:

    "Over under round and round, shaft of cedar piercing ground! Phallic staff draw sun to earth, bring our magic now to birth!"

* Note: The dance should be done with each person taking a different colored ribbon and counting off by twos. Ones will go in one clockwise direction, and twos in counterclockwise. As the dance begins, each person should alternate going over and under another. This creates the weaving of the ribbons. When the ribbons have finished, everyone takes a moment to place them on the ground, perhaps securing them with a small stone, reflecting on the community energy, and visualizing fertility coming to each individual and the whole.

Our theme for May requires fertile ground for an abundant life. The sankalpa we so deliberately chose for January is beginning to show signs of life due to our continued efforts through the winter months to diligently eliminate what stands in our way and cultivate more of what supports this goal. So celebrate with those who have supported and continue to support your journey. Life is meant to be joyous.

Tracey's Personal Reflection

Over the years, I've participated in and hosted many a Maypole celebration. Beltane is a festive holiday, and coming out of the long, cold winter months, it is most definitely a beautiful time of celebration with the earth and amongst other like-minded humans. Although I've admired Kemetic spirituality for a long time, I've never focused on a ritual specifically designed towards Wepet-Renpet. However, I've practiced many other Kemetic and pagan rituals for this and other times of the year, all of which have felt true and real.

Erecting a Maypole isn't always the easiest of endeavors. I've been known to start wrapping ribbons around local trees instead of going through the lengthy process of cutting one down, only to re-erect it again. Besides, I enjoy working with a natural tree rather than tearing it down. This feels more communal with nature to me.

I've found that, even though Beltane and Maypole traditions are steeped in paganism, many Christian, Buddhist, and Hindu friends enjoy the community endeavor and the fun of the dance. Try it out. Or, go with the full Kemetic ritual offered.

Maypole created with a local tree during a retreat in 2015

May Daily Yoga Practice:
For Opening the Throat Center

This practice is for all levels, and no yoga experience is required. However, it is always recommended to consult a doctor before beginning any new physical program. Remember to modify anything for particular conditions that you may be experiencing, and to always follow your breath for the truth about a feeling that arises.

Yoga Posture Sequence for Opening the Throat Center:

This month, the fifth chakra's focus on the throat and neck area allows us to open up our sharing and communication in preparation for the festival. As we begin this month, witnessing the seeds of our sankalpa blossom into reality, the invitation is to express ourselves openly and authentically, sharing our unique gifts with others.

Always allow the pace to be slow and mindful.

The element ether is omnipresent, so know that as you practice, you are in communion with Spirit every step of the way. Trust in this divine connection to put you exactly where you need to be in every moment.

Single Posture Practice: Fish (*Matsyasana*)

Lie on your back and stretch your body. Lengthen the legs forward, bringing the inner thighs together. Slide the arms under the hips with palms facing down. Be careful to keep the arms straight and work the shoulders underneath so the chest is open. Pull the belly down towards the floor. Press into the forearms and lift your head and chest. Puff up the chest, drop the head back, and lower it gently towards the floor. The legs, hips, elbows, forearms, and crown of the head remain on the floor as the chest and sternum lift. Gaze at the wall behind you, taking several deep breaths.

To release, maintain core muscle use, press into the forearms, and lift the head, bringing the chin towards the chest. Then lower to the mat and release the body.

Breathing Practice: Surrender Breath

This one seems easy, but if the energy to the fifth chakra is blocked, it can be challenging. You inhale through the nose, pause, open your mouth, and sigh with the exhalation. The sound should be audible, and you don't have to be shy about it. The more sound, the better. Remember that you are working to open the energy in the throat center. I recommend doing this in rounds of three.

You can do this once and see how it feels. Notice if the sound was deep or soft. Try it again, allowing your voice to come forward. If you are still holding back, do a few shoulder shrugs by inhaling and lifting them to your ears, then exhaling and dropping them with a sigh. Try the surrender breath again and see if the voice is more audible.

Practice opening your throat throughout the yoga sequence, particularly whenever you feel the energy has built up somewhere and needs to be released.

Mudra & Meditation:

Come to the easy-seated pose or Lotus seated pose. Place hands on lap, palms up. Touch thumb to middle finger for the *Akasha mudra*. Spend time in meditation/reflection, focusing on the area of the throat-center. Remember that the fifth chakra has a front and back opening. During meditation, focus on the area at the back of the neck, specifically the "Mouth of God" at the base of the skull, where a small indentation is found. Draw energy into that area and allow it to circulate throughout the neck and throat.

When you are ready, close the practice by bringing your hands to your heart, bowing your head, and closing with an intention or prayer, honoring how you will bring forth your sankalpa and share it with the world.

Hatha Yoga Sequence:

Supported Reclining Fish with Ujjayi Breaths	Easy Seated Pose Alternate Nostril Breathing	Seated Easy Pose Dropping Chin to Chest	Neck Stretches and Twists to Both Sides	Optional Neck Circles or Semi-Circles	Hero with hands interlaced behind back
Cobbler	Child's Pose	Table with Cat/Cow	Sphinx with Neck Turns	High or Low Cobra or both	Locust (with hands clasped behind back)
Sphinx with half Frog Legs	Child's Pose	Downward Dog	Ragdoll with Neck Releases & Bounces	Mountain	Waterfalls with Surrender Breaths
Warrior II	Goddess Pose	Goddess Legs with Twists	Standing Straddle Bend with Surrender Breaths	Bridge	Inverted Straddle
Fish	Happy Baby	Corpse - Final Relaxation	Easy Seated or Lotus	Meditation	Closing

* Note that the pre-recorded practice may differ from the sequence above.

Short 15-minute Practice:

- Surrender Breaths
- Six movements of the cervical spine: right and left lateral bends, twisting to both sides, forward and back bends
- Hero with hands clasped behind the back in Yoga Mudra
- Cobra with neck movements
- Bridge
- Shoulder-Stand
- Corpse

May Recap

The fertile landscape of May can or cannot be a reality for you, depending on whether you have been making the right effort. The purification aspects of this month allow you to look at anything still standing in your way of being your Highest and Truest Self. The 5th chakra connection ensures that we continue to move forward, sharing what we have been working on with the world.

We can no longer lurk in the shadows because our Highest Self has something to share with the world. Remember, we are here for a divine purpose. Allow the energies of May to provide you with a well-needed boost of energy, as you step out—maybe for the first time, in a bigger way in the world.

Go you!

June

Light

June Energies

Light. The sun brings our planet light. Without it, there would be no life. This star governs our entire solar system. In the yoga tradition, solar energy is equated to the sun god, *Surya*, the creator of the universe and the source of all life. He is the supreme soul that brings light and warmth to the world, and each day, he is said to travel across the sky in his golden chariot to *Aruna*, the dawn. But the sun, as a god, has been honored since the "literal" dawn of time. Egyptians call him Ra. To Greeks and Romans, he is known as Apollo, and to the Sumerians, he is known as Enki. The North American Lakota call the sun Wi, although Father Sun is also a notable reference for many Native American peoples. And then the Nordics refer to her as the Goddess, named Sunna, a rare reference to the sun as feminine energy.

Many other cultures refer to the solar deity as a sun disk or solar light. In the middle of Lake Titicaca in Peru and Bolivia sits Isla del Sol, or Island of the Sun. The origin story of the Incas begins here, known as the "birthplace of the sun." Here in Peru, there are also many stories of the" Golden Sun Disc" and its significance in the entire landscape of humankind. Even today, when the sun's rays cascade down through the clouds, millions of people honor this as a symbol of God and creation.

June brings the longest day of the year, and many cultures around the world celebrate this halfway mark of the year with festivals and celebrations. The days leading up to the Summer Solstice and immediately after offer the most sun and sunlight available. Usually, the weather is warm, and there is a great sense of vitality and vibrancy.

Not surprisingly, June's birthstone is the Pearl, a symbol of health and longevity. The flower of the month is Honeysuckle, symbolizing gratitude, something that we should be feeling at this time of year when everything is ripe for the picking, including anything that we have been working on manifesting.

June is the sixth month of the year, and the number six (6) is representative of responsibility, service, and family. These are also very spiritual qualities. As the sixth month of the year, June is also linked to the 6th chakra, located at the center of the head or cerebral plexus. This third-eye center is associated with intuition and insights, and the 6th chakra's element is "Light." The location of the third eye is the Pineal Gland, a tiny, light-sensitive organ in our brain that controls over 100 bodily functions. That is quite a responsibility for a small organ.

Our zodiac signs for June are Gemini, the twins, social and creative, and the talented Cancer, the crab. The crab has a very hard exterior, with a soft inside. This has often been my understanding of very hardworking men and women. They feel that they must put on a hard front to be successful in the business world, yet they can be the kindest and most intuitive people in reality. Cancer is a water sign, which attributes itself to the moon and the feminine. However, as Ariel Guttman says in her book *Mythic Astrology*, "The key idea here is that the sun is turning back, beginning its progress into the world of the Night force or collective humanity, which is the *yin* or feminine component of the consciousness and civilization."

Interestingly, there is a lot of *yang* or masculine energy heightened in June, while there is an opposing pull towards the *yin*, feminine energies. Since June is named after the Roman Goddess Juno, wife of Jupiter, it's easy to note that the intense energy of this month needs to find balance. This is why, as the halfway point of the Gregorian calendar, this month also represents a balance of opposites, which presents itself again in the activation of the 6th chakra, as will be discussed later in the chapter.

Holidays and Holy Days

The most significant day in June is the Summer Solstice or *Litha*. Summer Solstice is the day when the sun is at its most powerful and daytime is the longest in the Northern Hemisphere. It is the pinnacle of Solar energy, when the Sun God is in full power, activating the greatest growth on the planet. Everything is bursting with life at this time of the year, and local produce, herbs, and spices are available in bulk. Most of the seeds that were planted are now arriving at us in full manifestation. As such, this is the time of year when our food has the richest energy of prana or chi (life force). Eating a lot of local foods is a way to stay healthy, vital, and vibrant, with more solar qualities.

Just about every civilization and spiritual path celebrates the sun and the Solstice, in one way or another. It's quite possible that, universally, this is the most honored day of the year, worldwide, since the dawn of humankind on our planet.

The next three holidays for June are steeped in masculine energy, often equated with the sun and solar energy.

Father's Day is celebrated on the third Sunday in June. This is Dad's day. Mom has had her day for a while, but what about dear old dad? This holiday is a relatively new one, created in 1910 by Sonora Smart Dodd. President Lyndon B. Johnson issued a proclamation in 1966, finally designating the third Sunday in June as Father's Day. But it wasn't until 1972, during President Richard Nixon's administration, that Father's Day was officially made a permanent national holiday.

D-Day and Flag Day, both associated with patriotism, also fall this month, bringing quite an intense masculine energy. June 6, D-Day, commemorates a historical and bloody battle of 156,000 male troops from the US, Britain, and Canada who stormed the beaches of Normandy, France, during World War II. Of those, approximately 4,000 died. On this day, silence is taken for the men lost in battle, and for our country.

Flag Day on June 14th is celebrated from sunrise to sunset, where the American flag is raised in respect for our nation. This energy is all significantly patriarchal, although certainly many brave women also serve our country today.

Chakra Connection

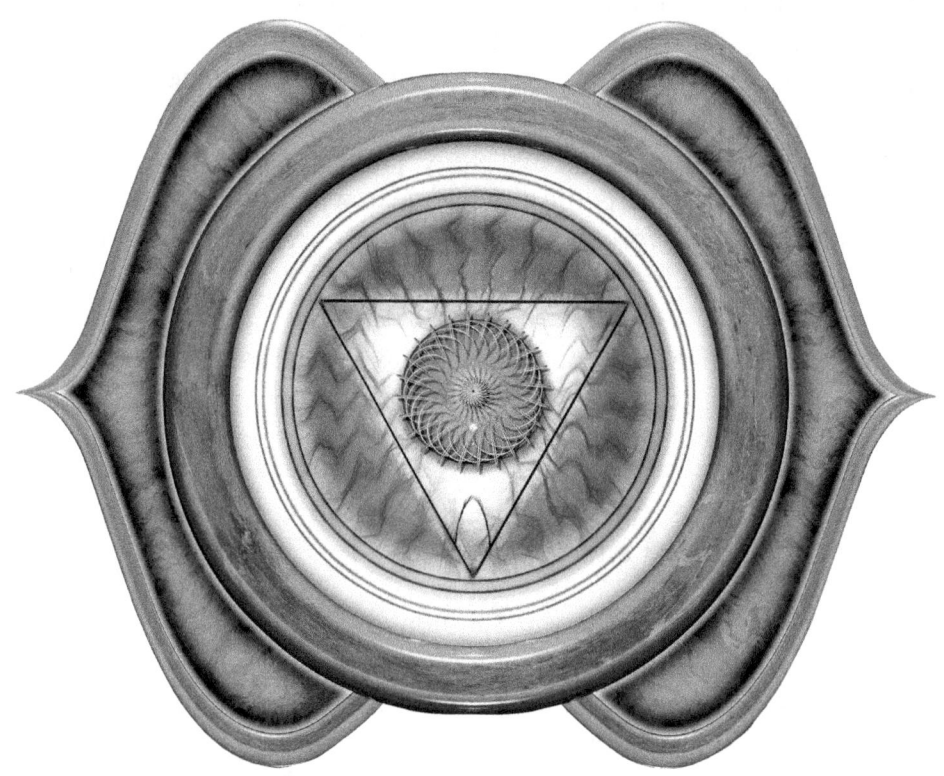

6th Chakra

Sanskrit: *Ajna*
Meaning: To perceive or command
Location: Third-Eye, Brow

When we reach ajna, our development within our humanity is completed, and we reach the bridge to Divine Consciousness. We do not need to seek the truth because it is right in front of us. To recognize it, a person needs to open pure consciousness and clear thoughts.

May's chakra is the 6th, or Ajna, in Sanskrit, meaning to perceive or command. The physical location is the third eye or center of the forehead, and the actual command center is the pineal gland. Since the element of the 6th chakra is that of light, it makes sense that the light-sensitive organ, the pineal gland, is also in this location. This organ translates variations of light to hormonal messages that are relayed to the human body. Approximately 100 bodily functions have daily rhythms that are influenced by exposure to light. This certainly feels significant.

As we move into these upper chakras, the areas get smaller. The physical location is a triple-confluence area where three main nadi points come together: *ida*, the feminine downward current; *pingala*, the masculine upward current; and shushumna, the central channel aforementioned. This termination point is why yogic breathing is so much more effective when done through the nasal passages. *Pranic* energy all comes together here and inspires consciousness to then move upward. This is why the ancient yogis declared this the area for clairvoyance and intuitive powers.

As the fifth chakra opens truthful communication, the sixth chakra allows us to see clearly what is true on a grander scale. As we tune in to our psychic world or higher dimensions of consciousness, we start to tap into the mystical realms. Everyone has this ability. How do we attune to this energy, and how do we determine if we are working appropriately? See the companion Workbook for more questions, but consider these few journal prompts on your sixth chakra:

> Dreams & Imagination: Do you recall your dreams? Do you have a good imagination? Able to see and imagine alternatives and other realities?
>
> Clairvoyance: Do you have flashes of insight or visions that you cannot explain?
>
> Pattern Recognition: Are you aware of patterns that need to change for yourself?

After you have answered these questions or others, contemplate what you need to work on and formulate a plan. Perhaps you need to work with meditation more to enhance the opening of your perception. Having a dream diary where you log your dreams upon awakening can help you remember and see patterns in them.

Moon Phases

Let's talk sankalpa. Where is that special intention at this moment? June's energy is the highest light and most intense taskmaster energy of the year, so if we need another big push to make things happen in a big way, this is the month to do so.

Dark Moon:

If your sankalpa is still not showing up for you by now, you may need to re-evaluate if it is indeed your highest intention, and if you have been putting all the right energy into it since January. If you determine your January sankalpa is still the correct one, then you will have the energy that you need to push forward now in June. If you determine that it is not the right energy, then this is a great month, placed right at the center of the year, for you to make a detour in another direction and to set an altogether new sankalpa. The night of June's dark moon offers a brilliant opportunity for such significant introspection.

Do not feel bad about changing direction, by the way. Many stories and mythologies discuss this theme. A pop-culture reference is the character of Rocky Balboa, a Sylvester Stallone boxing character from Philadelphia, PA. In the original movie, which won Best Picture for Stallone in 1976, Rocky aspires to win the title role of heavyweight champion of the world. He works hard towards this goal and finds himself in the boxing ring, where he could win the title. Yet halfway through the fight, he realizes that he cannot beat the current champion. He changes his directive to "finishing" rather than "winning."

This theme is an important one. The hero reroutes based on many things, but humility is the cornerstone. He chooses not to give up and walk away from something he will not come out winning. Instead, he decides to let his ego go and walk a truer path. Rocky finishes this fight and still feels as though he came out on top. Consider this if you have to reroute your sankalpa, for it is not the end of the world, and this encounter may be just what your ego needs to learn something very important in your journey.

New Moon:

On the phase of the New Moon, work from the insights you gained over the dark moon about your sankalpa and any course-correcting or path changes that you need to make. Once you are clear, it is time to get moving and push energy into this intention. Use the night of the new moon to activate this.

<u>Waxing to Full Moon</u>:

Pull out all of the stops during the waxing to full moon stages. Don't give up. Create whatever boundaries you need to move forward. This is a significant time for work. Perhaps there is a big aspect of your sankalpa that you have been waiting to dive into. Do it now. If you have been floundering with old habits, fears, or doubts, leap forward into the unknown and trust your instincts that you are doing what you need to do and that the Universe will likewise support you.

<u>Waning Moon</u>:

Even the waning moon phase will have a lot of energy to it this month. We don't have long nights, and the days are longer, so even though the nights may be darker, it is only for a brief time. Of course, we don't want to burn the candle at both ends and wind up sick or depleted. So, make sure to rest and nurture even though you are putting massive energy into your dreams. Bring in your third eye this month and visualize and see what you are working towards, already happened, and in the present tense. Daydream, visualize, make vision boards, and work with your sight to create a vision of your future that supports you in the highest light possible.

Do not tire of working with the vision of what you see for yourself this month. It can sometimes be challenging and feel like an uphill battle, but remember that the tortoise eventually won the race through a slow and steady pace and perseverance. If you are truly meant to do what you feel you are, it will manifest. The key is to be clear on the intention.

Faith Tradition: Native American

"The first peace, which is the most important, is that which comes within the souls of people when they realize their relationship, their oneness, with the universe and all its powers, and when they realize that at the center of the universe dwells Wakan Tanka, and that this center is really everywhere, it is within each of us."

– Black Elk, *The Sacred Pipe*

Native American tribes, especially those of the Great Plains (Lakota, Cheyenne, Blackfeet) and Southwest (Zuni, Pueblo), revered the sun as a sacred life-giver, embodying the Great Spirit or a divine force central to their spirituality. Their relationship with the sun was practical, spiritual, and cosmological, reflecting a deep understanding of celestial cycles. Tribes meticulously observed the sun's movements, employing structures such as Medicine Wheels (e.g., The Bighorn Medicine in Wyoming) or solar markers (e.g., Fajada Butte in Chaco Canyon) to denote solstices and equinoxes, synchronizing ceremonies with cosmic cycles. The Cahokia people (Illinois, 1000 CE) built Woodhenge, where the sun's solstice rise aligned with temple mounds, indicating solar respect.

The sun is called by various names across tribes, reflecting its sacred role. Wi (pronounced "wee") is the primary name for the sun, meaning "sun" or "light," per Black Elk in *The Sacred Pipe*. *Tunkasila,* or "Grandfather Sun," is another Lakota name. For the Hopi, it is *Tawa*, and for the Blackfeet, *Naatosi*. Native American stories about the sun, passed orally through generations, explain its origins, role, and spiritual significance, often tied to solstice ceremonies.

A Lakota myth recounts Wakan Tanka sending the Wi to gift the buffalo to the people via the White Buffalo Calf Woman, who teaches the sacred pipe and Sun Dance. The sun's light guides the buffalo, ensuring food and spiritual connection.

Although every ancient culture in the world honored the sun, with many having Solstice markers on sacred sites, this midway point of the year will work well with a ritual and symbol of the Native American traditions.

Symbol: Medicine Wheel

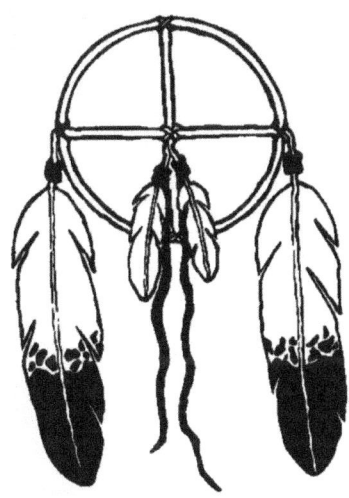

The Medicine Wheel is a sacred symbol and physical structure in many Native American Indian cultures, particularly among Plains tribes like the Lakota, Cheyenne, Blackfeet, and Crow, as well as other Indigenous groups across North America. The Medicine Wheel is deeply connected to the sun's light, its seasonal movements, and its role as a life-giving force. Over 150 Medicine Wheels exist across North America, primarily in the Great Plains and Rocky Mountains, with 70% in Wyoming, Montana, and Alberta, per archaeological surveys.[44] The largest physical Medicine Wheel, constructed as a stone mandala, is the Bighorn Medicine Wheel at Medicine Mountain at an elevation of 9,640 feet. For hundreds of years, it has marked rites of passage and ceremony by many diverse peoples.[45]

It represents the circle of life, encompassing cycles of birth, growth, death, and renewal, as well as harmony between humans, nature, and the cosmos. It symbolizes balance, interconnectedness, and the Great Spirit.

It is divided into four quadrants, often associated with the four directions, the four elements, the four seasons, and the four life stages: elder, adult, youth, and child. Medicine Wheels are used for ceremonies, prayers, vision quests, and healing rituals, often during significant times like the summer solstice.

---

[44] *American Antiquity*, 1990

[45] *Encyclopedia of Secret Signs and Symbols*, page 462

June Altar

- **Altar cloth:** Indigo or dark blue, the color of the sixth chakra

- **Flower:** Honeysuckle

- **Candle:** Indigo or white, and as many of them as you like - bring on the light!

- **Crystal/Stone:** Pearl is the stone for June. If you do not have a pearl, Indigo Gabbro (Mystic Merlinite) is a perfect substitute.

- **Symbol:** Medicine Wheel picture, drawing, or actual wheel that you made or purchased

- **Essential Oil/Incense:** White Sage, Native Americans use for illumination & purification

- **Herbs:** Ceremonial White Sage, Sweetgrass (Native Americans consider this "Hair of Mother Earth" for its connection to Earth as the Creator, Basil, the birth-month herb, and lavender, another herb of the month.

- **Other items (optional):**
  - *The Modern Mystic's Wheel of the Year* Book, Workbook, and Oracle Deck
  - Native American items: a drum, feathers, Medicine Wheel, dream catcher, buffalo skin, peace pipe, rattle, etc.
  - Picture of Black Elk or other Native American Elder or Medicine Man/Woman
  - Picture of the sun
  - Bring light to your Sankalpa this month by keeping items that remind you of it on your altar.

Angel/Ancestor: Medicine Man/Woman

In the Native American tribes, a Medicine Man or Medicine Woman is a healer, a visionary, a leader of ceremony, and sometimes a shape-shifter. Often through trance-like states, the Medicine Man/Woman gains knowledge of the world through its plants and animals. These spiritual leaders are known as holy people, similarly revered as in other traditions, a priest or shaman.

The Cherokee Medicine Person, Didanvwisgi, uses herbs for healing and performs divinations to counter witchcraft. The Navajo Hatałii create complex "Blessingways" to restore balance. Lakota Wičháša Wakȟáŋ (sacred man) or Winyan Wakȟáŋ (sacred woman) leads the tribe in the Sweat Lodge ceremony.[46] And the Hopi Skala focuses on spiritual healing.

Although each tribe's Medicine Man or Woman may go by a different name, their common theme is guiding the community through spiritual endeavors, communing with Great Spirit.

The most direct way to commune with a Medicine Man or Woman is to seek permission. Research a local tribe and contact the tribal leader or cultural center. Respect any protocols they may have, such as gifting tobacco. And if you are invited to attend a ceremony or ritual, strictly adhere to the guidelines presented to you.

Although invoking ancestral Medicine Men or Women is restricted to initiated practitioners, Lakota Medicine Man Black Elk may guide you through a Vision Quest or a dream.

<u>To Engage with Black Elk, Follow These Steps</u>:

1. Find a quiet, natural place and sit with gratitude
2. Offer thanks to the Earth with a blessing of tobacco, sage, or water
3. Meditate on Black Elk's words, like "As you walk upon the sacred earth, treat each step as a prayer" or "All things are our relatives; what we do to everything, we do to ourselves. All is really One."
4. Humbly ask Black Elk for guidance in your own words, ending with "Aho!" Which means "Thank You."

---

[46] *The Lakota Ritual of the Sweat Lodge,* Raymond A. Bucko (1998)

It's crucial to recognize that cultural sensitivity prohibits novices from invoking or directly performing specific rituals and ceremonies. Always respect and honor tribal beliefs and systems, as performing without permission violates protocols. When in doubt, seek permission.

June Ritual: Vision Quest

The Sun Dance and other ceremonies are sacred, often closed to non-Natives since the 1993 Lakota Declaration and 2003 ban by the White Buffalo Calf Pipe Keeper[47]. Respectful observation is allowed at some public dances, but participation or filming is restricted, per World History Encyclopedia. Although the Sun Dance may feel like the perfect ritual for June, due to this cultural sensitivity, we will look to another Native American rite: Vision Quest.

A Vision Quest is a rite of passage for Native Americans. After certain tribal ceremonies are performed, a young man leaves the community to fast for four days and nights, alone, communing with nature, seeking a vision for his role in this life, his soul's purpose. Different tribes offer different takes on Vision Quest, but the idea is that the youth comes back to the community a man, having had a vision, assisted by nature, of his Higher Self.

We can perform our own Vision Quest as simply or grandly as we are comfortable with. Perhaps you take a day to go off into nature, which for you might be a small park in your local area. Maybe you bring a biodegradable lunch, or perhaps you just pack water. You can also take a weekend or a longer trip to enter a National Park or a large natural area where you can immerse yourself completely in nature. This would require many more supplies, as most people today are not able to take off as the indigenous peoples did, with little to no luxuries. Instead, you will want to pack some important items that will secure your safety and security while still allowing yourself to plug into all that nature has to offer.

Take time to plan this accordingly and in the manner that you are comfortable with. Then, allow yourself to follow the signs of nature to guide you to something. Some people may stop and meditate until they have a vision. Others may do a walking meditation until they find a gift from Great Spirit. There is no perfect right or wrong way, as long as you allow yourself to be guided, naturally.

What you find on the way, you can then look up the meaning of. If an animal or part of an animal (bone, feather, teeth, skin, etc.) finds you, then the spirit of that animal may be one of your totems at the time. Jamie Sams' expertly thought-out *Medicine Cards* power animal deck can assist you in understanding the meaning of any animal totem that comes to you.

---

[47] *Notes from the Frontier*, 2019

For many, getting into nature is imperative to their spiritual life. Walking in the woods is as spiritual as sitting in a church or temple, but it could provide even more mystical experiences for the Modern Mystic.

Great Spirit is always talking to us; it's just that we aren't attuned to listening. So, for June, pause and go on a Vision Quest to explore the next step for us on this spiritual journey, or to listen for the signs that you are on the right path. See the workbook for more valuable insights on this month's journey.

Tracey's Personal Reflection

Many years ago, I led a Vision Quest with a yoga retreat, where I guided our group into a nature reserve area. It was big enough to get into, yet not large enough to get lost in. I guided our group to a clearing and had them meditate on being open to Great Spirit and following the natural signs. If a bird called, they were instructed to follow the sound of that bird. If a light or a movement of trees caught their attention, go to the light or the tree. Following nature without second-guessing or having a goal of where they wanted to be allowed them the time to discover what Wakan Tanka wanted to share with each of them. Although some people were scared to embark on this journey, this was an important step for many of the people on retreat.

What happened was nothing short of magical. Each person found an animal totem or part of nature that spoke to them. We came back and discussed the various meanings of each of these components of nature, and created their own animal totem shield/Medicine Wheel to take home to continue to embrace these qualities in their life, to help guide them in the next step of their journey to their Highest Self.

The Medicine Wheels created during the 2014 retreat after Vision Quest

June Yoga Practice:
Opening the Third Eye

This practice is for all levels, and no yoga experience is required. However, it is always recommended to consult a doctor before beginning any new physical program. Remember to modify anything for particular conditions that you may be experiencing, and to always follow your breath for the truth about a feeling that arises.

Yoga Practice for Opening the Third Eye:

The sun and light are energizing qualities. Tempering them with the lunar qualities this month focuses the energy more into that of light, rather than fire. For this reason, it is important to go slowly, mindfully, and never to rush or go very fast. When yoga practitioners move into Sun Salutations and start to kick up energy, it is natural to start going fast. For this, I recommend stopping after every salutation to note, be mindful, and slow down the heart rate before resuming.

We are working with this energy to open our ajna point for connection to our intuition, so let's remember that this endgame is what makes this practice so much more different than a regular *vinyasa* or *asthanga* practice that might be more fiery.

Single Posture Practice: Yogi Eye Exercises (*Tratak*)

The Yogi Eye Rolls are perfect to open the energy of the ajna chakra. If you're performing them for the single posture practice, first take the eyes from ear to ear, pausing at each side. Then go up and down, pausing at each extreme. After performing the horizontal and vertical movements, take the eyes in a clockwise direction, and then counterclockwise. The number of rolls is up to you, but go at least once, and maybe up to three times in each direction.

After performing this one posture sequence, sit in meditation on your sankalpa, waiting for a vision if you're progressing wisely or need to adjust that intention for the second half of the year.

Breathing Practice: *Nadi Shodhana*

Alternate Nostril breathing is a core breath practice for yogis. As previously mentioned, the ida and pingula nadis enter through the nostrils and terminate at the third eye. By stimulating these nadis in this breathing practice, we are igniting the spiritual centers, moving pranic energy upwards, irrigating the male and female points at the nostrils that push the energy to the ajna center.

This is one of the main yoga breathing exercises recommended for daily use. There are several benefits to the breathing practice: balancing the nervous system, improving respiratory function, reducing stress, enhancing focus, boosting the immune system, and more. You can utilize this breathing practice daily.

There are many ways to perform Nadi Shodhana; we will start with a simple version. However, if you know a different method, please feel free to use that.

Sit comfortably, and bring your right hand up to your nose. Using the fingers to close off each nostril, one at a time, we will coordinate the breath. Take an inhale through both nostrils, then use the thumb to close the right nostril, exhaling through the left nostril. Pause, then switch to have the pinkie finger close the left nostril, exhaling through the right. Pause, then inhale through the right nostril, and toggle it closed, opening the left for the inhalation. Repeat for several minutes. Go slowly, and remember to pause after each inhalation and after each exhalation. To complete, exhale through the right nostril, and place both hands in the lap to feel the flow of energy upwards.

Mudra & Meditation:

Come to the easy-seated pose or Lotus seated pose. Bring your hands up to heart-level and touch all of the fingertips together, keeping the palms open. You can bring this up to the third-eye center if you like, or keep it at the heart. This is the *Hakini mudra* to awaken the ajna chakra.

Spend time in meditation/reflection, paying particular attention to any visions that arise. Then close the practice by bringing hands to heart, bowing head, and closing with an intention or prayer.

Hatha Yoga Sequence:

Seated Easy Pose for Nadi Shodhana	Seated "Making the Sun" in both directions	Lateral Body Stretches	Seated Spinal Twists	Child's Pose	Table
Cat/Cow	Downward Dog	Ragdoll	Mountain	Standing "Making the Sun"	Half Sun Salutations
Sun Salutations 2X	Mountain with Eye Rolls	Chair	Chair Balance	Tree	Warrior I
Warrior III or Airplane	Warrior II	Half Moon Balance	Standing Forward Fold	Tip-Toe	Cobbler
Seated Spinal Twist	Seated Forward Fold	Corpse - Final Relaxation	Easy Seated or Lotus	Meditation	Closing

* Note that the pre-recorded practice may differ from the sequence above.

Sun Salutation Variations:

"Making the Sun" is the first option. Start with your hands at your heart in prayer, then inhale the prayer upward towards the sun. Pause at the top, then exhale, opening your arms down and around the body, finishing with the hands back in prayer. Repeat several times, then change the direction by inhaling your arms out and around the body, above the head, and touching your hands together in prayer to bring it to your heart. You can take it three or more times in each direction, feeling the warmth of the sun entering your entire being. Again, pause at the end of several rounds to reflect.

The progression from "Making the Sun" to the next sequence of Half Sun Salutations can be performed or skipped, depending on how you feel. Likewise, after several half salutations, if you feel like skipping the full sun salutations, do so. Or, return to "Making the Sun." These three progressive movement series should be practiced in this order to accommodate day-to-day energy levels.

Half Salutations Sequence:

1. Mountain pose, inhale arms overhead, exhale, bowing to the earth.
2. Bring your hands to your shins, inhaling halfway up and gazing forward, and then exhale, bowing deeper to the earth.
3. Inhale, coming back up to standing with arms extending to the sky, and exhale, bringing your hands to your heart.
4. Perform 2 – 3 times, pausing each time in Mountain to reflect on sensations.

There are many sequences for Sun Salutation/Surya Namaskar from different schools of yoga. None is more correct than others, so if you feel comfortable with the method that you know, please work with that. The suggested namaskar here is similar to what many refer to as "Surya Namaskar A."

Sun Salutation Practice:

1. Mountain pose, inhale arms overhead, exhale, bowing to the earth.
2. Bring your hands to your shins, inhaling halfway up and gazing forward, and then exhale, stepping to Downward Dog.
3. Inhale to lengthen to Plank Pose, and then exhale to either Low Plank Pose or Caterpillar, where you bring knees, then chest, then belly to the floor.
4. Inhale to either Low Cobra, High Cobra, or Upward Facing Dog, where from Cobra you lift the knees and hips off the floor.
5. Exhale back to Downward Dog.
6. Inhale, looking at the hands, and on the exhalation, either step or just to the front of the mat.
7. Inhale to half lift with back straight, and then exhale, bowing to the earth.
8. Inhale, coming back up to standing with arms extending to the sky, and exhale, bringing your hands to your heart.
9. Perform 1 – 2 times, pausing each time in Mountain and in Downward Dog to reflect on sensations.

It is always recommended to modify postures and sequencing if you find yourself gasping for breath or overheating. Sequences like these namaskars are meant to create *tapas* or heat, but not done fast and furious. Pacing is slow and steady, always linking the breaths to the movement.

Short 15-minute Practice:

- Nadi Shodhana
- Making the Sun
- Eye Rolls
- Half or Full Sun Salutations (2X)
- Tree Pose
- Tip-Toe
- Cobbler
- Corpse

June Recap

The sun is our light in the sky. June, with the Summer Solstice energy, equates to much solar activity, vitality, and light. We are halfway through the year, and halfway through working with our sankalpa. Using the energy we have this month, tempered by our intuitive activations of the third eye, we check in at this midpoint and assess our progress. If things aren't going as we'd planned or hoped, we need to pivot and shift in the right direction. We need our intuition fully awakened to know if we are being true.

It's all on the line.

The chakra energies are intensifying and changing. Next month, we move to the crown of the head and celebrate the wisdom that we've acquired from our practices in life.

July

Wisdom

July Energies

July begins with heightened energy coming off the Summer Solstice. In the Northern Hemisphere, we are in the throes of summertime and celebration. Many people plan vacations and time off around this time of year because the weather is warm and children are finally done with their school year. If you are a teacher, a child, or even a parent, this may be your favorite time of year.

The number seven (7) means transformation, spiritual growth, wisdom, and understanding. It is equated to the 7th chakra, Sahasrara, which translates to "Thousandfold," a reference to the thousand-petaled lotus flower, reflecting deep wisdom and spiritual illumination.

July begins with the talented Crab, Cancer, and moves into Leo the Lion midway. Those born under Leo are usually known as natural-born leaders, charismatic, and very outgoing, often placing them at the center of everything. Another well-known title for the lion is "King of the Jungle," where he reigns supreme over all others in the animal kingdom. Leadership is a key element of July, a quality that most world leaders share along with wisdom.

The ruby, a stunning gemstone used worldwide by nobles and royalty, has the metaphysical property of vitality. The flower of the month, the water lily, represents majesty and can also symbolize purity, a quality associated with heightened spiritual states of being.

July is named after the Roman Emperor Julius Caesar, perhaps the most iconic and well-known ruler of ancient Rome. Julius Caesar reformed the original Roman calendar to the Julian calendar due to an inconsistency with the solar calendar. In truth, they are only about thirteen days different. Julius Caesar is responsible for many accomplishments during his tenure as emperor, including beginning the Roman Empire, which was at one time the largest in the world. It was by his intellect and political savvy that Julius was able to bring new life to Italy and create a legacy that is still on the lips of many today. There is no doubt that July, Julius, and Wisdom go together.

Throughout history, many kings and queens, heroes and emperors, and those who came first in their field fell under the sun sign of Leo. We know of Julius Caesar, but also Napoleon Bonaparte, the famous French Emperor with stunning military victories, Benito Mussolini, ally of Hitler who sought to establish his own Italian Empire, Fidel Castro, Cuban Revolutionary and President, Herbert Hoover,

31st US President, Bill Clinton, 42nd US President, Barack Obama, 44th US President, Queen Elizabeth, Mata Hari, famous German Spy during WWI, Neil Armstrong, American Astronaut known as the first man on the moon, Orville Wright, inventor of the first successful airplane, Amelia Earhart, first aviatrix to fly solo across the Atlantic Ocean, Tom Brady, New England Patriots' football player currently known as the best quarterback that ever lived, and, of course, Madonna, the Pop Star.

It is easy to see that too much Leo energy can become a misdirection of power. That is quite a list! Yes, Leos seek the limelight and often come up as winners. But we can see that empty and short-lived victories happen when the energy is not of a higher vibration.

Akin to the energy of fire, the strong energies accompanying July can easily become forceful. This may be why many people gravitate to vacationing and relaxing this month. Those who don't can experience extreme burnout, which comes easily with this much energy, and when not tempered with the opposing qualities of rest, rejuvenation, and nourishment.

Holidays and Holy Days

Our theme of wisdom comes from living and learning. July's main holidays spotlight this well. First up, July 4th, Independence Day for the United States of America. In 1776, fifty-six men, the forefathers of the USA, signed the Declaration of Independence, freeing the thirteen American colonies from British rule. These men had the wisdom and foresight to create the foundation of arguably the most celebrated of Nations in the world—the land of the "free" and home of the brave. Now, 250 years later, America is still considered to be the greatest government platform, source of great power, generosity, inclusivity, and democracy. Our forefathers were smart men.

Like Independence Day, France celebrates the unity of the French people on the 14th of July, known as Bastille Day. In 1789, in Paris, the French National Guard stormed the Bastille, a political prison and fortress symbolizing royal authority, leading to the overthrow of the monarchy in favor of more liberal ideals.

Historically, at this time, we see people pulling away from monarchs and dictatorships for governments aligned with the collective. We see people looking back at how they were treated and realizing that enough is enough and that the time has come for different policies. It takes great wisdom and strength to reach these radical new ideas.

We also have some big birthdays in July. Sikhs celebrate the birthday of their 8th Guru Har Krishnan on July 27th. His Holiness the Dalai Lama celebrates his birthday on July 6, 2025. Tenzin Gyatso is a living *Bodhisattva* of compassion and a global advocate for peace. His birthday in July is auspicious and fits our theme, faith tradition, and symbol for the month.

Islam also celebrates a special Holy Day, the Day of *Arafah*, which is Muhammad's farewell sermon, signaling the completion of the message of Islam. Muhammad is known as a prophet, political leader, and founder of the Islamic religion.

Mormons celebrate Pioneer Day on July 24, commemorating Brigham Young and the first group of Mormons who entered Salt Lake City, Utah, back in 1847.

Many Native American Indian tribes celebrate Green Corn Ceremonies in late July and early August, which is marked with celebrations and religious ceremonies that celebrate the harvest, but more importantly, to hold council meetings to forgive minor misgivings, burning waste, and purifying the body—all aspects of great wisdom and mastery.

Asalha Puja or Dharma Day occurs on the full moon of the eighth lunar month, Asalha, and usually occurs in July, sometimes in June. This Buddhist holiday commemorates the Buddha's first sermon after enlightenment, the Turning of the Wheel of Dharma, delivered to five ascetics at Deer Park, Sarnath, in the 5th century BCE. This sermon introduced the Four Noble Truths and the Noble Eightfold Path, symbolized by the *Dharmachakra*, marking the start of Buddhism.[48] It celebrates the founding of the *Sangha* (Buddhist community), with the ascetics becoming the first disciples.

Guru Purnima is also observed on the full moon day in *Ashadh*. Purnima is the day Hindus venerate the masters' lives with heartfelt gratitude for all the knowledge passed down for thousands of years. Guru Purnima is known as *Vyasa Purnima* for Buddhists and Jainists. They celebrate this holiday with festivals for spiritual and academic teachers who have removed their students from darkness and ignorance. In yoga schools, Lord Shiva is known as the first yoga and the first teacher, or *Adi Guru*. This knowledge is said to go back 15,000 years. This day of worship to one's beloved teacher acknowledges the prevalent energy of the month and closes it out with a perfect blend of celebrations of various wisdom teachings from various faith traditions.

---

[48] *The Heart of the Buddha's Teaching,* Thich Nhat Hanh, 1998

Chakra Connection

7th Chakra

Sanskrit: *Sahasrara*
Meaning: Thousand, lotus flowers with a thousand petals
Location: Crown of the head

This chakra symbolizes obtaining supra-mental consciousness of the truth that one is all, and all is one. It is the most sublime chakra of pure consciousness; formless and with form, it is nothing and it is everything at the same time.

Until recently, the seventh chakra was the final known energy center in the Hindu chakra system. Many other chakra systems, including Tibetan, Mayan, Cherokee, and others, are known and used, but haven't been as broadly studied and shared in written text as that of the Hindu system, where the story goes that the spiritual energy rises from the base of the spine to the crown of the head towards liberation. Here at the crown or seat of the seventh chakra, the individual consciousness, *atman*, meets with spirit, *Brahma*.

The seventh chakra is known in the physical as Mt. Meru, or Lord Shiva's Divine Seat. As the first *yogi* and first teacher, and a god in part of the Hindu trinity, Shiva, the destroyer, is wisdom incarnate. He is said to have instilled knowledge in his pupils. For any austere yogi or yogini, the awakening of the crown chakra can move him or her to experience the mystical with regularity. For the layperson, our cumulative knowledge throughout life is how the seventh chakra is understood.

For many yoga practitioners, moving energy upward to the crown chakra is the penultimate step of his/her spiritual practice. How can we begin to understand this energy center? See the companion Workbook for more questions, but consider these few journal prompts on your seventh chakra:

> Knowledge: How do you know what you know?

> Divinity: Do you have a strong spiritual connection?

Many yoga teachers say that our work is never quite finished at the crown chakra, and that we continue to amass wisdom and mastery throughout our lives. This certainly feels true. And although we have several more chakras to go, we focus on the energy of wisdom for the seventh as it connects, literally, to the pituitary gland in the human body. The pituitary is known as the "Master Gland" in the endocrine system, as it regulates hormones for all of the other glands in the body.

Moon Phases

New Moon:

New Moon means putting new energy into your knowledge base. Time to institute a new course of study. Take that online program that you've been looking at, or enroll in a community course at your local college. Perhaps you have been thinking about going back to school full-time or advancing in your career by taking a necessary training or workshop. New Moon to Full Moon phases are excellent times to do this in July, especially as it relates to your sankalpa and helping move it forward.

Waxing to Full Moon:

Since we are talking about assimilating knowledge (new or previously learned), this month is extraordinary for putting together your amassed wisdom into a professional paper, blog, or newsletter to share with the world. Publish a "teaser" about your sankalpa to share what's coming in July.

Waning & Dark Moon:

Meditation and Divinity are qualities that fall under the roof of this month, so keep a strong spiritual connection throughout this month and use the waning moon or dark moon times to reconnect to the spark of Spirit through prayer and meditation. You may be working with Universal energy daily now anyway, so there may not need to be a time to sit back and be with Spirit on any particular day, because you are inviting that quality into your everyday experience. And if you are not, maybe you can also step up that game now.

Faith Tradition: Buddhism

"The wise ones, ever meditative and steadfastly persevering, alone experience Nirvana, the incomparable freedom from bondage."

– Gautama Buddha, *Dhammapada*, Verse 23

If you look at the map of the Earth Chakras now made famous by Modern Mystic, Robert Coon, you will see that the planetary location of the 7th chakra is Mount Kailash, Tibet. Tibetan monks are renowned for their purity, wisdom, and spiritual connection. These Buddhists live a life dedicated to attaining liberation, which can only be found through austere practices that they work on daily in the high-vibrational mountains of the Himalayas.

The Buddha reached enlightenment after forty-nine days of uninterrupted meditation. Buddhist monks spend a lifetime honoring Buddha's path and teachings by removing themselves from society, living pious lives in monasteries, and dedicating every waking moment to attaining enlightenment. While this may seem like a dream lifestyle to many Modern Mystics, it doesn't usually work for most in our current culture.

The country of Thailand bridges this issue by requiring all males to enter into Monkhood for at least one year of their lives. This secures that each Thai male will immerse himself in the Buddhist spiritual tradition and thus make it a primary consideration in his life. Well, if they can do it for a year, perhaps, just perhaps, we can try it for a month.

<u>Three Primary Schools of Buddhism</u>:

- <u>*Theravada*</u>: This school is also known as the "Way of the Elders" and is the oldest surviving Buddhist tradition. It emphasizes the original teachings of the Buddha and is prevalent in Southeast Asia, including countries like Sri Lanka, Myanmar, and Thailand.

- <u>*Mahayana*</u>: This school, meaning "Great Vehicle," is known for its emphasis on the bodhisattva ideal (beings who have achieved enlightenment but vow to help all others reach it). Mahayana Buddhism is widespread in China, Japan, Korea, and Tibet.

- *Vajrayana*: Also known as "Diamond Vehicle," this tradition developed from Mahayana and is strongly associated with Tibetan Buddhism. It's known for its tantric practices and its focus on achieving enlightenment in a single lifetime.

Symbol: Dharmachakra

The Dharmachakra, often called the "Wheel of Dharma" or "Wheel of Law," is a sacred symbol in Buddhism, representing the teachings of the Buddha and the path to enlightenment. The Dharmachakra is an eight-spoked wheel, signifying the Noble Eightfold Path, the Buddha's teachings, and the cyclical nature of existence, guiding practitioners toward liberation from suffering. Its meaning encompasses several layers, rooted in the Buddha's first sermon, the Turning of the Wheel of Dharma[49], delivered after his enlightenment, when it is said that the Buddha set the wheel in motion.

The Wheel's turning symbolizes the Buddha setting these teachings in motion, spreading wisdom to end suffering (*dukkha*).

<u>Eight Spokes Correspond to an Aspect</u>:

- Right View (understanding reality)
- Right Intention (compassionate motives)
- Right Speech (truthful communication)
- Right Action (ethical conduct)
- Right Livelihood (harm-free work)
- Right Effort (cultivating positive qualities)
- Right Mindfulness (awareness)
- Right Concentration (meditative focus)

---

[49] *Dhammacakkappavattana Sutta*, 5th century BCE

July Altar

- **Altar cloth:** Violet, color of the seventh chakra

- **Flower:** Bouquet or bowl of Water Lilies

- **Candle:** Purple or violet

- **Crystal/Stone:** Rubies, as a gemstone, can be pricey, but you can find raw rubies quite easily, and they are not generally too expensive. Amethyst, a beautiful purple stone that also invokes the energy of calm, spiritual awareness, and inner peace, is a perfect substitute for the month.

- **Symbol:** Dharmachakra picture/drawing or a wise old owl

- **Essential Oil/Incense:** Cedarwood, Tibetans use in temple rituals for insight and spiritual protection

- **Herbs:** Ceremonial White Sage and Rosemary, an herb of remembrance and wisdom.

- **Other Items (optional):**
  - *The Modern Mystic's Wheel of the Year* Book, Workbook, and Oracle Deck
  - Since July's theme is Wisdom, place any textbooks, spiritual texts, scripture, or books for any course of study that you are either currently undertaking or are interested in taking on your altar this month.
  - Picture/Statue Options: (1) The Buddha, (2) your Higher Power, God, Goddess, Source Energy, Great Spirit, (3) Picture of your teacher or teachers who have influenced you on your spiritual journey. When working with the Buddha, it is appropriate to place his image in the Eastern quadrant of the home; however, it can sit at the center of the altar.
  - Push wisdom into your sankalpa this month by nourishing its presence on your altar.

Angel/Ancestor: Hermit or Monk/Nun

There are important distinctions between Hermits and Monks, both of whom follow Buddhism. You may choose to align with one versus the other for personal reasons, and so, the information is provided herein.

Hermits seek a life of solitude. Often living in remote places such as caves and forests, they prioritize self-guided meditation over alignment with a particular secular order. Monks, on the other hand, live in a monastic community (sangha), strictly following rules. The Hermit life aligns with the early Buddhist ideals. The Buddha himself withdrew from his life as Prince Siddhartha to meditate in solitude and renunciation, seeking the way to enlightenment. Monks practice the Buddha's teachings, which spotlight his Middle Path, a way he discovered after realizing that the Hermit life didn't provide him with all the answers that he sought. Note that only men can be Buddhist Monks. For women, the appropriate term is Nun.

Since we don't live in caves, but rather live engaging with society through work, family, and community, embodying the Hermit poses challenges. However, many people have carved out secluded lifestyles and may wish to take this further for the retreat ritual.

For others, the Monk may be a more accessible route. We already learned that Thai males must be monks for at least a year. This reinforces Buddhism's emphasis on everyday life. Some decide to stay and become ordained, committing fully to the monastic life. Novices take temporary vows, often shaving their heads and eyebrows and wearing traditional saffron robes, symbolizing detachment from worldly things.

Decide which to align with for this month: Hermit or Monk? If you chose one over the other and realize it isn't working for you, change to the other option. It's all a work in progress.

Hermit:

- Find a secluded spot, preferably in nature, for the duration
- Abstain from connection to the outside world in any way
- Commit to Buddhist self-study and meditative practices
- Have a plan in place to re-engage with society at the end of your time

Monk/Nun:

- Connect with a local Buddhist community (in person or virtually)
- Attend all appropriate meditation classes and ceremonies
- Continue self-study on days when the community doesn't offer any events
- Find ways to be of service
- Do your best to avoid social media, TV, and other outward distractions

July Ritual: Retreat

Vassa is the three-month rainy season retreat for monks, also known as the Rains Retreat or Buddhist Lent. During this time, monks and nuns remain in monasteries to study and meditate, a tradition since the Buddha's time. It's a time for intensive spiritual practice, reinforcing the Buddha's teachings, or Dharma. Its purpose is to deepen meditation, study, and utilize ethical discipline, fostering progress toward enlightenment or nirvana by minimizing worldly distractions.[50] Vassa is a structured period of intensive practice, with meditation and prayer as core activities, alongside study, chanting, and communal rituals.

If there's a local Buddhist community nearby, you may be able to study and learn along with the sangha there; otherwise, you can create your own template, including meditation, prayer, and study. Some practices to incorporate daily, or as often as you can, for the month are:

Meditation:

Meditation is the cornerstone of Vassa, utilized for cultivating mindfulness and concentration (the Dharmachakra's 7th & 8th spokes), purifying the mind of impurities to attain insight and tranquility. Meditation deepens the understanding of the Four Noble Truths and fosters progress toward enlightenment. Many types of Meditation exist, and each person will have his/her own methods that will work best for him/her. If you have no mediation experience, try each of the styles listed here to determine which one fits best for you. If you are still unsure, go back and try each one more consistently, as it does take regular practice to see any real results. Here are a few options:

- Breath - Observe the breath by concentrating on the four parts: inhalation, retention after inhalation, exhalation, and retention after exhalation. Note any sensations that arise and pass. Notice any thoughts that come and go. Do not try to change the breath, but instead be a witness to it.
- Candle Gazing - using a candle, sit comfortably and observe the flame. Notice what you see, feel, or understand. Keep the eyes soft and diffused.
- *Metta* (Loving-Kindness) - Cultivating compassion for all beings, starting with oneself, often combined with insight meditation, focusing on the breath, a thought, or the body to understand the nature of suffering, attachment, and impermanence.

---

[50] *The Heart of the Buddha's Teaching,* Thich Nhat Hanh, 1998

* Watch Rev. Dr. Tracey's *Metta* Meditation Here: https://youtu.be/ZGIo7lp6gAs.

Prayer & Chanting:

Prayer and chanting express devotion to the Three Jewels: Buddha, Dharma, and Sangha, reinforce ethical vows, and cultivate mindfulness for Buddhists. Mantra is the reciting of sacred mantras. Some to use are:

- *Om Mani Padme Hum* (translates as "Om the Jewel in the Lotus")
- *Om Ah Hum Vajra Guru Padma Siddhi Hum* (carries the entire blessing of the teachings of Buddha)

Devotional prayers to the Buddha and his teachings are a part of Vassa that you can incorporate. One such homage to the Buddha is:

- *Namo Tassa Bhagavato Arahato Samma Sambuddhassa*, a "Homage to the Blessed, Noble, Perfectly Enlightened One."

Dedications of merit can be recited after offerings or meditation: "May this merit benefit all beings."

Study of Scriptures:

Monks study Buddhist texts, focusing on the Four Noble Truths and the Eightfold Path. There is much information available about these teachings, both free online as well as in published books and translations. Look for local "Dharma Talks" with monks or other Buddhist practitioners in your area, as they can reveal hidden meanings within the texts often missed or misinterpreted by laypeople.

Ethical Discipline:

Monks adhere to 227 rules, while nuns adhere to 311. This could be a bit to manage for someone not on the Buddhist life path. However, we can commit to honoring several ethical disciplines for the month. Some things to consider are from the Eight Precepts. They are abstaining from killing, stealing, sexual activity, lying, intoxicants, eating after noon, entertainment and beautifying the body, and using luxurious furniture.

Almsgiving and Lay Support:

Lay Buddhists offer food, robes, or supplies daily, supporting monks who cannot cook during Vassa. This is a beautiful option for those wishing to support their local Buddhist monastery.

It is important to note that Vassa is primarily a monastic practice. This doesn't mean it is not welcome, but ask for permission before joining any activities at a local Buddhist temple. Honoring in a personal way at home, even by studying the Buddha's teachings, is a highly noble endeavor for this month's ritual practice.

Planning a month-long Buddhist retreat is also a possibility; however, this does require much planning and foresight. Luckily, there is always next July if you realize that you resonate with Buddhism this month and wish to take a deeper dive next year.

Tracey's Personal Reflection

Over the years, I've attended and hosted many retreats. In my earlier years with yoga, I visited The Kripalu Center for Yoga in Stockbridge, MA. This former ashram now hosts yoga workshops and R&R retreats, both of which I've attended there. One of my favorite parts of staying at Kripalu was the silent breakfast on Sunday mornings. I was so moved by this practice that I brought it into my local retreats over the years, which, unfortunately, was not equally appreciated by all of the participants. This little practice creates internal space while in a busy sangha —something significant in quieting all the busyness.

Another facet of practice that I strongly bonded with over the years is the mantra meditation. There's something incredibly profound about chanting sacred prayers in the language in which they were originally written, especially in Sanskrit, which is the oldest known language in the world. It is often referred to as a "perfect language." Many Buddhist texts are written in Sanskrit, as well as other languages. *Om Mani Padme Hum* is one of the first mantras that I was taught. I was introduced to this through the beautiful songstress, Deva Premal, from her 1999 CD, *Love is Space*. Since then, I've been lost in this mantra thousands of times, suspended in time with the sheer love of the Divine Essence being the predominant force.

Receiving *Sai Sin* (white thread) in Thailand by a Buddhist Monk's assistant (as Monks aren't allowed to touch women)

At the time of writing this book, I am 57 years old, and I just purchased another important spiritual text. I am always learning, always seeking a deeper connection to Spirit and my Highest Self, and always finding that the layers go even deeper. Meditation and retreat are essential for my personal spiritual journey, and also help me to be a better person in my life.

July Yoga Practice:
To Move Energy up to the Wisdom Center

This practice is for all levels, and no yoga experience is required. However, it is always recommended to consult a doctor before beginning any new physical program. Remember to modify anything for particular conditions that you may be experiencing, and to always follow your breath for the truth about a feeling that arises.

<u>Yoga Posture Sequence to Move Energy to the Crown Center</u>:

This month, we will move the energy from the first chakra up to the seventh in our all-level Hatha yoga sequence. By the end of the class, you will feel that all seven primary chakras are aligned. You can return to this practice as often as you like for the rest of the year and use this as a baseline for understanding your daily energy cycles.

Meditation is a foundational element to the 7th chakra, our faith tradition of Buddhism, and opening to deep wisdom, this month's theme. All postures should be practiced in a meditative way, focusing on deep breathing and on being present in the moment. Do not wiggle or move about. Find your seat and become one with the pose.

<u>Single Posture Practice</u>: Rabbit or Hare (*Sasangasana*)

From the hands and the knees, bring the crown of the head down on the floor. Interlace the fingers behind your back, squeeze your shoulders inward, and lift the arms over your head (like rabbit ears). Press the shins firmly down into the floor to support a grounding, ensuring that you are not crunching your cervical spine. Your hips should align directly over your knees. If bringing the arms over the head is difficult, keep the hands on the floor to support you in the posture.

To release, bring the hands to the floor, and put the hips back on the heels, resting the head and arms on the floor for Child's pose (*Balasana*).

Breathing Practice: Central Channel Breathing

By now, you understand that the seven major chakras are aligned on top of each other in a central energy channel, referred to as the Sushumna Nadi. This channel, where the subtle chakra energy centers reside, needs constant flushing and cleansing. This breathing practice will guide you into that.

Take a moment to visualize the Central Channel as a hollowed-out tube through the center of your body, with open ends at the first and seventh chakras. Think of a white light coming down from the Spiritual or Heavenly realms, or the Universe or Natural realms, and hitting the top of the head, awakening this opening in the Central Channel. Visualize light streaming down the channel to the base of the spine, opening the door at the bottom for the light to flow out, and down into the earth below you.

On the next inhalation, visualize the light coming up from below you in the earth, to the base of the spine, and upward through the channel to the crown of the head. On the exhalation, visualize the light moving back down through the central channel to the base of the spine, and out into the earth. Each inhale moves the light up, and each exhale moves the light down.

If you have issues visualizing, notice how this "feels" when you think of the energy moving up and down the central nadi. Repeat this until you feel that you have successfully moved energy up and down the channel, freeing it from any blocks or lower vibrational energy.

Mudra & Meditation:

Come to a seated pose, and bring the hands to *Jnana Mudra*, the Seal of wisdom, by bringing your index finger to the thumb and extending the other fingers. Allow for a silent meditation in which to connect to Spirit, listening for any advice or knowledge that the Divine may wish to share with you. When you are complete, bring your hands to prayer and bow.

* Note: This mudra is similar to our 4th chakra Vayu mudra, but differs in that the tip of the index finger is touching the thumb. Jnana Mudra is also known as *Gyan* Mudra, and these two are literally the same gesture with the same meaning. In fact, there are even other names for this famous yoga mudra.

Hatha Yoga Sequence:

Corpse – Guided Relaxation	Seated Central Channel Breathing	(1) Seated ½ Forward Fold	(1) Seated Forward Fold	(1) Child's Pose	(1) Downward Facing Dog
(2) Cobbler	(2) Animal Stretch with movement	(2) Seated Straddle	(3) Seated Twist	(3) Upward Boat	(3) Cat Cow with Leg Lifts
(4) Yoga Mudra	(4) 5-Pointed Star	(4) Warrior II	(4) Proud Warrior	(5) Standing Straddle with Yoga Mudra	(5) Mountain with Neck stretches
(5) Lion	(6) Eye Rolls	(6) Tree Pose	(6) Tip-Toe	(7) Dolphin Pose	(7) Rabbit Pose
(7) Headstand	(7) Child's Pose with Prayer Hands	Knees to Chest	Corpse - Final Relaxation	Silent Meditation	Closing

* Note that the pre-recorded practice may differ from the sequence above.

Begin in a supine position, lying on your back. Perform a guided relaxation starting with your right big toe, relax that, and then move all the way up to the crown of the head, one body part at a time. You can look for a guided body relaxation online, or pre-record yourself walking you through it. When you are complete with this, take a full body stretch, roll over, and come to a seated position or the Central Channel Breathing.

1st Chakra Poses:

This sequence will allow us to open up the first chakra. Visualize the color red, or that you are sending energy to open the base of the spine and the first energy center.

2nd Chakra Poses:

Move your awareness to the second chakra in the hips and visualize the orange color you are sending to open this chakra.

3rd Chakra Poses:

Move your awareness to the third chakra in the solar plexus and visualize the yellow color you are sending into the chakra.

4th Chakra Poses:

Take your awareness to the fourth chakra in your heart-center and visualize a green color you are sending to the chakra.

5th Chakra Poses:

Take your awareness to the fifth chakra in the throat and visualize a light blue color that you are sending to the chakra.

6th Chakra Poses:

Take your awareness to the sixth chakra at the Third-Eye and visualize an indigo light you are sending to the chakra.

7th Chakra Poses:

Take your awareness to the crown of the head and visualize a violet color you are sending to the chakra.

Close the practice in an extended relaxation, Yoga Nidra, or silent meditation to dwell in the energy liberated towards the crown of the head. Witness any insights that come while you bask in this state.

If you've never tried Yoga Nidra, known as yogic sleep, head to the secret page on the website that you opened with the Cipher and look for a short version of the practice there. If you can't find it, send an email to OneYogaCenter@gmail.com, kindly requesting the link.

Short 15-minute Practice:

- Central Channel Breath
- Forward Fold
- Cobbler
- Seated Twist
- Yoga Mudra
- Neck Stretches
- Eye Rolls
- Headstand
- Corpse

July Recap

Wisdom is an accumulated item. Practices and life lessons teach us what we understand about the world. If we never move to different areas, we limit our ability to accumulate knowledge and stifle our personal growth. Every faith tradition has a wisdom practice, often something that the founder taught to his/her disciples. There are more commonalities between traditions than differences. To truly understand any spiritual practice, we must look beyond what we have been taught and go deep into meditative places to reveal the truth.

Always be open to learning. Approach every opportunity from the mindset of a novice, a newcomer. Forget all that you think you know. Remember that Socrates said, "The only true wisdom is knowing that you know nothing."

Since this is merely the seventh month of the year, we understand that five more months are coming until we reach a full wheel cycle. It is good to amass knowledge, but as we move forward, we must move into the unknown, the uncomfortable, and the mystical to realize true wisdom.

August

Liberation

August Energies

The dog days of summer are in full swing in the Northern Hemisphere. "Dog Days of Summer" nods to Sirius, also known as the "Dog Star," the brightest star in the constellation Canis Major. Sirius means "scorching" or "burning," and is 23 times brighter than our sun, even though it appears much smaller. Sirius is a significant star in spiritual circles, believed to be a portal to higher dimensions, guiding humanity toward an awakened and enlightened path. This seems fitting for the theme of liberation this month.

In August, the weather is typically hot and dry; however, this time of year corresponds to the beginning of the monsoon season in Ayurvedic health and wellness practices in other parts of the world. No matter where you live, the energy of August is intense, lending to vacationing and relaxing for most people, especially students and schoolteachers who have less than a month before the new school season begins. For those who follow the school-year calendar, August can feel quite ominous with the stress of the impending change.

August is named after the first Roman Emperor, Augustus Caesar, from the original Roman calendar. As the eighth month of the year, the number eight corresponds to the energy of achievement, ongoing abundance, and opportunities. In the grand scheme of numbers, eight is close to the end of the hero's journey, so in August, we celebrate the hard work and achievements by letting go of the constant work and manifesting by allowing ourselves to relax a little. It's a very liberating experience!

The number eight (8) has many meanings, from success and abundance to infinity, renewal, and transcendence. It's considered a "lucky" number, as in the eight ball in pool. If you flip the number on its side, it then becomes the infinity symbol, another wheel-type structure, reminding us that there is an everlasting loop of life, never-ending, yet always changing form.

The beginning of August arrives on the back of Leo the Lion and his social energy from July, but by mid-August, we have moved into the earthly Virgo, the Virgin. In Mythic Astrology, Guttman says, "Virgo concerns transformation of personality from childlike or virginal state into a wiser, more mature individuality, represented by the fruition of the harvest."[51] This transformative energy is another

---

[51] *Mythic Astrology*, Guttman & Johnson, 1998, pg. 288

type of liberation: exalting one to a higher state from whence they came and opening up to greater wisdom and power.

This time of the year brings many different meteor showers, flying through the night sky. While meteor showers follow cyclical patterns, many believe they offer messages from Spirit, bringing insights and opportunities to manifest goals and desires. Work to send energy towards your sankalpa this month, with the energy of liberation behind it, and you may get a great breakthrough.

August's peridot birthstone reminds us to enjoy the beauty in life. The gladiolus is the flower of strength and integrity. These are important points for the month. While we have intense energies around us, we also have a slight inward pull, signifying enjoyment of the harvest.

Life is meant to be joyful, something many forget, especially when having challenges. August brings monsoons and hurricanes, and life can feel like we are caught in the middle of gale-force winds, whipping us around to and fro. Remember to stop and smell the roses. Remember to have fun and play. Be like a kid jumping in the puddles after a storm. This is what August is teaching us.

Holidays and Holy Days

August 1st is the pagan celebration of Lammas or Lughnasadh, the first Harvest festival and celebration of the wheat harvest. The planting of seeds in January, which began as thoughts and preparations, was planted in February and March. Those seeds started sprouting in April and May, and now, by August, have come to full fruition. Whether we are talking about our sankalpa or crops, this is a time to celebrate!

Matthew 4:4 says, "Man shall not live by bread alone." However, our ancestors honored the seasonal selections naturally grown in the area. Modern Mystics are committed to living by the earth's natural cycles, so if you've given up wheat, perhaps you could allow yourself a small privilege in August in some way that works with your particular dietary needs.

Often in August, *Janmastami* or Krishna's Birthday is celebrated. Krishna is one of the most beloved Hindu gods. He is worshiped as the eighth (a link to August) avatar of Vishnu, the preserver god, meaning that he keeps life going in the Universe. Krishna is most known as God in the Hindu epic, the Mahabharata, a 5th-century poem. This lengthy tale extols the mythology behind the pantheon of gods in Hinduism.

August's third holiday is *Eid al-Adha*. This Islamic holy day celebrates God's intervention in the sacrifice of the son of Abraham, but also in Abraham's willingness to listen to the word of God, even though it meant losing his son. In both these last two religious holidays, Janmastami and Eid al-Adha, the piety of man and devotion to God are celebrated. In their devotions, they find God's compassion and intervention before potential devastation. The clear moral is that true victory comes from self-sacrifice and complete faith in one's Higher Power, which is not something that just happens out of nowhere, but must, rather, be nurtured over time—the reward of which is attaining God's love.

In late summer, the Green Corn Festival is celebrated by various Native American tribes. Corn was the primary cultivated item for Native Americans, who then gifted it to the European settlers. It was the settlers who, in turn, gifted the Native American Indians wheat. The Green Corn Festival is a three-day celebration and a religious ceremony, with dancing, feasting, fasting, and ceremonies. Although different tribes may practice the Green Corn festival in their own ways, the commonality is that corn shouldn't be eaten until Great Spirit or Wakan Tanka gives his proper thanks.

According to Legends of America, during this event, tribal members give thanks to all things that contributed to a good harvest, including the corn, rain, and sun, among others.[52] During this celebratory time, tribes may perform cleansing rituals, celebrate baby naming, host ball tournaments, and hold council meetings. The Green Corn Festival is about harvest and renewal.

Ganesh Chaturthi honors the birth of Lord Ganesha, the elephant-headed Hindu god, remover of obstacles, and god of beginnings. And when obstacles are removed, we most certainly will feel liberated. It is celebrated on the fourth day of *Bhadrapada,* per the lunar calendar, which often falls in August.

---

[52] https://www.legendsofamerica.com/na-ceremoniGreen Corn Festivals

Chakra Connection

8th Chakra

Sanskrit: *Viyapini*
Meaning: That which is present everywhere
Location: Above the crown of the head (12-18")

Thought to be the first of the "spiritual chakras," this energy center is known as the "Soul Star."

The eighth chakra moves us out into uncharted waters. Known as the "Soul Star" chakra or Viyapini, this chakra takes us above the crown of the head and beyond the physical body. Since it's the first chakra that is not directly associated with the physical body, it can be challenging to understand. The ancient yogis studied and learned about the seven-chakra model, which has been the primary guide to the chakras for thousands of years. It has been a fairly recent occurrence that we have begun to discover these upper chakras that bridge the human body to the energetic bodies. It is exciting stuff!

The actual location of the eighth chakra is a bit of a debate in the energy communities. Some say that it sits just above the crown, and others say maybe 12-18" above it. Regardless, we know that we now move out and into the higher light resonance and vibrational field. The color is ultraviolet or magenta (with some sources saying silver), and this is where we link to our "Higher Self."

What is our true purpose on Earth? Why do we experience the many challenges we have gone through in this life? What are the recurring patterns for our souls? These are appropriate questions to ponder as we move into the higher realms of this chakra.

We want to understand and move into a greater place, ascending upward to the larger scope of who we are and in our Soul Star. Understanding the "grander you" is an incredible achievement in this life. Working diligently through your seven chakras to the point of unlocking the eighth is such an achievement. Just as August is linked to the number eight, symbolizing near completion, we celebrate achieving the connection to our higher self and becoming liberated from the lower self.

How might one connect to the energy of the eighth chakra? See the companion Workbook for more questions, but consider this journal prompt on your eighth chakra:

Soul: What karmic patterns/cycles do you need to work out?

Energy appropriately winds down in August, allowing us to carve out some time to contemplate and work with the eighth chakra, the first of the higher chakras. Do a quick review of the seven chakras, and notice what you have accomplished, and remember to honor all that hard work.

Moon Phases

Dark Moon:

The Dark Moon is the night to rest and relax, meditate, and contemplate all the hard work that you have done for the past seven months. Where do you stand with your sankalpa? Most likely, if you have been putting regular energy into it, much like the month's numerological identity of eight, you see considerable progress and near completion. But what if you don't? Remember, it is okay to be where you are. Consider what threw you off, and perhaps find a smaller thing to celebrate the completion of this month, so that you can feel good about what you accomplished.

New Moon:

When you consider the idea of liberation, what jumps out to you? Create a new moon intention for an area or aspect of your life that embodies the energy of liberation, and make a plan honoring that intention.

Waxing Moon:

Follow through with your plan during the waxing moon period and up to the full moon. And make sure that this plan and liberation intention align with your sankalpa.

Full Moon:

We know that the full moon offers a burst of energy towards anything that is our focus. With liberation as our theme, and understanding the significance of the objects in the sky as we move into the higher realms of our being, create a ritual this evening to assist you in liberating yourself from anything that has kept you stuck or has been holding you back. Look to this month's practices or any of the previous ones to help liberate you.

Waning Moon:

Waning moon time is when we begin to unplug and wind down, as you most likely need from the abundant energy of the past several months. Remember, there is great liberation in letting go.

Faith Tradition: Hinduism

"When a man is free from desire, his mind is not swayed; having abandoned attachment, he attains liberation, the supreme state of freedom."

– Krishna, Bhagavad Gita, Chapter 2, Verse 71

Hinduism's concept of liberation (*moksha*) is the ultimate spiritual goal, achieved through various paths, rituals, and festivals, many of which are prominent in August. The lotus flower underscores this pursuit, while August's festivals provide practical and devotional expressions of liberation's ideals.

Moksha is a central theme in Hinduism (as well as Buddhism and Jainism), referring to liberation or emancipation from the cycle of birth, death, and rebirth. It can be translated as freedom, release, or *nirvana*, representing the ultimate goal in a spiritual life.

Both Krishna's and Ganesha's birthdays are celebrated in August. Yet these are only two of a pantheon of Hindu gods and goddesses, the exact number of which is difficult to determine, but thought to be well in the hundreds or even thousands. The Rig Veda says, "Three thousand three hundred and thirty-nine gods have worshipped Agni," but this is most likely symbolic rather than a precise number.[53] However, in the epic poem the *Mahabharata,* composed between 400 BCE and 400 CE, Lord Krishna states in its well-known section titled *The Bhagavad Gita,* "I am the source of the gods and sages in every way."

While Hinduism has no single founder, it is considered one of the world's oldest religions, with diverse practices, some of the oldest spiritual texts, and a vast spiritual landscape. There are currently approximately 1.2 billion people worldwide who follow Hinduism. However, the reach of certain of its teachings through yoga schools and other spiritual centers cannot be determined. Certainly, the extent of Hinduism, which, remember, was the Buddha's original faith tradition, cannot be truly known. Most likely, it is far greater than we know.

Since he put it that way, celebrating Krishna's birthday in August, along with the concept of *moksha,* gives Hinduism an appropriate status as our month of liberation.

---

[53] *Rig Veda,* 3.9.9

Sacred Symbol: Lotus

The otherworldly lotus flower holds profound significance in Hinduism, symbolizing purity, spiritual awakening, and divine beauty, among other concepts. The lotus grows in muddy waters yet blooms pristine and untouched, symbolizing purity and detachment from worldly impurities (*maya*). It represents the soul's ability to remain untainted by materialism or sin while living in the world. This purity aligns with the pursuit of liberation.

The lotus embodies divine beauty and is associated with the creation of the universe. In Hindu cosmology, Lord Vishnu, the preserver, gives rise to a lotus from his navel, from which Brahma, the creator, emerges to form the world. Deities such as Lakshmi (the goddess of wealth), Saraswati (goddess of knowledge), and Vishnu are depicted holding or seated on lotuses, signifying their divine qualities.

Lotus flowers or petals are offered in *puja*, floated in water bowls, or used in *homa* (fire rituals), symbolizing purity and devotion. Think of the lotus as a Hindu "freedom flower," used in August prayers and festivals to show the heart's wish to be pure and join God forever.

August Altar

- **Altar cloth:** Ultra-violet/Magenta (or silver) altar cloth, the color of the 8th chakra

- **Flower:** A bouquet of Gladiolus or any magenta colored flowers

- **Candle:** Magenta candles

- **Crystal/Stone:** Peridot stone, prayer bead bracelet, or necklace. If you want to work with a magenta crystal, Rubellite/Magenta Tourmaline varieties will work.

- **Symbol:** Lotus in any form or color, natural or created

- **Essential Oil/Incense:** Pachouli, used in Hindu rituals for releasing and liberating

- **Herbs:** Ceremonial White Sage and a floral arrangement of dried wheat using grasses from the area, and tying them with a ribbon

- **Other items (optional):**
  - *The Modern Mystic's Wheel of the Year* Book, Workbook, and Oracle Deck
  - Items for Ritual: lotus flower, tulsi leaves, 2–4 incense sticks of sandalwood or your choice, a small oil lamp with ghee or sesame oil and a cotton wick, or a candle, offerings such as sweets, fruit, or homemade butter/milk, a small cup of clean water, spoon for *achamana* (purification, small handbell to invoke Krishna's presence, cloth for wiping the idol, *Kumkum* (red powder), sandalwood paste, and conch shell
  - Pictures or statues of any Hindu gods or deities, but especially Krishna
  - Continue to up-level your sankalpa by keeping something on your altar that inspires you

Angel/Ancestor: Sage

The ancient sages, or rishis, are known far and wide for their profound wisdom and insights into the practices that lead the human person to liberation. Through devotion, austerities, and rituals, the Sage has brought us some of the most enlightening wisdom pieces the world has ever known.

Rishis composed the Vedas, the world's oldest written text and the foundation of Hinduism, in the Vedic Period (1500–500 BCE). These texts are said to be channeled directly from God, and thus not of human origin.

Sages gave us the world's oldest self-development tool: yoga. Whether it's meditation to still the mind, breathing practices to channel life-force energy, mudras that further channel appropriate energy, or the classical postures that are said to prepare the body for the grueling task of liberation and ascension that the world has come to define as being yoga, this extensive system continues to provide humanity with a way to work towards Oneness. In this book, we practice yoga monthly. Therefore, one could say that we link with their wisdom every month. So, we will work through our ritual to take this month to the next level.

There are living sages who are accessible globally. Often found in temples or ashrams, they may be known as *gurus* (teachers) or *sadhus* (wandering modern ascetics). One can visit a temple or an ashram to work with various gurus. Extensive research should be conducted before attending an ashram setting so that you are prepared for the rigorous schedule and expectations. Due to the negative aspects sometimes associated with gurus, it's also suggested to discover the true person behind the teachings and ensure that they are of integrity in their position.

For yoga practitioners (yogi or yogini) already dedicated to the practice of yoga, one can connect with ancestral sages through meditation and chanting, following the moral and ethical principles outlined in the *Yoga Sutras*, and humbly calling in these masters to be with you, particularly during your practice or, if you are a yoga teacher, during your classes.

The *Gayatri Mantra* is said to be one such chant of universal prayer to assist in alignment with ancient *rishis*.

Gayatri Mantra:

Om
(Represents the divine cosmic vibration)

Bhur, Bhuvah, Svaha
(the physical, astral, and celestial planes of existence)

Tat Savitur Varenyam
(That, the most excellent, the source of all life)

Bhargo Devasya Dhimahi
(We meditate upon the divine light and radiance)

Dhiyo Yo Nah Prachodayat
(May that light illuminate our intellect)

Om, Shanti, Shanti, Shanti
(Om, peace, peace, peace)

Even those who are not dedicated yoga practitioners can reverently ask for guidance from the sages and rishis. Intention is the key. Never practice as an authority, but rather with humility and respect.

August Ritual: *Krishna Puja* & *Bhakti* Yoga

In Sanskrit, puja translates to homage, worship, reverence, or adoration. Hindus create elaborate rituals around holy days and deities to celebrate and honor them. One of the paths to liberation (moksha) for a yogi is *Bhakti* Yoga, the yoga of devotion. Devotees surrender to deities like Krishna, Vishnu, or Shiva daily, achieving liberation through loving devotion. One way this devotion is expressed is through the use of sacred mantras that repeatedly invoke the name of God. It is an act of mysticism, whereby the lover and the beloved (God) become one.

Due to the tenderness and truth required to engage in this loving act with the divine, you must be all in. Surrender and being open are requirements. Lord Krishna is the respective deity for the puja, fitting perfectly for his birthday month and exaltation as perhaps the supreme god of Hindus. However, if you feel that there is another deity, perhaps Ganesha, that you wish to honor, please work accordingly to your heart.

A Krishna puja combines devotion, ritual offerings, and prayer, typically performed at home on a small altar or in a temple, focusing on Krishna's qualities as the divine lover, protector, and source of all gods.

Preparation:

Perform the puja at dawn or dusk, when energies are calm, or during Krishna Janmashtami for Krishna's birth. Select a clean, quiet corner of your home. Set up a small altar facing east or north, covered with a clean cloth (white or yellow as Krishna's colors).

Items Needed:

- Statue or picture of Krishna
- Lotus flowers
- Tulsi leaves
- Fresh flowers
- 2–4 incense sticks of sandalwood or jasmine
- Small oil lamp with ghee or sesame oil and a cotton wick, or a candle
- Offerings such as sweets, fruit, or homemade butter/milk
- A small cup of clean water
- Spoon for *achamana* (purification)

- A small handbell to invoke Krishna's presence
- A clean cloth for wiping the idol
- *Kumkum* (red powder)
- Sandalwood paste
- Conch shell

Set up the altar by placing the Krishna idol/image at the center, elevated on a small platform or cloth. Surround him with flowers, snacks, and a candle, as if you were decorating for a special friend coming over.

Cleanse yourself and the space by bathing or washing your hands, feet, and face. Wear clean, modest attire crafted from natural fabrics. Clean the area of the altar by sprinkling water mixed with turmeric or sandalwood, or lighting incense to purify the atmosphere.

Puja Ritual Steps:
(follow these steps with devotion, focusing on Krishna as the divine source)

1. Sip water three times from your right palm, chanting: "*Om Keshavaaya Namah*" (Homage to Krishna), purifying body and mind.

2. Sprinkle water on the altar items, saying "*Om Shuddhi*" (purification), to sanctify them.

3. Ring the bell gently, inviting Krishna's presence, and chant: "*Om Shri Krishnaya Namah, Avahayami*" (I invoke Lord Krishna). You can also say, "Come, Krishna," and imagine him joining you.

4. Visualize Krishna arriving, smiling with his flute, adorned with a lotus.

5. Offer a small cloth or lotus, saying: "*Om Shri Krishnaya Asanam Samarpayami*" (I offer a seat to Krishna)

6. Gently pour water over the idol (or sprinkle if using a picture), saying: "*Om Shri Krishnaya Snanam Samarpayami*" (I offer a bath to Krishna)

7. Place a small cloth (yellow/blue) or garland of lotus/tulsi flowers on the idol, saying: "*Om Shri Krishnaya Vastram Samarpayami*" (I offer clothes to Krishna)

8. Light incense sticks, wave them clockwise before Krishna, saying: *"Om Shri Krishnaya Dhoopam Samarpayami"* (I offer incense to Krishna)

9. Light the oil lamp or candle, wave it clockwise, saying: *"Om Shri Krishnaya Deepam Samarpayami"* (I offer light to Krishna)

10. Offer sweets, butter, milk, or fruits, placing them before Krishna, saying: *"Om Shri Krishnaya Naivedyam Samarpayami"* (I offer food to Krishna)

11. Chant Krishna's mantra to deepen devotion, focusing on his role as the source of all, repeating it 108 times:

    "Hare Krishna, Hare Krishna,
    Krishna Krishna, Hare Hare,
    Hare Rama, Hare Rama,
    Rama Rama, Hare Hare"

Hare is another name for Vishnu, meaning "He who removes illusion." Krishna and Rama refer to the Supreme Godhead, meaning "He who is All-Attractive" and "He who is the Source of All Pleasure"

12. Wave the lamp or a camphor flame clockwise in front of Krishna.

13. Offer lotus or tulsi flowers, placing them at Krishna's feet, saying: *"Om Shri Krishnaya Pushpam Samarpayami"* (I offer flowers to Krishna)

14. Prostration (*Namaskara*) - walk clockwise around the altar 3 times (or turn in place if space is limited), saying: *"Om Shri Krishnaya Pradakshinam Samarpayami"* (I offer circumambulation to Krishna). Bow or prostrate before Krishna, saying: *"Om Shri Krishnaya Namaskaram Samarpayami"* (I offer salutations to Krishna)

15. Partaking of *prasada* - take a small portion of the food (*prasada*), considering it blessed by Krishna, and share with family/friends

16. Thank Krishna for his presence, saying: *"Om Shri Krishnaya Visarjanam Samarpayami"* (I bid farewell to Krishna)

17. Extinguish the lamp safely, store reusable items, and dispose of used flowers respectfully.

Simplification:

If time or resources are limited, or the pronunciation of all the mantras seems daunting, light a lamp, offer a lotus or another flower, and chant Hare Krishna.

It is perfectly fine to say the English translations of the chants and mantras. This may be a much more accessible way for you to feel connected to Krishna and the puja.

Tracey's Personal Reflection

Bhakti Yoga is one of the five main styles of yoga, along with Jnana (yoga of knowledge), Karma (yoga of action), Hatha (forceful yoga, known for its postures and breathing practices), and Raja (the "Royal" yoga, which includes facets of all of the others). It is said that any one of these modalities can be the vehicle to enlightenment for a dedicated yogi. In my advanced 500-hour yoga teacher training, I taught all five of these styles, allowing each trainee the time to see which style felt most authentic for him/her. The section on Bhakti Yoga was always well received, with most of my students thoroughly enjoying this way of connecting to the divine.

As I've already shared, I love chanting mantras. But Bhakti Yoga goes beyond singing. According to Kirtan artist, Krishna Das, "Bhakti Yoga isn't something you join. It's love. It means falling in love." Das is a devotee of the Indian Saint, Neem Karoli Baba (Maharajji), who grew up "a middle-class Jewish kid on Long Island," as he says. He met spiritual teacher Ram Dass after returning from a pilgrimage to India, having spent time in the presence of Maharajji. Fascinated by Ram Dass' stories, Krishna Das set out to meet Maharajji himself and quickly became one of his most beloved disciples.

To hear Krishna Das talk about Maharajji is nothing short of deeply moving. The love for his guru emanates from his entire being and takes form in the mantras that he guides others in. I've been in kirtan, the group chanting call-and-response format, with Krishna Das many times. I cry every time.

NYC, Nov 2018

Princeton Univ., May 2015

The first time I heard the mantra "Baba Hanuman" from his CD *Breath of the Heart*, it hit me like a ton of bricks. It literally stopped me in my tracks, and I fell to my knees, crying with joy and in love with blessed Hanuman—and I didn't even know who he was at the time. That's Bhakti.

August Yoga Practice:
Connecting to the "Soul Star"

This practice is for all levels, and no yoga experience is required. However, it is always recommended to consult a doctor before beginning any new physical program. Remember to modify anything for particular conditions that you may be experiencing, and to always follow your breath for the truth about a feeling that arises.

Yoga Posture Sequence for 8th Chakra:

For the 8th Chakra practice, we will spend more time in Meditation in the beginning, and learn how to move the energy upward and out of the crown/7th Chakra, to connect to this "Soul Star" which holds the records of our life's purpose for this life, and perhaps for several lifetimes, along with karmic lessons.

There should be a focus on stillness and being in this practice. Resist the urge to move, wiggle, and feel around. The postures included in the long sequence are meant to assist you in being more comfortable sitting longer and being still. Your central nervous system is the command center that controls body movements, and the spinal cord is a pathway for messages to the body. The thalamus, a part of the brain, has extensive nerve connections and relays to the brain. All of these poses are designed to assist energy in moving upward through the central channel, along the spine, through the brain, and higher energy centers, and to the 8th star, and then, back toward that chakra through the body.

This will be a more challenging chakra to work with, so stop the overthinking, lower brain, and allow the practice to align you with the higher brain's abilities.

Single Posture Practice: Making the Sun & the Moon

This can be performed seated on the floor, in a chair, standing, or even in certain postures. The hands start in Prayer or *Atmanjali* Mudra at the heart center.

As you inhale, reach the prayer upward through the center line of the body and towards the 8th chakra. Pause, then exhale, opening the arms out, down, and around the body, repeating. This is "Making the Sun."

After several rounds, change direction by inhaling the arms out, and up to the 8th chakra, pausing, then exhaling and bringing them down to the heart, for "Making the Moon." Visualize the energy flowing through the chakras and up to the 8th chakra, then back down again and into the earth to the physical form your soul chose to inhabit in this lifetime.

This "pose" is considered a moving meditation.

Mudra & Meditation:

Come to the easy-seated pose or Lotus seated pose. Place your hands into your heart to Prayer or do Anjali Mudra. Bring the prayer up above the head towards the 8th chakra/Soul Star. Release the hands back to the heart. Perform Central Channel Breathing up and down the spine, this time going above the head and into the 8th chakra. Focusing on connecting with the Soul Star and its bright Magenta color. Breathe that light down through your spine to your root and back up again through the crown to the Soul Star. Allow your being to open up to the Akashic Records, the records of all time, to assist you in revealing your Life Purpose.

Spend as much time here as you need. You can build energy to this chakra every day, and you will find that the Akashic Records begin to open up to you with continued focus.

Breathing Practice: *Kumbhaka* Breath Retention or 4,4,8

From a comfortable seated position, keeping the spine erect, take several deep breaths to center yourself in the moment. When ready, take a long inhalation to a slow count of four. Hold your breath for an equal count of four. Then take a slow exhalation to a count of eight. Repeat this pattern, focusing on the pause between the inhalation and exhalation. If 4,4,8 is too long for you, try 3,3,6. If you are a seasoned practitioner and can do more, try 6,6,12.

After some time, allow yourself to take slow, deep inhalations, pause for longer periods of time, feeling the rest and space in the pause, before exhaling. You have control over how long you hold, but you can encourage yourself to be present in the moment and in the pause. Notice that in the seeming void, everything is…

Hatha Yoga Sequence:

Seated Easy Pose for Khumbuka Breath	Neck Stretches & Head Rolls	Cobbler	Seated 1/2 Forward Fold	Body Rolls	Seated Cat/Cow
Seated Spinal Twist	Seated Pigeon	Child	Hero	Tratak/ Eye Exercises	Thymus Tapping
Lotus	Central Channel Breathing	Meditation	Alternate Nostril Breathing	Corpse	Closing

* Note that the pre-recorded practice may differ from the sequence above.

Short 15-minute Practice:

- Seated Easy-Pose with Kumbhaka breath
- Neck Stretches
- Body circles
- Eye rolls
- Thymus tapping
- Akashic Record Meditation
- Corpse

August Recap

After seven solid months of hard work and dedication, where are we? Do we use the energy of the month to move us forward, or do we slow down and pause to reflect? August can be versatile that way.

As we consider the concept of liberation, we move beyond the physical limitations of our human form.

What, if anything, is still holding us back from being the vast and timeless True Self?

What soul patterns can we unlock to free up and liberate us?

We do this work now because from September through December, we usher in a time of celebration and homage to the many people and things that have assisted us in this journey. The journey is not complete, but we are moving closer to achieving our goal.

September

Friendship & Community

September Energies

September launches us into the final third of the year, and thus, another shift is underfoot. The number nine (9) in numerology represents completion and letting go, and with a connection to the 9th chakra, we enter into a strange synergistic mix of finality and newness. The mixture of holidays in September can also lend to a confusion of energy, and yet, there is a sublime recollection that in seeming opposites, there is unity and wholeness.

Growing up in the United States, September signaled a return to the school year. Although some places begin earlier, the school year is the working calendar for most people, even long after they and their children have completed active years in school. Recall what it felt like at the beginning of school every year when you suddenly found yourself back in touch with friends that you had not seen all summer long, and forging new friendships as you changed grades, moved into different classrooms, and met people who just transferred into the district. Friendships were forged, and your tribe or community came together by the end of the month. This represents the energy of September.

September's birthstone, the sapphire, symbolizes truth, and the flower, aster, symbolizes patience; two endearing qualities for friends and communities, both reflected in the Hebrew text, the *Torah*:

> Exodus 20:16:
> *You shall not give false testimony against your neighbor.*
>
> Genesis 29:20:
> *So Jacob served seven years to get Rachel, but they seemed like only a few days to him because of his love for her.*

When investigating the zodiac influences for September, we begin with Virgo, associated with the Goddess Astraea, a symbol of Justice, then move to Libra, or Scales, as the only mechanical instrument of the zodiac, held by Astraea.

As pointed out in *Mythic Astrology*, Virgo's theme is that of the transformation of the childlike or virgin state to the more mature. The book goes on to say, "This personal transformation must take place so that we can re-orient ourselves from personal to universal concerns."[54]

---

[54] *Mythic Astrology* pg. 288

Then we look to Libra's scales and see a connection to the Egyptian Goddess Ma'at, who famously placed a human soul and a feather on each side of the scale to determine if the soul must reincarnate or not.

Both of these stories of Virgo and Libra indicate a need for transcendence from the mundane and a seeking of our soul for meaning and truth, which is a beautiful connection to the 9th chakra or "Stellar Gateway," where our soul descends into our body.

We came to discover something in this life. We came to learn and to become better people. All of this self-discovery, however, means nothing without others to live and work with. This need for friendship and community sits at the heart and soul of our desires, because at the end of the day, we are all One.

Holidays and Holy Days

September offers an array of holidays showcasing roots from several different traditions, many with connections to our theme of community and friendship. The first Monday in September is the US holiday Labor Day, when the American labor force celebrates the hard work it has collectively put in. It is a national tribute to our work ethic. Here we can see our country come together as a community to enjoy this day.

We can see from both *Muharram* (the Islamic New Year) and *Navaratri* (the Hindu "Nine Nights of the Goddess") that these are celebratory days when communities come together. *Muharram* is a solemn holiday often marked by participation in processions, prayers, and religious gatherings, with a focus on remembrance and reflection. Navaratri is an annual holiday celebrating the Goddess Durga's victory over the demon Mahishasura, and thus the victory of "good over evil." Durga is celebrated in her three forms: Kali (destruction), Lakshmi (wealth, beauty), and Saraswati (wisdom, knowledge, learning).

Likewise, the pagan holiday *Mabon*, celebrated on the Autumn Equinox around the 20th, marks the second harvest. Similar to Ostara in March, we find an equal day of light and dark on the opposite side of the year during Mabon, yet instead of the planting of seeds beginning, we now see the fruition of the seeds planted in the harvest. Together, we then celebrate with festivals and feasts during Mabon, in community and friendship.

On the 29th, the Feast of the Archangels, specifically Archangel Michael, is celebrated. It is known that Archangels are always close by, but we must invite them into our lives, and in doing so, we create a relationship with them. Many people have often found that they have become some of their very best friends.

This brings us to the two Jewish holidays that often fall in September: *Rosh Hashanah* and *Yom Kippur*. Rosh Hashanah is known as the Jewish New Year, formerly known as "Feast of Trumpets" or "Day of Shouting." The Feast of Trumpets is first spoken of in Leviticus 23:23-25. At this time, the Israelites had been brought out of Egypt and had built the Tabernacle. God gave instructions for Moses to tell the Israelites. God tells Moses the exact time the Israelites are to celebrate and how the people should celebrate. This feast was a call to the Israelites to stop work and honor God.

Yom Kippur is known as the "day of atonement," where Jews practice fasting and prayer, also usually spending the entire day in synagogue. This place of worship is where Jews congregate to celebrate their faith. The synagogue is vital for Jews in maintaining their identity and fostering a sense of belonging.

Chakra Connection

9th Chakra

Sanskrit: *Vyomanga*
Meaning: Heavenly Being or Sky Being
Location: Above the 8th Soul Star chakra

Known as the "Stellar Gateway," "Mouth of God," or "Seat of the Soul," it is the exact entry point and exit point of the soul into the body.

The 9th month and the 9th Chakra are associated with Ascension energies and soul programs. It is said that our soul has a plan and waits for the perfect moment in which to incarnate into this world. We, as Consciousness, want to experience life, grow, and be the best beings that we can be. To do this, we must traverse various landscapes in this life, some of which can be quite arduous and challenging. But we do this to expand our awareness and continue our spiritual development. To summarize: we signed up for this—all of it.

Viktor Frankl's book *Man's Search for Meaning* reminds us of this. This memoir of Frankl's account of surviving the Nazi death camps explains how he and others survived their experience because they had a drive to press on to find meaning in their life. We must continue to strive to be better people because our world needs us to. He explains in the last two sentences of his book:

> *Since Auschwitz, we know what man is capable of.*
> *And since Hiroshima, we know what is at stake.*[55]

Consider a significant event in your life. Your soul created a situation for you to explore that challenge for a reason. Somewhere, embedded in that pain and suffering, is the key to your purpose in this lifetime.

The ninth chakra is the highest chakra above the body. The 10th, 11th, and 12th locations will be explained in the coming months. Suffice it to say that when looking at the body, we go no higher, physically, than that of the ninth chakra and that of our soul's divine plan and program here in the world.

Referring back to Viktor Frankl and the story of the many mighty people in the Jewish community, we ponder why a soul would choose to spend time in Auschwitz and die in a concentration camp. More so, why would *so many* souls collectively choose that tragedy? Perhaps to awaken a whole group of others, incarnated at that time for the needs of the many, and for uplifting the whole.

How can we better understand our ninth chakra? See the companion Workbook for more questions, but consider this journal prompt on your ninth chakra:

Soul: What life lessons did I choose to come into this body to learn?

---

[55] *Man's Search for Meaning* page 154

Don't despair if the answer to this question doesn't come right away. You may want to go back through the sixth chakra's pattern recognitions to determine what keeps coming up for you, and the larger explanation for why that is happening.

In many shamanic traditions, the appearance of a bird serves as a reminder to view a situation from a "higher" perspective. Consider how you can do that this month so that you can see the entire picture.

Moon Phases

With the theme of friendship and community this month, we need to break out of our comfort zones and spend time with other people. If you have a small circle of friends, consider how you can expand that circle to include more people and a wider community in which you can thrive. Many people are uncomfortable with this idea, but it's a time to explore potential larger circles of people, or at least to spend more time with those in your small one. We are always learning and growing, and the more people we meet, the more opportunities we have.

Dark Moon:

The dark moon would be a good time to reflect on the people you surround yourself with. Do they support you? Do they offer you an opportunity to be authentically you? Or do you find your True Self hiding in the shadows when around most people in your circles? You want to be authentic to connect to your Highest Self, so make a list of the people that you share space with all the time. Work may be non-negotiable, but you can still limit the time you spend there with negative people. If you spend a lot of time with people whom you've outgrown spiritually or otherwise, you can see how to limit this time, still honor and love them, yet open yourself up to spending time with those who are on your new wavelength.

As far as your sankalpa is concerned, this month, ask yourself if the people that you surround yourself with are in alignment with that committed goal. And, if not, that should tell you all that you need to know about them or your sankalpa. Whatever you choose to do about creating more alignment, make sure that you are clear.

New Moon:

Use the new moon to help set your boundaries regarding people whose energy is detrimental for you to be around. Sometimes we outgrow our relationship with a particular person or group of people. This is not to mean we are "above" them or "better than" them. You may have heard the phrase "your vibe attracts your tribe." What is your vibe? And who is your tribe? And are they serving your highest self and the highest good of all? These are important questions to ask and to set into motion for you this month, around the new moon and into the waxing moon.

Waxing Moon:

Start plugging into and exploring the groups, communities, and people who light you up inside! If you did your work on the dark and new moon, you are ready to open up to the right vibrations and the right people. Get cracking!

Full Moon:

On the full moon, plan a big gathering. Check out the ritual this month for some ideas or create your own, with new friends or old—whoever you're feeling aligned with.

Waning Moon:

Now that you've invited more people into your inner circle, how's it going? Did you get a little overzealous? Did you join too many social media groups or attend too many events? Where did it go awry? Begin the process of releasing again. Go through your social media accounts and remove people that you do not know or are not real friends with. If there is mutual respect and sharing happening with someone, you will know. If not, you have to ask why you are still connected.

Everything is energy, especially things in the digital world. The waning moon is also a good time to release groups or communities that you are no longer actively a part of. Step down from positions in groups that no longer resonate with you, but always do so kindly.

Faith Tradition: Judaism

"When a single soul is elevated through Torah and *mitzvot*, the entire community is uplifted, for all Israel is bound as one in the divine light of the *Shekhinah*."

– Rabbi Isaac Luria
(Aphorism compiled by Chaim Vital in *Etz Chaim*[56])

With the energy of friendship and community, we bow to our Jewish friends for their bond with each other in September. History books tell many tales of the hardships the Jewish people have endured. Of course, many people bore hardships, but the attempted annihilation at the hands of the Nazi's is such an extreme event that our collective consciousness will always understand the pure evil that it represents. Somehow, through strength and community, many Jews survived these atrocities and strived to overcome the devastating history that they shared.

Judaism is one of the three Abrahamic religions (along with Christianity and Islam). About 15.7 million people practice Judaism worldwide, with 7.2 million living in Israel. The three predominant movements in Judaism are Orthodox, Conservative, and Reform Judaism. Orthodox is the most traditional branch, emphasizing strict adherence to Jewish law and tradition. Conservative Jews take a more moderate approach, seeking to conserve traditional practices while allowing for some degree of adaptation to modern life. Reform Jews use a more liberal approach, emphasizing ethical principles and individual interpretation of Jewish law. Beyond these three main styles of Judaism, there are several additional ones: Reconstructionist, Hasidic, Humanistic, and Secular. These different ways of faith allow Jews to worship God in a way that feels authentic to them, while still belonging to this vast and significant community.

Many Jewish holy days center on overcoming what appear to be insurmountable historical events through the grace of God. When considering bonds, friendships, and community, is there another group's faith tradition that cohesively represents this energy other than that of the Jewish people? With a couple of major Jewish holidays that often fall in September, we honor this faith in September.

---

[56] *Journal of Jewish Studies*, 2023

Symbol: Star of David

The "Shield of David," "Hebrew Star," or "Seal of Solomon," is a hexagram, consisting of two interlocking equilateral triangles to form a six-pointed star. As the Seal of Solomon, it is said to have been featured on a magical signet ring belonging to King Solomon, (builder of the Temple of Jerusalem, renowned for his wisdom, and considered to be a contributing writer of the Bible to the book of Proverbs and Ecclesiastes), giving him the ability to understand birds and animals, and to conjure up spirits to work for him.[57]

Energetically, the Star of David and its interlocking triangles represent, particularly in Jewish mysticism (*Kabbalah*) and spiritual interpretations, a dynamic balance of complementary forces that harmonize the spiritual and material realms, creating a unified whole. This alchemical symbol has been attributed to the Elixir of Life and finds itself within many magical mystery schools.

In Kabbalistic thought, the upward-facing triangle is linked to masculine energy, associated with the active, expansive qualities, while the downward triangle represents feminine energy tied to nurturance and receptivity. The energetic interplay is that of union. The Star of David thus embodies the energetic synergy that strengthens community through mutual support.

During the Nazi persecution, Jews were made to wear the star. When the war was over, Jews took it and used it more as a badge of honor, and it became known as the symbol for the Jewish faith.

---

[57] *Encyclopedia of Secret Signs and Symbols,* page. 152

September Altar

- **Altar cloth:** Gold, color of the 9th chakra

- **Flower:** Bouquet of Asters

- **Candle:** Gold candle at the center of the altar to light whenever doing work, holding the energy of Spirit

- **Crystal/Stone:** Sapphire stone, prayer mala bracelet, or necklace. Other possibilities for September are Honey Calcite or other gold colored stones like Pyrite, Golden Quartz, or Citrine, assuming that you do not own a gold bar—or two.

- **Symbol:** Menorah (a candelabrum with seven branches that was used in the ancient Jewish Temple in Jerusalem) or other symbols of Judaism, like the Star of David.

- **Essential Oil/Incense:** Myrtle, used in Jewish Sukkot celebrations, has a sweet, herbaceous aroma that symbolizes peace and community.

- **Herbs:** Ceremonial White Sage

- **Other items (optional):**
  - *The Modern Mystic's Wheel of the Year* Book, Workbook, and Oracle Deck
  - Anything given to you from a group that you belonged to or belong to that holds meaning: awards, medals of honor, gifts, etc.
  - Picture of your best group of friends, tightest family members, or another significant community that you are a part of
  - Picture of the Kabbalistic Tree of Life
  - Find a way to share your sankalpa with supportive friends and the community.

Angel/Ancestor: Archangel Michael

St. Michael the Archangel's name means "He who is like God." He is undoubtedly the most famous of all the Archangels, having been featured in the Bible and other texts many times and having churches erected in his honor. Most know of him as "the protector" or warrior angel, and call on him in times of challenge and strife. Often, when considering the army of Archangels, he is exalted as the general, leading the brethren to battle for humankind.

Doreen Virtue says, "Some believe that Michael and Jesus are the same Divine son of God because they have such similar missions…Michael is one of the two Archangels named in the canonical Bible (along with Gabriel). In the Book of Daniel, Michael identifies himself to the prophet Daniel as the protector of Israel. Michael protected Moses's body in Jude, and fought dragons (the historical symbol of evil or the ego) in Revelations. In the apocryphal Book of Enoch, Michael is called the "prince of Israel," who teaches and protects the prophet Enoch."[58]

To further ground his presence in Judaism, Michael appeared to Abraham and is considered the Archangel who assisted Moses in receiving the Ten Commandments. Basically, when stuff is going down, you want Michael with you.

Michael's symbol is the sword of light, which can be used to remove any lower or unwanted energy, and, as Virtue says, "detach us from the grips of fear." His color/ray is sometimes thought to be blue, and other times purple. Steve Noble calls his flame "electric blue."

In a world where energy is constantly changing, having protection and the highest light around one is a valuable tool.

<u>Prayer Invoking Archangel Michael</u>:

"Dear Archangel Michael, surround me and my loved ones with your blue light in all directions of time and space so that no lower vibrational energy may enter our field. Guide us to only interact with beings aligned with the highest light and integrity. And so it is. Amen."

---

[58] *Archangels 101*, page 2

Once you've invited Archangel Michael into your life, he will always be with you, like a trusted friend. However, it's not unrealistic to create this daily prayer to him, thus ensuring that this busy angel is aware of your continued interest in his special gifts in your life.

September Ritual: Kabbalistic Tree of Life Meditation

This meditation will guide you through the Tree of Life, the *Kabbalistic* map of the ten *Sefirot*, visualized as a ladder of divine energies from the earthly (*Malkhut*) to the divine (*Keter*). The theme of ascension reflects the soul's journey upward through these attributes, balancing energies (like the Star of David's interlocking triangles, per your prior query) to connect with God's presence.

The meditation will take 15–20 minutes and is suitable for beginners. It can be done alone or in a group to resonate with community strength. It incorporates visualization, breathwork, and Hebrew mantras, drawing from Kabbalistic practices to foster spiritual elevation.

Preparation:

- Choose a time and place, ideally dawn or dusk, when energy is calm
- Find a peaceful, clean space, free from distractions
- Set up a small altar with a candle, a Star of David image, or a Tree of Life diagram, facing east (toward Jerusalem)
- A cushion or chair for sitting upright, ensuring ease during meditation
- Optional: a journal to record insights post-meditation
- Cleanse yourself by washing your face and hands, or taking a quick shower to purify your body and mind
- Wear comfortable, modest clothing

Set Intention:

Before starting, set an intention for ascension: "I seek to rise through the Sefirot to connect with God's light and strengthen my soul's bond with the community."

Meditation:

1. Grounding & Center: Sit comfortably, spine straight, feet flat on the floor, or cross-legged on a cushion. Close your eyes or soften your gaze toward the candle or Star of David image.

2. Take 5 slow, deep breaths: inhale through the nose (for 4 counts), exhale through the mouth (for 6 counts), visualizing roots extending from your body into the earth, anchoring you in Malkhut (Earth).

3. <u>Say silently or aloud</u>: *"Adonai ha-Aretz"* (Lord of the Earth, associated with Malkhut), grounding your presence.[59]

4. <u>Entering Malkhut</u>: Visualize a warm, golden light at the base of your spine, representing Malkhut, the divine presence (*Shekhinah*) in the physical world. Feel connected to your community, embodying strength.

5. <u>Chant softly (or think)</u>: *"Adonai"* (3 times), inviting God's immanence. Affirm: "I am rooted in God's creation, part of a strong community."

6. <u>Ascending to *Yesod* (Foundation)</u>: Move your awareness to your pelvic area, visualizing a violet light for Yesod, the channel of divine energy and connection. Imagine a bridge linking you to higher realms.

7. <u>Chant</u>: *"El Chai"* (Living God, 3 times), activating vitality and flow. Affirm: "I am a conduit for divine energy, rising upward." Imagine a bridge to the sky, like a step up your spiritual ladder.

8. *Hod* <u>and *Netzach* (Splendor and Victory)</u>: Shift to your left hip for *Hod* (orange light, humility, gratitude) and right hip for Netzach (green light, endurance, ambition), balancing the Star of David's energies.

9. <u>Chant</u>: *"Elohim Tzva'ot"* (God of Hosts, 3 times for each), harmonizing discipline and drive. Affirm: "I balance gratitude and perseverance, ascending in harmony."

10. *Tiferet* <u>(Beauty)</u>: Focus on your heart center, visualizing a radiant yellow light for Tiferet, the heart of the Tree, embodying compassion and balance (like the Star of David's center).

11. <u>Chant</u>: *"YHVH Eloah v'Da'at"* (God of Knowledge, 3 times), evoking harmony. Affirm: "My heart shines with divine love, uniting my community."

12. *Gevurah* <u>and *Chesed* (Strength and Loving-Kindness)</u>: Move to your left shoulder for Gevurah (red light, discipline, boundaries) and right shoulder for Chesed (blue light, generosity, love), reflecting the Star of David's masculine/feminine energies.

---

[59] Sefer Yetzirah (~2nd–6th century CE)

13. <u>Chant</u>: *"Elohim Gibor"* (Mighty God, 3 times for *Gevurah*) and *"El"* (God, 3 times for Chesed), balancing restraint and openness. Affirm: "I balance strength and kindness, rising toward God."

14. <u>Binah and Chokhmah (Understanding and Wisdom)</u>: Focus on your left forehead for Binah (black or deep blue light, intuition, discernment) and right forehead for Chokhmah (white or silver light, insight, inspiration).

15. <u>Keter (Crown)</u>: Raise your awareness to the crown of your head, visualizing a dazzling white light for Keter, the divine source, pure unity with God.

16. <u>Chant</u>: *"Ehyeh Asher Ehyeh"* (I Am That I Am, 3 times), connecting to God's essence. Affirm: "I am one with the divine light, ascended in God's presence."

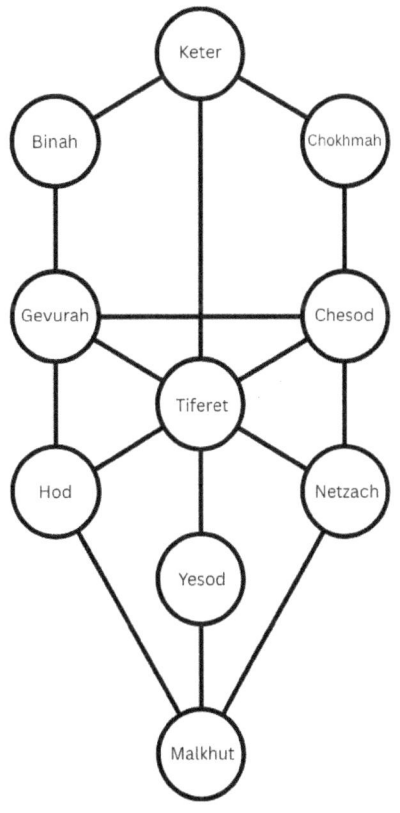

17. <u>Chant</u>: *"Sh'ma Yisrael, Adonai Eloheinu, Adonai Echad"* (Hear, O Israel, the Lord our God, the Lord is One, Deuteronomy 6:4), affirming unity.

18. <u>Slowly return awareness to your body</u>: breathe deeply (5 breaths) and open your eyes, grounding in Malkhut. Affirm: "I carry divine light back to my community, strengthened and uplifted."

19. <u>Closing</u>: Extinguish the candle safely, thanking God silently: "Thank You for guiding my ascent through the Sefirot." Journal any insights.

If you're not Jewish, practice respectfully, avoiding the commercialization of Kabbalistic symbols, and consult a rabbi for guidance if integrating into communal settings.

Tracey's Personal Reflection

I am 1/4 Jewish. Well, that depends on who you ask. My maternal Grandmother was a Jew, so according to the Jewish tradition, I'm a Jew. Don't tell this to my Father's Methodist Minister, who baptized me when I was a baby.

Over the years, I've attended many functions with my Mother's Jewish side of the family. It was always full, alive, and, well, loud. There were many times when I had to take myself out of the house to have a minute of quiet, only to find my Grandfather also sitting on the porch or taking the dog for a walk. I had a difficult time discerning if these family members were fighting or if a murder had just been committed. At the end of the day, they loved each other. And if any one of them experienced a challenge, the entire family was behind them, supporting in any way possible. That's just how they rolled.

Because I am being brutally honest, I must confess that I find the Hebrew language difficult and have tended to steer away from Jewish rituals and ceremonies because I find it too challenging to understand. My only critique of attending the synagogue during my doctoral investigations was that there was no English translation available, and I didn't understand what was being said, what was happening, or what I was supposed to do. Because of this, I felt a disconnection to this path, unlike other times in my spiritual journey. For whatever reason, Judaism hasn't resonated with me, personally. And I'm a Jew… sort of.

Grandmom (left) with two of her sisters and her niece

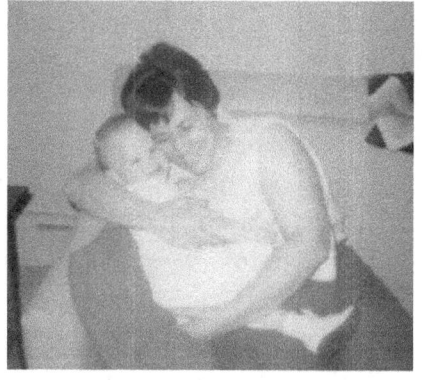

Baby Tracey with Grandmom, Rachel

I want you to know, this is okay. As I said earlier in the book, not all of the monthly practices will evoke feelings for you. You won't enjoy everything equally. But you can respect it, deeply, nonetheless, as I do with Judaism.

September Yoga Practice:
Igniting the 9th Chakra/Stellar Gateway

This practice is for all levels, and no yoga experience is required. However, it is always recommended to consult a doctor before beginning any new physical program. Remember to modify anything for particular conditions that you may be experiencing, and to always follow your breath for the truth about a feeling that arises.

<u>Yoga Posture Sequence to Ignite the Stellar Gateway</u>:

The "Mouth of God" is the location of our entry point into the physical body we currently inhabit to experience what we are. With its location as the highest one above the crown, our practice will ignite energy in our core to accelerate energy upward to the crown. We will focus on ascension and descension energies, the upward and downward currents in the body, similar to the 8th chakra.

The energy will be more active for the 9th chakra than the 8th, however, since it takes energy to ascend. However, due to the complex nature of this powerful chakra, a balance of rest and force is needed.

<u>Single Posture Practice</u>: Headstand (*Sirsasana*)

Headstand can be a challenging posture for many people, but luckily, we have the prep, which is more available for most.

Start on your hands and knees, placing your forearms on the floor. The elbows should be in alignment with the shoulders. Interlace your fingers and place the crown of your head down on the floor so that your hands hold the back of your head. Tuck your toes, lift your knees, and slowly walk your feet in towards your body. This is the "prep," so you can stay right here and focus on pressing the forearms into the floor so that the cervical spine has little pressure.

For those wishing to proceed, gather energy

into your core by pulling the abdominal muscles in and up, then slowly bring your legs up to the sky. Some people kick up or "pike," so if this feels available, give it a try.

I always suggest beginners have a wall in front of them, especially if you are trying to pike up, but even if not. There is something about having the wall there as a potential support that assists you in achieving the pose.

Mudra & Meditation:

Come to the easy-seated pose or Lotus seated pose. Place your hands on your lap, touching the index fingers to the thumbs for the *Gyan Mudra*. Gyan means knowledge or wisdom, and this gesture is said to connect the individual soul to Universal Consciousness.

Focus on the 9th chakra, Stellar Gateway, the gold color, and why your soul chose this life, this body, this family, these situations, in which to incarnate at this time. What did you come here to experience? And is your sankalpa in alignment with this choice?

Breathing Practice: *Bhastrika* or Bellows Breath

Bhastrika breathing is similar to the Breath of Fire except that we emphasize both the inhalation and the exhalation here. We are using this breath this month to push energy up and out of the crown of the head towards the 9th Chakra and our Soul's connection here on the planet, so that we can align with the right people and places in this lifetime.

To perform, you will want to stand or sit with your spine straight. Make sure that you have not recently eaten, or this will be difficult. Think of a bellows, the instrument that sends a concentrated air stream out when squeezed. It is used to stoke fires. As you inhale, sharply push the abdomen out. As you exhale, sharply squeeze the abdomen inward. This is a rapid and forceful breathing process, but in the beginning, you may want to go slowly to learn the movement of the abdomen. Perform 3 rounds of about 10 breaths each day.

This is a very energizing breath, so perform in the morning or during the daytime when you may need an extra pop of energy.

Hatha Yoga Sequence:

Seated Easy Pose – breath & Meditation	Making the Sun (Ascend/ Descend breathing)	Child	Table with Cat & Cow movements	Downward Facing Dog	Standing Forward Fold
Mountain	1/2 Sun Salutations	5-Pointed Star	Warrior II flow	Triangle	Sun Salutations/ Surya Namaskar
Bellow's Breath w/ Chair Pose	Standing Forward Fold	Child	Bridge	Shoulder Stand	Fish
Headstand	Knees to Chest	Supine Spinal Twist	Closing Postures (optional)	Corpse - Final Relaxation	Meditation on 9th Chakra

* Note that the pre-recorded practice may differ from the sequence above.

Short 15-minute Practice:

- Making the Sun with Ascending/Descending Breathing
- Sun Salutations (3X)
- Bellow's Breathing with Chair
- Headstand
- Corpse

September Recap

Friendship and community are significant aspects of our lives as human beings on this great planet. We cannot do everything alone, nor should we. The famous quote, "It takes a village," proves deeply true once you realize you're not Wonder Woman (or Superman) and can't do it all, all the time. We are all in this together, this life and on this planet, so we should honor each other and share sacred space regularly.

It is said that your vibe attracts your tribe. Who is your tribe? Do you need to finesse that? Do you long for more connection but are shy? Have you been hurt and have turned too far inward? Take a look at how you can connect or reconnect with others more in September.

October

The Harvest

October Energies:

October's shoulder season is one of the most sought-after months for weddings and special events, as the weather is usually a perfect blend. Along with May, this transition time before the severe cold of winter is a beautiful month for outdoor events. Many harvest festivals continue, and they are often better attended than previous ones as school is back in session and most people tend to stay closer to home, yet look for interesting things to do on the weekends. Of course, our ancestors weren't looking for interesting things to fill their time; they lived by the cycles of the seasons and the Wheel of the Year because they were more in touch with the earth. Although we honor the harvest during August and September in many cultures, we bring it as our presiding theme for October, when we see the final harvest of the season.

"Octo" means eight in Latin, linking to this month's original connection to the Roman calendar. Eight symbolizes material success and wealth, which aligns with the celebration of the harvest. Yet as the tenth month of our current calendar, there's a different energy, that of new beginnings. For those not familiar with numerology, two digits are broken down to one (most of the time), so for the number ten (10), we see $1 + 0 = 1$. And one is new beginnings.

Interestingly, the world-renowned fall foliage in the northeast, when the leaves change from dark green to yellow, orange, and reddish colors, before falling off the branches and into the earth to be transformed, symbolizes death. Death is about change. Therefore, we can reconcile the energy of new beginnings at this time of real transformation and embrace the concept of death and dying as a new stage in life, rather than the final one.

We come into the month on the balanced Libra's scales, then midway move into Scorpio territory. Now, this astrological sign is well known for being bold and strong, and that includes the watery realms of the emotions. Scorpio is often equated with the dangerous, scary animal that packs a powerful sting. It is no surprise that the Scorpio has been identified with the cycle of life, death, and rebirth itself, and often those of the sign will notice this recurring theme throughout his or her life.

In *Mythic Astrology*, Guttman and Johnson say that Scorpio holds the promise of "resurrection" and that its connection with the underworld goes back to Ancient Babylonia and the *Epic of Gilgamesh*, where Gilgamesh had to cross many mountains that were guarded by the scorpion-men on his way to the "other world."⁶⁰

For many, talk of death is scary territory. October brings this element, but as the final harvest, it should be looked upon as a celebration, one of final harvest as well as new beginnings. When we view the world as never-ending cycles, we realize that there is nothing to fear.

The flower of the month is the marigold, which symbolizes devotion. Marigolds are used in offerings to the spirit world during Day of the Dead ceremonies, and also decorate the festive sugar skulls used in Mesoamerican cultures. The bright colors of the flowers guide spirits as well as remind us that life is fragile. The stone of the month is Opal, representing inspiration and transformation, a known spiritual quality and property of death.

---

⁶⁰ *Mythic Astrology* page 312

Holidays and Holy Days

The Hindu holiday *Diwali* begins on the darkest night of the year, in the month of *Kartik*, which falls somewhere between October and November. Diwali is known as the "Festival of Lights," and is a five-day holy day that honors Lord Rama's victory over darkness, evil, and ignorance. With many people tending to focus on the darker aspects of October, celebrating the light overcoming the darkness is a reminder that all things shall pass.

The next two holidays need to be discussed together. Christopher Columbus is often credited for "finding" the Americas, and, as such, we celebrate Columbus Day on the second Monday of the month, sometimes on or around the twelfth or the fourteenth. However, we all know that this is a false statement, and that indigenous peoples inhabited the Americas long before Columbus came along. In 1972, President Nixon proclaimed this day Indigenous Peoples' Day to celebrate the Native American peoples and their culture. Unfortunately, much of their rich cultures were attempted to be wiped out in favor of the traditions of the early European settlers. Let us remember how they lived in harmony with the planet, something Modern Mystics strive to do more of today.

The Jewish holy day of *Sukkot* sometimes falls in October. It is the "Feast of the Tabernacles," a festival commemorating the last harvest. What happens after the final harvest when no more fresh food is available? Jews honor this holiday as a reliance on God for watching over them during the biblical time of Exodus, when they spent time in the desert, a barren place. The Sukkot is the temporary dwelling that the Jews made in the desert, which is similar to the marigold, reminding us of the delicateness of life.

Samhain is the pagan holiday now often confused with Halloween. Nowadays, children dress up in costumes, parade around school, and then go around their neighborhood in hopes of collecting a massive mound of candy. The roots of this holiday offer a much deeper meaning. Halloween, or 'All Hallows' Eve," is when we remember the dead and departed by lighting bonfires, dressing in costumes, utilizing divination techniques to communicate with the deceased, and more. Samhain is the official celebration of the last harvest, signaling the entrance into the darker half of the year. Many of the same celebratory activities occur during Samhain and Halloween, such as the lighting of bonfires, dancing, and feasting.

With Samhain, the focus is on the last of the harvested crops, not on the deceased. These are closely related holidays, but with different emphasis. All

Hallows' Eve is often thought of as a Celtic holiday, where the veil between worlds is thinnest.

The Mesoamerican holiday of honoring the dead, *Días de los Muertos,* is celebrated on November 1st. However, preparations for that day begin in October and culminate on All Hallows' Eve. But hold on, for in November we will honor our deceased in big ways.

Chakra Connection

10th Chakra

Sanskrit: *Vasundhara*
Meaning: Earth
Location: Approximately 12" below the Earth

Known as the "Earth Star" chakra, this is where we anchor our individual being into the heart of Mother Earth.

The Earth Star chakra rests in the Earth. After we move above the body to the 8th and 9th chakra, it may feel comforting to some to return to the Earth for the 10th energy center. Many say that it resides 12-18" below the feet in the earth and is believed to be the grounding point for the entire chakra system.

What else often rests inside the Earth? The remains of our ancestors do, of course. The phrase "ashes to ashes" is synonymous with what we refer to as the body's remains returning to the Earth after the soul essence departs the physical vehicle. The tenth chakra is said to refer to our legacy and nature. It's fitting to have the connection to our month of the harvest.

Even though both the tenth and the first chakras connect with the Earth, they have quite different energies. In the first chakra that we explored in January, we find grounding, foundation, and support for the rest of our spiritual journey. Now, much into that journey, we find ourselves at the tenth chakra, deeper physically into the earth than the first, but much higher up in the developmental chain than the first. So, how do we connect to a higher energy level while physically lower in the ground? We take our consciousness higher.

Healing the planet and being more aware of our carbon footprint are significant concerns. The Earth is a vital, thriving planet, but it is also in an intense cycle of hyperactivity and superstorms. We need to attend to each day with reverence and in harmony. Here we move into what we can do to elevate our days in communion with the Earth. How can we go "Greener?" How can we clean up the planet and eliminate waste? How can we be active participants in our planet's health and well-being? How can we reconnect to our roots with the advanced understanding that we must all move up together?

How do we know if we are connecting to the tenth chakra? See the companion Workbook for more questions, but consider this journal prompt on your tenth chakra:

> <u>Gaia</u>: Gaia is the network of Mother energy on the planet. How connected are you with that?

Moon Phases

This month's practices are geared towards focusing on the harvest as it relates to our sankalpa. This is it, The Harvest, celebrating the fruits of our labor. Even though the year has not closed, this is where we see what we have manifested, with just a couple of months of fine-tuning left.

Dark Moon:

Take time to meditate and reflect on what you have achieved. Your sankalpa may have come to full fruition, or you may have redirected the energy. Either way, this is a time to contemplate the work you've done and how far you've gotten.

New Moon, Waxing Moon & Full Moon for Ritual:

The Samhain bonfire ritual for this month can be scheduled for the night of the new moon or full moon. Note when each falls and which date is most appropriate for you. Neither is better than the other; however, there are some slight differences. The new moon is an obvious choice for new beginnings, and on Samhain, we celebrate the New Year.

However, the full moon brings heightened energy, and with the veil being thinnest this night offers a superb opportunity to connect with those in the Otherworld. Wherever you wish to put your full focus will determine which day to perform your bonfire. Of course, it is always best to do this festival on the actual night of Samhain on the 31st. Work with the energy as best you can to determine how it will work for you.

Waning Moon:

Use the waning moon time to release what no longer serves you in respect to your sankalpa, but also with whatever you're holding on to from your ancestry and bloodline that doesn't serve you, your family, your Highest Self, and the greatest good of all. Perhaps it's time to release this lower energy that has plagued your family, possibly for eons. Is there a consistent and recurring theme in your family line that you are ready to transform? Create a ritual to release.

One way to do this is to create a sacred space, make a Family Tree, and write the ways this theme showed up for each member. Read it aloud, committing that this energy stops with you. Tear it up and burn it in a separate fire from the

Samhain bonfire. Once they've cooled, bury the ashes left from the paper into the Earth, visualizing the roots of it going down to the Earth Star chakra for transmutation.

Faith Tradition: Celtic/Druid

"You will be the land, and the land will be you. If you fail, the land will perish; as you thrive, the land will blossom."

– Merlin in *Excalibur*

The ancient Celts were a diverse group of tribal peoples who shared a common culture, language, and religious practices in Central Europe around the 8th century BCE. They were located in the British Isles, including Ireland, Scotland, and Wales, and then into Gaul (modern France), Spain, and parts of Central Europe such as Austria and Switzerland.

The Celtic people encompassed all tribal members, including farmers, warriors, artisans, and nobles. Closely related, the Druids were a specialized group of priests, political and intellectual elites, and healers, akin to the Shamans known around the world in other cultures.

The ancient Celts and Druids followed the lunar/solar calendar, which they celebrated with four main fire festivals to mark the seasonal transitions:

1. Imbolc (Feb 1-2), marking the beginning of Spring
2. Beltane (May 1), celebrating growth and fertility
3. Lughnasadh (August 1-2), tied to the initial harvest
4. Samhain (October 31st), the Celtic New Year, marks the end of the harvest season and the start of winter. Samhain is the most significant festival, when the veil between the physical world and the Otherworld (spiritual realm) thins, allowing communion with ancestors, spirits, and deities like Brigid (for fertility) or Cailleach (for winter).

Today, it's estimated that over 120 million people are of Celtic ancestry, from the United Kingdom to America. While it is difficult to determine the number of Druids in the world today, it is estimated to be somewhere between 60,000 - 100,000. Many people will identify strongly with their Celtic heritage, but not with Druidry. And then, some identify as Druids, yet are not of Celtic origin.

Apologies for any confusion that this modern neopagan faith tradition may pose. If you are of Celtic heritage, go with that. If you want to explore this month through the lens of a Druid Priest, have at it! Just explore the meaning.

Symbol: World Tree

The World Tree (*Crann Bethadh*, meaning "the feeding tree"), often an oak, is a central Druidic symbol of the cosmic axis connecting heaven, earth, and underworld, with branches reaching skyward and roots delving deep into the Mother Gaia. It was a sacred gathering place for rituals, embodying community strength and spiritual balance.

The World Tree reflects Samhain's theme of endings and beginnings, as its seasonal shedding of leaves and acorns parallels the harvest's completion and the promise of new growth, aligning with Druidic beliefs on reincarnation. The World Tree was a focal point for Samhain gatherings, where Celts feasted on harvested crops, shared stories, and divined the future, strengthening community bonds. During Samhain, the World Tree served as a spiritual portal to the Otherworld, facilitating communication with ancestors and spirits through harvest offerings, as the thinned veil heightened spiritual access.

The World Tree is found in several other cultures and goes by many names. For the Norse, it was *Yggdrasil*. Buddhists know it as the *Bodhi* Tree. And in Kabbalistic imagery, it is the Tree of Life—to name a few.

October Altar

- **Altar Cloth:** Brown or copper colored, the color of the tenth chakra

- **Flower:** Marigolds

- **Candle:** Brown

- **Crystal/Stone:** Opal stone, mala bracelet or necklace, or Smokey Quartz as an alternative or supplement

- **Symbol:** Figure or picture of the World Tree

- **Essential Oil/Incense:** Heather, used in Celtic harvest rituals

- **Herbs:** Ceremonial White Sage

- **Other items (optional):**
  - *The Modern Mystic's Wheel of the Year* Book, Workbook, and Oracle Deck
  - Cornucopia of nuts, plants, and harvest items
  - Wheat bundles or bowls
  - Ritual offerings (see ritual page)
  - St. Brigid's cross
  - The Harvest is here, so celebrate the progress with your Sankalpa, continuing to honor it and what you've sown by keeping it on your altar.

Angel/Ancestor: Druid

The priestly cast of the ancient Celts is the Druids. They were priests, judges, and healers in tribes across Britain, Ireland, and France, guiding people with nature's wisdom. Due to a lack of Druid text, it is difficult to pinpoint the origins and dating of these mystics. There are speculative beliefs that the Druids descended from the *Tuatha Dé Danann*, the mythical beings of Irish folklore. It is said that these magical former beings retreated to the fairy realm after losing in battle to the Milesians (mythical human ancestors).

The earliest historical references to Druids include writings by Roman Emperor Julius Caesar, who claimed they conducted rituals, sacrifices, and divination.[61] In addition to Caesar's testimony, there is archaeological evidence of Celts and Druids, such as bronze figures, gold coins, and, of course, the many circular temples and burial sites that litter the area.

The most notable of these ancient stone circles is Stonehenge. Seated as it is in the English countryside of Wiltshire, it is the most iconic one in the world. The largest stone circle, Avebury, sits approximately 23 miles away. Both of these sites have been linked to the Druids, along with the famous Carnac stones in France. While the exact methods of construction are debatable, they're mostly regarded as ceremonial temples.

Stonehenge is known for its alignment with the sunrise during the solstices. Thousands of people converge upon the landscape to witness the rising of the sun above the large sarsen "Heel" stone on June 21st. The astronomical significance of this event suggests that the builders created the monument to celebrate these markers of the solar calendar.

While walking amongst these famous sites certainly promotes a connection to the Druid ancestors, there are other means to connect with these ancient Celtic priests. The word Druid is derived from Celtic *dru-wid-s,* combining *dru* ("oak" or "firm") and *wid* ("to know/see"), meaning "oak-knower."[62] So, find a local oak tree, get comfortable underneath to meditate, and connect with nature. Perhaps bring mistletoe as an offering.

---

[61] *Gallic Wars*, Julius Caesar, 50s BCE

[62] *The Oxford Dictionary of Celtic Mythology,* James MacKillop, 1998

<u>With Humility, Ask</u>:

"Druid elder, seer, wisdom-keeper, I seek to connect to your knowledge of harmony with the natural world. Align me with nature so that I may respectfully celebrate the cycles supported by the sun, moon, and stars upon this great Earth. So mote it be."

October Ritual: Samhain Bonfire

Creating a Samhain bonfire involves preparation, safety, and ritual elements to honor the Celtic/Druid harvest celebration. This guide is designed for a small backyard or adaptable for a larger community event.

<u>Preparation</u>:

- Choose a Safe Location and Time (Sunset on October 31 is optimum)
- Select an open, flat area at least 10–15 feet from flammable objects
- Check local fire codes and obtain permits if needed
- A site near a tree enhances authenticity, but keep it 50+ feet away for safety
- Gather Materials: matches or fire starter, dry hardwood logs, kindling
- A portable or permanent fire pit
- Offerings: Harvest items like apples, nuts, or bread
- A candle
- A small World Tree image or an oak branch
- A bowl for offerings
- Safety Gear, such as a bucket of water, sand, or a fire extinguisher
- Wash hands/face or bathe to purify, and wear comfortable clothes
- Build the fire structure in the fire pit
- Send invitations to individuals you wish to invite

<u>Steps of Samhain Bonfire</u>:

1. <u>Form Circle</u>: Participants form a circle around the unlit fire pit, facing the center. Place the World Tree symbol (or oak branch) and offerings (apples, nuts) on a cloth near the pit.

2. <u>Light the Candle</u>: symbolizing divine light, and hold it while saying: "Brigid, Cailleach, spirits of the Otherworld, bless this fire and our harvest." Pass the candle to light the kindling.

3. <u>Chant</u>: "Fire of Samhain, burn bright, guide our ancestors tonight," invoking protection.

4. <u>Place Offering into the Fire</u>: Each participant places an offering (such as an apple, nuts, bread, etc.) into the fire or a bowl, saying, "We thank the Earth

and ancestors for this harvest." Visualize the World Tree channeling gifts to the Otherworld.

5. <u>Share stories or names of loved ones who've passed, saying</u>: "We honor [name], your spirit joins us at Samhain." Reflect on community strength, as the fire mirrors the World Tree's unity.

6. <u>Gaze into the fire for insights (a Druidic practice), asking silently</u>: "What wisdom does Samhain offer?"

7. <u>Thank the deities and spirits</u>: "Brigid, Cailleach, ancestors, we thank you for your presence." Extinguish the candle (keep the bonfire burning safely).

8. <u>Collect cooled Ashes</u>: (when safe) to scatter on a garden for fertility, or leave offerings under a nearby tree (not the fire site).

9. <u>Share a small harvest feast</u>.

10. <u>Stay until the bonfire burns out</u>: naturally allow the fire to burn out or extinguish with water/sand, ensuring no embers remain.

Samhain bonfire ceremonies can be deeply reverent. Don't rush the steps. Stay present, and honor whatever comes up. As the veil is thin at this time of year, it is not uncommon for the spirits of ancestors and dearly departed to show up. Watch for their presence.

Tracey's Personal Reflection

It's hard to recall just how many bonfire ceremonies I've hosted or attended, including those for Samhain. I would guess that over twenty years, during which I followed the pagan Sabbats ritualistically, that it would be safe to say forty or fifty, at the very least. In addition to bonfire ceremonies, Samhain was always one of the most important holy days for me and my circle. We felt that it was always easy to complain or focus on the lack of, so we wanted to ensure that we spent time celebrating what we had achieved and what went well for us. Samhain, as the final harvest, is all about that. It's the whole reap what you sow stuff!

In addition to my many years of conducting Samhain rituals, I do have a direct connection to Celtic/Druid ancestry. Remember my Jewish Grandmother from last month? Well, I've traced her husband, my Grandfather's, roots back to the early 1000s in England. Then the records stop. I've been to England four times so far. It is another place that feels like home. All three times I've gone to Stonehenge, and I love the energy there. But, there's nothing like some of the lesser-tourist stone circles, henges, long barrows, and, of course, the famous Glastonbury Tor. Something deep within me draws me to these Druid places. I feel at home. And I don't feel the need to perform any big rituals or ceremonies, I simply know that I need to sit on the Earth and connect to her, root to root.

Avebury Stone Circle, July 2022

Connecting with Stonehenge, June 2024

October Yoga Practice:
Rooting into the 10th Chakra/"Earth Star"- Vasundhara Chakra

This practice is for all levels, and no yoga experience is required. However, it is always recommended to consult a doctor before beginning any new physical program. Remember to modify anything for particular conditions that you may be experiencing, and to always follow your breath for the truth about a feeling that arises.

<u>Yoga Posture Sequence for Connecting to the Earth Star</u>:

The energetic focus of the practice is to dive into the earth, but on a deeper level, and with the understanding that this is to drive energy upward again. Here in the tenth chakra, we are embodying a deeper sense of who we are meant to be and what legacy we will leave behind. We also want to remember to honor our ancestors, whose bodies have returned to the earth.

After the practice, come to a seated pose or into Lotus posture. Place both hands on your lap, with the fingers of your right and left hands pointed towards the earth for the *Bhumisparsha mudra* or "touching the earth." Spend time in meditation/reflection, perhaps on your sankalpa and what you've harvested. Then close the practice by bringing your hands to your heart, bowing your head, and repeating your intention or prayer.

<u>Single Posture Practice</u>: Mountain Pose (*Tadasana*)

Standing with legs hip-width apart. Press into all four corners of the feet, evenly. As you press downward into those points, pull upward through the center of the foot, like a suction cup, and allow that energy to draw the body upward. The more you push downward, there is an equal and opposing energy moving upward. To center this, draw the abdominal muscles inward toward the spine, and lengthen the tailbone downward. Allow the heart-center to remain open with the shoulders down and back. The arms rest at the sides of the body, with fingers also pointing downward.

To create full and clear alignment, stand next to a

mirror and align the ankles with the knees, the knees with the center of the hip, the hips with the shoulders, and the shoulders with the ear, all in one straight line.

While standing in full Mountain posture, imagine roots growing downward from the feet into the earth, spreading out, and creating an energetic connection to Mother Earth/*Pachamama*.

While connecting to the Earth, say your sankalpa, either aloud or inwardly. Feel it resonate within your being. Notice anywhere in your body where you feel charged or a lack of charge as you repeat this intention. Focus on your breathing and stay as long as you wish.

<u>Breathing Practice</u>: Squat Breath

Squat. Standing with feet hip-width apart, and toes turned out to the sides. Keep your feet flat on the floor and allow the knees to open as you squat towards the floor. Press deeply into the feet at all four corners, evenly, while drawing up with the arches of the feet. This is the *pada bandha* or foot lock. Feel rooted and allow the tailbone to descend downward, feeling the energy from the main central channel of the chakras opening up to the Earth Star below it. Feel the energy of the Earth Star chakra waking up, rising through the chakras at the same time it descends. There is a toric field of energy flowing out and around the body, through the Earth Star, the seven chakras in the body, and out again.

On the inhalations, press into the feet, rising back up to Mountain pose. The arms can continue to rise upward in "Making the Sun," then pause at the top of the inhale. When exhaling, begin to squat again, allowing the arms to flow downward. Repeat several times, syncing breath and movement.

<u>Mudra & Meditation</u>:

Find a comfortable seat on the ground. Bring your hands into *Bhu Mudra*, bringing your index finger and middle finger to rest on the surface of the earth while the pinky and ring fingers come into the palm, and the thumb presses them down. Close your eyes and become aware of your connection to the earth beneath you. Continue to feel roots growing downward from your body, and connecting into Gaia, Mother Earth, and finally the Earth Star chakra. Connect with the energy of the 10th chakra, feeling its energy reaching upward through the roots to connect to your body in this moment. Continue to breathe, connecting to your ancestors, to the legacy of your family, and to the One-Earth Being in which you are a part.

Hatha Yoga Sequence:

Mountain - Standing for Meditation	Standing Forward Fold	Cobbler	1/2 Forward Fold	Seated Twist	Child
Table with Cat/Cow	Twisting Cat/Cow	Downward Facing Dog	Low Runner's Lunge	Leg Stretch	Sphinx
Crocodile	Downward Facing Dog	Warrior I with Yoga Mudra Hands	Humble Warrior (head to foot)	Standing Forward Fold	Mountain
Squat Breath Flow	Bridge	Inverted Legs Up with Block Under Hips	Full Body Stretch	Happy Baby	Corpse - Final Relaxation

* Note that the pre-recorded practice may differ from the sequence above.

Short 15-minute Practice:

- Standing for the Meditation
- Squat Breath
- Humble Warrior
- Bridge
- Legs-Up on block
- Corpse

October Recap

Through the Earth, we connect with our legacy and with all of nature. Who we are and what we came here to do is reflected in our sankalpa, which we should be seeing the fruits of during "The Harvest" we now celebrate.

Nothing is wrong.

Celebrate what you have achieved thus far in your journey. You've worked hard, and you deserve to enjoy the fruits of your labor. Nobody and nothing can take that away from you. And this month, you get to decide what you want to take with you moving forward.

November

Remembrance

November Energies:

No matter where you are in the world, November invokes the energy of ancestral remembrance. As the eleventh month of the year, November has a significant numerical energy, known as a "Master Number." Although the name originates from the Latin *Novem,* meaning nine for the ninth month of the year, where it was originally placed when the calendar began with the Spring Equinox in March, we now view it as the last month in autumn and the eleventh month of our calendar year.

In Numerology, a Master Number carries potent energy, amplifying the qualities of its base digit to a higher spiritual level. The number eleven, a Master Number, embodies intuition and insight. It unlocks access to the subconscious, revealing hidden truths. As a single digit, one signifies new beginnings and transformation. But when doubled to eleven (11), it elevates awareness, empowering us to grasp the deeper energy driving change and uncover the true purpose behind it. There is also much discussion about the number eleven being linked to Angels as an "Angel Number," and that when seeing this pattern of 11:11, angels are around, trying to give you a message.

Solara Anani, visionary of the 11:11 doorway, has a different message about the number pattern 11:11. Solara began to see the truth of this number when she was young. Her message states, "11:11 is not another Stargate; it is our bridge to ascension. It is our doorway Home."[63]

In her book of the same name, Solara continues to describe 11:11 as our time of completion, empowerment, and embodiment of our Highest Truth and Oneness. She says that when you see the repeated numbers of eleven followed by eleven, no matter if it is on a digital clock, a sign, a license plate, or any other means, that it activates a "pre-encoded order in our cellular memory banks." This order reminds us of who we truly are and begins to guide us on our way home.

It is significant to mention that this is no doomsday prophecy, but rather a calling to awaken from our disconnected slumber and move from duality to Oneness, a concept shared in many spiritual traditions. How is that for the theme of remembrance!?

---

[63] *11:11*, Solara Antara Amaa-Ra, 1992 Star-Borne Unlimited, Charlottesville, VA.

Energetically, eleven signals a time that completion is near. If you contemplate the energy that you've been sending to your sankalpa for the past ten months, you realize that, for this calendar year, at least, the time for completing this task is coming to a close. After ten months of consistent focus on the subject, we should be seeing the light at the end of the tunnel.

In the Northern Hemisphere, November weather is turning colder, and the trees are mostly bare of leaves, signaling the next phase of the cycle: death. With the harvest complete and no new life on plants, fresh foods are no longer available. The days are getting shorter, the nights longer, and there is an inward pull that brings about a stockpiling of energy, like a squirrel furiously gathering nuts for the impending winter.

We come into November on the water sign Scorpio, who have a knack for never forgetting, and then head into Sagittarius, or the Centaur, mid-month. The Centaur is half-man, half-horse. The story of the king of centaurs, Chiron, is that he was a philosopher, teacher, and master healer who was accidentally wounded in the foot by one of Hercules' poisoned arrows during a fight that he was not a part of. He could not heal himself nor die, as he was immortal. So, he chose to give up his immortality and die, a profound act of sacrifice driven by his desire to alleviate his own suffering and the suffering of others.

The story goes on to say that Zeus had punished the Titan Prometheus for giving man fire by tying him to a rock and allowing an Eagle to eat his liver daily, which would regenerate due to his immortality. Zeus decreed Prometheus could be freed only if an immortal surrendered their life. Chiron, moved by compassion and aware of Prometheus's sacrifice for humanity, offered his immortality to take Prometheus's place in the underworld so that the great awakener could return. The self-sacrifice that Chiron exhibited projected him into the stars, to be honored by man for eons to come. His death and ascent to the stars symbolize spiritual transformation, akin to the cycle of death and rebirth. For this sacrifice, he will be remembered in the time memorial.

November's flower is the Chrysanthemum, a flower of compassion. The birthstone is Topaz, symbolizing joy. In a month of remembrance, the qualities of compassion and joy surely align.

Holidays and Holy Days

November comes in with a day of remembering ancestors on the 1st. This is commemorated in Mesoamerica (an area of the southern part of North America, Mexico, and Central America) as the "Day of the Dead" or "Día de los Muertos." The origins of honoring the dead date back to indigenous peoples. According to some, the Nahua people of Mexico held rituals honoring the dead in August, where the families of those deceased prepared food, water, and tools to aid the dead on their journey to Chicunamictlan, the land of the Dead, where they then had to travel through nine levels on a journey to Mictal, their final resting place.

It was important to provide the Dead with the necessary supplies for this arduous journey. The Nahua people can be traced back to the Aztec, Toltec, and even the vast Mayan civilization, which dates back to around 250 CE, in Mexico. The Olmec civilization is the first known in the Mesoamerican territory, but unfortunately, little information has survived of their culture and practices. It is most likely that this ancient civilization, which dates back to at least 1200 BCE, also practiced aiding the deceased to their final resting place, but we cannot be completely sure.

The movement of the Day of the Dead, or "Día de los Muertos," to October most likely occurred due to Christian influences and the concurrent events of the Christian holy days All Saints' Day and All Souls' Day. All Saints' Day is a feast day of observing the lives of many Catholic saints on November 1st. All Souls' Day, observed on November 2, is a day of remembrance and prayer for the deceased, particularly those who are in purgatory, a temporary state of purification for souls who have died in God's grace but still need to be cleansed of imperfections.

A closely related holiday in La Paz, Bolivia, is the "Day of Skulls," also known as *Fiesta de las Natitas*, a unique and vibrant celebration honoring the deceased by decorating and venerating human skulls, which are believed to house the spirits of the departed. During this holiday, people bring their own skulls to the cemetery for blessing and celebration. This is celebrated on November 8th.

The first Sunday in November is Daylight Saving Time, an event used by less than 40% of countries, according to timeanddate.com. The reason for the change is to make better use of natural sunlight in areas of the world whose days become shorter as the nights become longer. Many believe that this goes against the natural rhythms of the world and should not be touched. There has been great debate about this event for years, with recent headway made towards eliminating it in the USA. Alas, only time will tell if this false change of time will be eliminated. In the meantime, we shall do our best to work with this strange occurrence, understanding that those who are sensitive to energy may need several days to adjust.

November 11 is Veterans Day in the United States, a day we honor the men and women who died serving our country and providing for our freedom. And to that freedom, the second Tuesday in November, the United States holds for Election Day, when our Democratic country votes for the individuals that we feel will foster the ideals that we hold most dear, and support our Nation's longevity and prosperity. Regardless of our individual political feelings, our Nation is still one of democracy, not Dictatorship. Ideas such as freedom and liberation are watched by the world over by countries with extreme poverty, oppression, lack of inalienable rights, brutality, war, and mass destruction. The world looks to America. U2 songster Bono said, "America is built on an idea. It's a place that offers grace for every welcome that is sought."

Bono continued to say, "America is a song still being written." That's right. We aren't done. Our idea is still unfolding. And with the right intentions, we can course-correct where we went astray and, in the process, save the world. We are the land of the free and the home of the brave. And our time of being distracted by all the small stuff is over. Let's start, individually, to take steps to unify and find common ground. If more of us took that proactive approach, then we would collectively get our groove back. But not by going backwards, rather by finding that new way, that higher way, on the road paved with love and Oneness.

In the United States, Thanksgiving is celebrated on the fourth Thursday of November. We celebrate this as a day when the pilgrims of Plymouth Colony and the Wampanoag Indians sat down for a weeklong harvest feast in 1621. The Indians taught the pilgrims how to cultivate corn, avoid poisonous plants, catch fish, and extract soap from maple trees, which held healing properties.[64] The result of the successful corn harvest was this feast, which was later considered a national holiday by President Abraham Lincoln in 1863. Perhaps, in a month based on remembrance, we should ponder the irony of how we continue to celebrate a day when the Indians assisted us in surviving in the new world, yet have forgotten how we stole their land and resources and forced them to live in small areas we labeled "Reservations."

---

[64] https://www.history.com/topics/thanksgiving/history-of-thanksgiving

Waxing philosophical about Thanksgiving aside, we come to *Mawlid al-Nabi* or Muhammad's Birthday. This can often occur in November, but because of the following of the Islamic lunar calendar, it may not. The Muslim faith was founded by the Prophet Muhammad, to whom, one night, while in meditation, the Archangel Gabriel came and whispered the words of the Qur'an. This text became the basis of the Islamic teachings. The teachings of Islam seek to help those living chaotic lives. Many people don't know that the Qur'an is the Old Testament, including the stories of Adam and Eve, Noah, Moses, Abraham, Joseph, Mary, and Jesus. Again, we see much conflict where we should see similarities.

As November connects to the number eleven, symbolizing inner growth and a higher path, it is time to reflect on some of these erroneous ideals that perhaps we have been holding onto for far too long.

Chakra Connection

11th Chakra

Sanskrit: *Hasta* & *Pada*
Meaning: Hands & Feet
Location: Both Hands and Both Feet

While there is no formal Sanskrit name for the chakras in the hands and feet, some new sources use the Sanskrit words for hands (*hasta*) and feet (*pada*) combined with chakra. However, it should be noted that there is no ancient or formal text revealing those names.

The eleventh chakra is called the "Spark of Inspiration," reflecting its role in bridging divine or cosmic insights with practical expression, amplified by the numerological significance of 11 as a Master Number. Energy Practitioners are well-versed in these centers, as we use our hands for healing sessions in our daily work.

The chakras in the hands and feet are where energy transference and transmutation of physical energy occur. Those who practice yoga may be familiar with hasta and pada bandhas, the locks/energy centers of the hands and feet. This is the same thing as the eleventh chakra.

Ancient yogis realized the power in this place when they discovered the various hand gestures (mudras). They learned that by applying light pressure and holding two or more fingers together in different positions, energy changed, and often physical healing occurred.

For the yogi, the feet provide significant support as they connect the physical being to the earth for grounding. This is only the case in standing postures, of course. But for those who practice yoga asanas, the physical poses, we understand how important the placement of our feet can be to the success and the stability of any posture.

How do we know if we are connecting to the eleventh chakra? See the companion Workbook for more questions, but consider these journal prompts on your eleventh chakra:

> Energy: Do you feel energy in your hands and feet?

> Physical Body: Do you enjoy walking barefoot on the earth?

Moon Phases

Dark Moon:

Dark Moon in November is for taking the time to contemplate the people in your life who have passed on to the next realm, who've either inspired you or contributed to the path that you are on, and to what the meaning is behind your sankalpa. Intention is everything when discussing energy, and honoring those whose magnificence stood out to you and contributed to who you are is a significant tool in refining your goals. Appreciation and gratitude are two aspects that cannot go unattended.

New Moon:

Create something to honor those people, or a single person, who was a driving force in your life and who is now deceased. You might write a poem or a letter to them. You could create a song for them. You could choose to perform a ritual or ceremony for them, or even visit their gravesite or a memorable place where you both spent time together.

Waxing Moon:

A Gratitude Journal could be something to do on the waxing moon. Each day, express gratitude for a person in your life and for what their presence and love have given you. Love is of a very high vibrational frequency. So when you express your gratitude in some way, you're spreading that energy and increasing your own positive vibrations.

Full Moon:

There is a Wiccan ceremony called a "Dumb Supper," which is hosted around Samhain/Day of the Dead, but can be performed on the full moon of November. Simply prepare a meal and set an empty seat for the dearly departed (or one empty seat for each person). You could place a picture of them or one of their items on the seat. Put a plate of food down for them and yourself. Then, sit quietly and have your meal. The "dumb" in this supper refers to being quiet.

<u>Waning Moon</u>:

You can still take the time to be grateful for those who have crossed over during the waning moon. All of the moon phases can assist you with a piece of the story. Perhaps if you are carrying any grief over the loss of a loved one, waning moon energy can help you release that heaviness.

Use the waning moon time to plan the rituals for this month. Any time in November is suitable, though the Day of the Dead may be considered to see if it aligns with your intentions. It comes as the first day of the month, so unless you read ahead, you'll be crafting your special remembrance rituals at any time this month. And, it's all good.

Faith Tradition: Mesoamerican

Ximihtoti inhuan moachtonhuan.
"May you dance with your ancestors."

– Nahuatl natives in Teotihuacan

As previously mentioned, Mesoamerica refers to the region of the lower part of North America, Mexico, and Central America. Many differing countries contribute to this region, but there is also a conglomerate of faith traditions linked here as well. Roughly, these refer to the indigenous cultures of the area from about 2000 BCE through the Spanish conquest in the 16th century.

Although this is a diverse people, they share common ideologies such as a cosmology of a multilayered universe, worship of a pantheon of gods related to war, creation, fertility, and others, belief in an animating vital force through all living things, and rituals based around the calendar/Wheel of the Year.

Main Faith Traditions Comprising Mesoamerica:

- Aztecs: Ruled central Mexico from Tenochtitlán, dominated until the Spanish conquest in 1521.
- Mayans: Thrived in southern Mexico, Guatemala, Belize, and Honduras, peaking during the Classic Period (250–900 CE) in cities like Chichén Itzá and Tikal.
- Toltecs: Centered in Tula (Hidalgo, Mexico), were a Nahuatl-speaking people revered by the Aztecs as cultural ancestors. They thrived roughly from 900 to 1150 A.D.
- Olmecs: Of the Gulf Coast (modern Veracruz, Tabasco), considered Mesoamerica's "mother culture," laid the foundations for later faiths. The Olmecs thrived from 1500 to 400 BCE.

Symbol: Sugar Skull

Skulls are synonymous with fear as they are understood worldwide, across cultures and belief systems, to be the ultimate symbol of death. Sever the head from the body, and death is surely imminent. They were kept as trophies of war, regarded as a reminder of God's judgment, and often believed to contain life-force and oracular powers.[65]

However, in Mesoamerica, the skull takes on a different vibe altogether. Known here as Sugar Skulls, they are vibrant, edible sculptures crafted from sugar and used as offerings and decorations during *Día de los Muertos* on November 1–2, celebrating deceased loved ones. Here, they embody the joyful embrace of life and death, echoing Mesoamerican views of ancestral connections, and a reminder to celebrate life.

---

[65] *Encyclopedia of Secret Signs and Symbols,* page 574

November Altar

- **Altar cloth:** Pink, the color of the eleventh chakra, and healing

- **Flower:** Chrysanthemums

- **Candles:** Pink or black, pink for the chakra color, and black due to its connection with respect for the dead

- **Crystal/Stone:** Topaz jewelry or the raw stone. Other pink crystals are nice additions this month, especially Rose Quartz and Pink tourmaline. If you are working with black, you may want to bring in some Black Tourmaline or Obsidian. Both of these stones offer the metaphysical properties of protection, but Obsidian is also widely known to have been used throughout Mesoamerica.

- **Symbol:** Colorful Sugar Skulls

- **Essential Oil/Incense:** Copal, Burned by Mesoamerican cultures to honor ancestors, copal's resinous, sweet aroma evokes a sacred connection to the past.

- **Herbs:** Ceremonial White Sage, tobacco, and cacao. The latter two were widely used throughout Mesoamerica in ritual and ceremony.

- **Other items (optional):**
  - *The Modern Mystic's Wheel of the Year* Book, Workbook, and Oracle Deck
  - Pictures of the dearly departed
  - Clothing or other items of the dearly departed
  - Family Tree, Ancestry, and other bloodline research
  - Respectfully thank your ancestors for being with you on your journey, and present your Sankalpa to them, asking for their blessings.

Angel/Ancestor: Elder

There may not be anything more endearing than a culture's Elders. These wise senior figures of any tribe or group hold the history of the past. By weaving stories of the past, they keep the precious memories alive and bear witness to the vast changes that have occurred over their years.

If you've been given the gift of having a Grandmother alive, you most likely have a memory of a time when she shared a story with you about her past, and in the process, realized how it linked to your present, and your family's future. Yes, our seniors encapsulate a timelessness, not in their physical appearance, but in the very fabric of a family's crest. The Maya were known to weave their history, mythology, and cultural narratives into their fabrics, using textiles as a medium to preserve and express their heritage. These encoded weavings are a mix of both art and history.[66]

We are a part of our family's story, but we are also here to create a story of our own. Each of us is here to carve out our own path. But when we do so with the wisdom and counsel of our elders, we will most assuredly succeed. For was it not them who created the Wheel? And yet we still try to make it better. Perhaps if we stop long enough, we can learn more from our seniors. Giving them a voice when so many other parts of them are failing can mean more to them than we can ever imagine.

November's theme is "Remembrance." What a time to connect to your family's elders and hear their stories! If you're in a committed relationship, spend time with your partner's elders. They'll surely know a piece of history that may enlighten you to the nature of your significant other's habits.

If your family has all passed over, or you have no family to sit with, this is a great month to dive into your ancestry. Whether it is through ancestry.com, DNA testing, or researching your family tree in their country of origin, dive into all things Elder wisdom, ancestry, and legacy this month.

Even if you think you know the story, you'll be surprised to learn some hidden gems along the way.

---

[66] *Maya Textiles of Guatemala,* Margot Blum Schevill, 1993

November Ritual: *Ofrendas*

An ofrenda is an offering made to the dead. It can include candles, marigolds, food, tobacco, toys (if for children), or other items. You can place ofrendas on an altar, which is traditionally done, for the dead. You can also place them somewhere in the home where they lived, where they passed away, or a certain place that was special to both of you.

It is not uncommon to see ofrendas on the roadside where a horrible tragedy may have occurred. Floral crosses, candles, pictures, stuffed animals, and other items often accompany the place where the person's soul was thought to have left the body.

Creating the ofrenda can be an uplifting, joyous endeavor or a solemn, respectful one. The way that one goes about remembering the dead is personal and needs to be meaningful to you. So, do what feels right and what you think will best honor those whom you are remembering in this ritual.

Perhaps linking this ritual to a Wiccan Dumb Supper or a Day of the Dead festival feels supportive. Take time to plan the events of the ritual during the waning stage of the moon.

You may recall when the Princess of Wales, Lady Diana, died in 1997. The fence around the royal palace in London, along with other places where she was known to reside or spend time, was lined, several feet deep, with ofrendas to Diana. The offerings of stuffed animals, pictures, poetry, and heartfelt letters were never-ending, a testament to the people's love of their Princess.

It's easy to see how a simple yet poignant ritual transcends cultural and religious boundaries. And since everyone knows someone who has transitioned before us, this is a perfect way to embrace a practice.

Tracey's Personal Reflection

In September 1997, I was headed to England on a trip through the UK. Days before our departure, Lady Diana died in a tragic accident. We had planned to see London first, but decided to reroute our trip plans and head straight to Wales, then Ireland and Scotland, before traveling through England to London. By the time we got back, the memorials left in front of Buckingham Palace were astounding. I'd never seen anything like it. Thousands upon thousands of these "Ofrendas" poured out several feet deep from the fence. People were still crying as they dropped more offerings. Their show of love for her was something that I'll never forget. And to date, I've not seen any other gesture quite like it.

Before then, I didn't know much about Diana as a woman or a Princess. I'm not the little girl who ever wanted to be a Princess, so when the world watched that royal wedding with wonder, I was busy doing something that I felt was more entertaining. But as I stood there in front of the palace gates, it struck me that I wanted to understand more about this woman and why she was so loved throughout the United Kingdom.

This led me to research her and add her picture to my famous "Wall of Fame," as it was jokingly called at my yoga studio. On the wall hung assorted photos of people who inspired me to be a better person, or who contributed in some way to the betterment of the world. They were people who I felt were authentic in their quest, not simply doing an obligatory job.

That's the beauty of the ofrenda. It's a beautiful memorial for those left behind, but it also inspires others so that their legacy lives on in surprising ways.

Love from Diana's Ofrendas was palpable

November Daily Yoga Practice:
Hasta & *Pada* Chakra Awakening

This practice is for all levels, and no yoga experience is required. However, it is always recommended to consult a doctor before beginning any new physical program. Remember to modify anything for particular conditions that you may be experiencing, and to always follow your breath for the truth about a feeling that arises.

Yoga Practice to Activate the Chakras of the Hands & Feet:

The chakras of the hands and feet, or hasta and pada chakras, respectively, are major centers where energy transmutation takes place. As mentioned, energy workers naturally have an awakened sense of these chakras in the hands when they perform or facilitate healing sessions. You don't have to be initiated into a practice to feel the energy in these centers; you merely need to become conscious that this is where energy alchemy takes place.

As you practice, become ultra-aware of the energy in your hands and also in your feet. The feet in many postures anchor the body to the earth. Drawing energy upward from the Earth Star (10th chakra) and the root (1st chakra) is an essential part of this energy transmutation. Without the connection to the physical matter on the planet, how can we begin to work with it? Like an electrical cord, once the base is plugged into the socket, the energy begins to flow, and something miraculous happens: we have light or power.

The single posture, Downward-Facing Dog, is a perfect way to ignite the energy of the hands and feet chakras.

Single Posture Practice: Downward-Facing Dog (*Adho-Mukha Svanasana*)

From hands and knees, tuck the toes under. Push the yoga mat forward with the fingers and allow the hips to glide backwards towards the feet, keeping your eyes forward and spine long. Pull the belly in and on an exhalation, push into the ground, lifting the hips towards the sky. Keep the knees slightly bent and push the chest back towards the thighs and legs. The lower back keeps its natural arch, so connect to the sitting bones and lengthen them to the wall behind you. Start to lower your heels and straighten your legs to the degree that you can keep your back in the proper arched position. The shoulders will naturally lift towards the ears, so connect to the armpits or outer edge of the upper arm (Deltoid muscle) and rotate it downward towards the earth. Allow the head to hang loose and bring the gaze towards the navel.

I've been told that there are over 100 alignment cues for Downward Facing Dog. This is a posture that we can return to over and over, still discovering nuances that we never felt before.

Modification/Variation: Table pose (*Goasana*)

Come onto your hands and knees. Align the wrists directly under the shoulders so the arm bones are straight. Spread the fingers wide like starfish and plug down into the knuckles of the fingers while drawing energy up through the center of the palm and up the arm bones. Look back and make sure leg bones are aligned under hip bones, too. Feet should be flat, pressing into the top of the toenails and shins to get weight slightly out of the knees. Keep spine straight, gazing forward passed the tip of the nose.

Breathing Practice: *Pranic* Ball Breath

Stand for this breathing practice. Place your right hand on your heart center or *Anahata Chakra*, and your left hand on your solar plexus or *Manipura Chakra*. This creates a balance of the vital life-force of the male/female and left/right sides of the body. Allow your feet to be flat on the floor and ground down into the four corners of the feet while pulling up through the center arch of the foot, like a suction cup.

When ready, take a deep inhalation, filling the abdomen up to the chest. Pause and hold your breath. Then, taking a long exhalation, release the air from the chest down while squeezing the belly inward. Repeat, focusing on the energy of the hands and the feet. Perform this part of the breath until you feel the hand and foot chakras activating.

Then, bring your hands, cupped and fingers not touching, in front of you and imagine that you are holding onto a ball of energy. Attempt to feel the energy ball in your hands. When you do, inhale the ball upwards, body relaxed. Exhale the ball downwards and back in front of you.

You can inhale the ball to the left or right and exhale it back in front. When ready, inhale it away from you in any direction, and then exhale it back in towards you. Feel your connection to the pranic energy ball and see if you can allow it to grow bigger by spreading your hands further apart, yet still feeling the ball's presence.

Mudra & Meditation:

Padangustasana is considered a yoga posture and not a hand gesture or mudra. However, this "Yogi-Toe-Lock" creates a binding grip of the fingers around the big toe, which connects both the hands and feet chakras.

To perform this pose/mudra, interlace the index and middle fingers around the big toe, using the thumb to hold them down around the base of the toe, strongly. You can perform this in a seated posture, such as Cobbler (*Bandha Konasana*), or standing, balancing on one leg with the other leg extended for *Utthita Hasta Padangustasana*. While in the pose, breathe deeply, connecting to the energy transference from the hands to the feet and back again.

Hatha Yoga Sequence:

Seated - Meditation	Pranic Ball Breathing	Making the Sun	Seated Forward Fold	1/2 Forward Fold	Animal Stretch
Lateral Bend	Cobbler	Foot Massage	Mountain with Pada Bandha	Yoga Mudra	Making the Sun
Pranic Breathing	Standing Forward Fold	Table	Cat/Cow	Child	Hero
Neck Rolls	Self-Reiki Healing	Supine w/ optional more Reiki	Supine Cobbler	Corpse - Final Relaxation	Closing

* Note that the pre-recorded practice may differ from the sequence above.

Short 15-minute Practice:

- Mountain with Pada Bandha
- Pranic Ball
- Making the Sun
- Yoga Mudra
- Self Healing
- Corpse

November Recap

November is all about remembrance. Express your gratitude to all who came before you and supported you in any way for being the person that you are today.

There is a humble quality to this month's reverence. Whether you choose to be quiet and reflective or joyful and celebratory is up to you. Remember that we heal through our hands and how we reach out into the world. Your heartfelt sankalpa came to you for a reason. You need to share something with the world, and you are closer than ever to bringing it forward. For those who came before us, often those who paved the way and have left this plane of existence, we respectfully honor and bow to you, and bring a part of you with us forward in healing the world.

December

Hope

December Energies

The last month of the year is full of energy, love, and cheer. As Yule and other festive holidays approach, the atmosphere brims with hope and vitality. With holiday decorations and crispness in the air, the weather turns to the official start of winter in the Northern Hemisphere. There is an essence of purity as we breathe in the newness of falling snow and admire the white lights that perk up homes and store windows. This may be the final month of the Gregorian calendar, yet we are going out with considerable positive energy.

The number twelve breaks down numerically to the number three (3), which represents creativity and love. We've been here before, back in March, when our theme was Rebirth. Now that we are in the final month of the year, and are cycling back to the number three, we have an opportunity to close out the year with the culmination of spiritual fulfillment, another meaning of three: the trinity. A trinity is a triadic structure, three interconnected principles, deities, or aspects that denote divine or cosmic unity, balance, or process in many spiritual traditions. It often symbolizes creation, preservation, and transformation (or destruction), reflecting the cyclical nature of existence.

Nearly every spiritual tradition has a three-part cosmology. Taoists consider the Trinity the three pure ones: Yunshi (cosmic origin/creation), Lingbao (harmony and teaching), and Daode (moral order). *Jains* see the Trinity as correct sight, correct knowledge, and correct conduct. Celtics refer to her in her Trinity as Maiden, Mother, and Crone. Christianity is famously known for the Father, the Son, and the Holy Spirit. Hindus have Brahma, Vishnu, and Shiva. Q'ero Shamans have the Snake, Puma, and Condor. Mesoamericans used Heaven, Earth, and the underworld. Buddhists use the Buddha (awakened guide), Dharma (the path to enlightenment), and Sangha (a supportive community). In Kemetic spirituality, Osiris (the underworld), Isis (magic and motherhood), and Hathor, representing the sky and victory, are used. Native Americans use the sky (Wakan Tanka), the Earth (Make), and the underworld or spirits. And the Norse work with Odin, the "All Father," representing wisdom and creation, Thor, the protector and preserver, and Freyr, for fertility and renewal.

While Jews rebuke the Trinity, *Kabbalists*, the mystical, esoteric Jewish sect, understand the Tree of Life to be formed from three emanations of All That Is: Nothingness, Wisdom, and Understanding.

Islam's Sufi Mystics embody the trinity in several ways. The Sufis' three realms of human, angelic, and divine are traversed by devotees in their spiritual aspirations. The Phoenix, Sufism's rebirth symbol, embodies the transformative cycle of life (existence), death (*fana*), and rebirth (*baqa*). During Ramadan, Sufis progress from *Sharia* (law), through *Tariqa* (path), to *Haqiqa* (truth), embodying the rebirth cycle of the Phoenix. As we saw in March, even the famous Sufi "Whirling" breaks down to three parts: the preparation phase, the whirling itself, and the closing rituals.[67]

Some faith traditions do not honor the Trinity. Instead, they believe in a monotheistic belief system in God. If we really want to find a connection for those faith traditions in December, we look to their origins. *Decem*, which is Latin for "10." In numerology, ten breaks down to the number one, corresponding to when this month was originally the tenth month in the former Roman calendar. So there we have it: the number one for a sole God-source.

Our astrological friends for December begin with fiery Sagittarius, whose worldly concerns take precedence, then move into the stabilizing energy of the Goatfish or Sea-Goat. Capricorn activates at the Winter Solstice, the shortest day of the year, when darkness reigns.

Guttman and Johnson explain this time expertly in *Mythic Astrology*, "And in the journey of individual consciousness. The point of greatest contact with universal consciousness has been reached, the collective wisdom has been assimilated, and the individual begins a symbolic return as a transformed being: the self has become the Self. This is why all gods who represent the higher Self—including Christ—have births celebrated at the winter solstice."[68]

How fitting to come to our final month of the year with an understanding that the journey is perfectly completed with the Goatfish. Remember that in January, we discussed the Goatfish's connection to rebirth at the beginning of the year, and now we see how this creature brings us full circle at the conclusion.

December's birthstone is the turquoise, perhaps one of man's oldest talismans for good luck, and also represents friendship. The Poinsettia flower symbolizes good cheer and success, an appropriate symbol for December's festive season and the culmination of our sankalpa.

---

[67] https://ghayb.com/the-reality-of-sufism/

[68] page 333

Holidays and Holy Days

The Abrahamic religions all celebrate major holidays this time of year, but remember that for some, following the lunar calendar may challenge these actual dates.

The lesser-known Islamic Holy Day of *Dar al-Masnavi* (Rumi Wedding Night) commemorates the death of the Sufi mystic on December 17th. He is said to have then obtained union with God, the only Beloved. The traditional celebration on this eve is that of the 'Whirling Dervish,' the ritual we observed in our book back in March, when we originally discussed Islam and the number three. Now we revisit it through an assimilation of knowledge.

Yule, the Winter Solstice, occurs on or around December 21st and is the longest night of the year. From this day forward, the light begins to strengthen and brighten just a little more each day. Not that there is anything negative about the darkness, but there is a hopeful quality that reigns supreme when the light regains its brilliance. Similar to the conversation about the trinity, all spiritual traditions discuss the light, which was our theme for June, and the highest energy of the sun during the Summer Solstice. But since that day, the light began its slow dimming until this darkest day at the Winter Solstice. Now we feel the cyclical stage of light come around again, and it couldn't feel more brilliant and perfect to end the year with a renewed hope for what is coming.

Christians celebrate the birth of Jesus Christ on December 25th. Everyone knows the story of the Savior who was born in a manger in Bethlehem, of virgin birth to Mary and Joseph, the saint who raised him as his own, even though the baby was God's son. The fact is that historians disagree on the actual date of Christ's birth, with some accounts considering that he may have been born somewhere around 6 BC. In 2018, an article in *Live Science* magazine by astronomer Dave Reneke argued that due to the placement of The Star of Bethlehem in the sky for this famous birth, the rare occurrence of Venus and Jupiter conjunct would have occurred somewhere around June 17, 2 B.C.[69] In any event, the fact that probably the most famous birthday in the entire world is incorrect bears little significance to the over two billion Christians on the planet. We will, most assuredly, continue to celebrate the birthday of Jesus Christ on December 25th for many years to come, despite the theories that suggest otherwise.

---

[69] https://www.livescience.com/42976-when-was-jesus-born.html

Our Jewish friends often celebrate *Hanukkah* in December. This "Festival of Lights" is an eight-day-long festival commemorating an improbable victory of a Jewish band known as the Maccabees in reclaiming their land and Temple from the Greek Empire. The story goes that once the Maccabees won victory in 164 BCE, they sought to relight a lamp called the "eternal flame," but only a day's worth of consecrated olive oil could be found. The intention to light the flame was so deep that the priests did so anyway, and miraculously, the lamp burned for eight days straight until they were able to refill the oil. The emphasis of *Hanukkah* is on the light guiding us through the darkness, another beautiful story of hope.

Chakra Connection

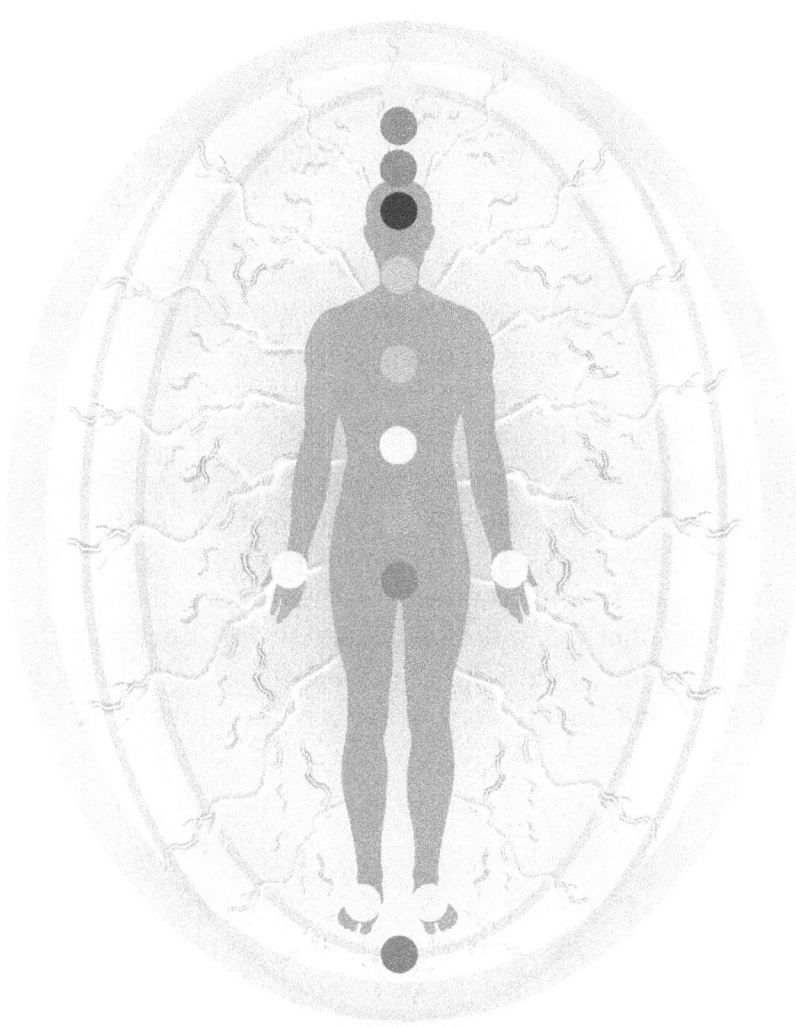

12th Chakra

Name: Cosmic Energy Egg

Location: 32 secondary chakra points and the Cosmic Energy Egg

Through the 12th chakra, we might discover the boundaries of our being and connect to the boundless, One Consciousness.

And so we have reached the 12th chakra. I bow to Cyndie Dale's Encyclopedia, called *The Subtle Body,* for much of this information. Here she details thirty-two different points that she calls the "Secondary Chakra System" in the body. These points correspond to organs, joints, and other areas of the human system, binding it all together in one cohesive energetic unit.

She discusses the "Energy Egg," which is a set of energy lines encircling the body, exploring the boundaries of our entire being, and constituting the end of the human self. Here, we might discover the boundaries of our being and connect to the One Consciousness.

How might one go about this? See the companion Workbook for more questions, but consider these journal prompts on your twelfth chakra:

Energy Egg: Do you feel energy around you?

Oneness: Are you fully connected to your Divinity or Higher Self?

The 12th chakra can feel unattainable if there are still major issues to work through in the lower chakras. Go back and spend some time with those areas that still require more attention and do the work. Look at things from the new perspective of being connected to your own divinity and the Creator of the world.

Moon Phases

Hey, how's that sankalpa going? Remember that there's no shame in falling short of your expectations because energy shifts. We need to adjust to the constant changes. Hopefully, however, you are on a new trajectory, having culminated a full year of working in harmony. Let's check it out.

Dark Moon:

On the dark moon night, go within and reflect through meditation, prayer, journaling, or other methods that work for you. Look back at your journal from this year and assess where you found your energy to be the highest and lowest, what worked for you at what point, and what still needs work. Concentrate on connecting to your true and Highest Self to discern where you should focus your efforts for the conclusion of the current year and thus the segue into the new. Then you will be poised with the right effort on the night of the new moon, the last one of the year.

New Moon:

The New Moon in December is the final one of the year. Go back to January and remember what we said about the dark moon the evening before. We want to be very clear about what energy we are putting forth into the new year. As this is the last new moon, it will be a gateway to the next Wheel of the Year.

Waxing to Full Moon:

The waxing to full moon stage is all about concluding the year on a high note. If things have shifted during the year, what can you do at this point to gain a positive perspective and finish the year feeling good about all that you accomplished? Can you put the finishing touches on a major project? Can you celebrate your festivals with the knowledge that you have gained much wisdom? Are you ready to put a new you out into the world?

Whatever it is, just do it. Do it with the heightened awareness that you are bringing forth your deepest and truest longings and intentions to share your gifts with the world. Enjoy having something important to share and embody it with all that you are.

If the full moon falls on or around Yule, then Hallelujah! Create a special event to commemorate this auspicious moment and to align with friends, family, and community in a way that inspires hope for the new year.

Faith Tradition: Norse

"Don't Waste Your Time Looking Back. You Are Not Going That Way."

— Ragnar, legendary Viking

Old Norse, as a belief system, historically shows up around 500 BCE, with roots that are likely much older from an oral tradition. The *Poetic Edda*, from which much of Norse folklore is derived, was written down 1000-1300 CE. This is the primary source of information about the ancient gods and humankind.

In the poems of the *Edda* lay the runic alphabet, or *Futhark*, previously thought to originate from the Germanic era, 400-800 CE. It is now considered possible to trace the runic language back to shortly after the last ice age, approximately 11,000 years ago, which would make this much older than Hinduism or any other known written knowledge.[70] Without laying claim that the Norse religion is the first formalized one to have existed, it may be the oldest in written form that we have to date.

The story of the Futhark takes us to their god, Odin (*Woden*), the predominant god of Old Norse mythology. It is said that when Odin originally sought knowledge, he sacrificed himself on Yggdrasil, the world tree. This is famously displayed in the Hanged Man tarot card in the traditional Rider Tarot divination deck. Yggdrasil is said to be the center of the Universe and to contain the nine worlds, including that of humanity, the gods and goddesses, giants, elves, elemental worlds, and the dead. According to the *Edda*, Odin hung himself for nine nights on Yggdrasil to gain the knowledge and magic of the runic language.[71]

There are twenty-four runes in the Futhark, separated into three *Aetts*, or divisions. Together, the Futhark tells a story of creation and destruction of the world. According to Freya Aswynn in her book *Northern Mysteries and Magick*, the first aett describes the god and all other beings coming into existence, the second aett describes the necessary antagonistic forces, and the third aett gives an overview of the human condition.[72]

---

[70] https://www.ancient-origins.net/opinion-guest-authors/northern-mysteries-current-futhark-and-mystery-schools-viking-age-005971

[71] https://norse-mythology.org/cosmology/yggdrasil-and-the-well-of-urd/

[72] *Northern Mysteries and Magick* page 91

In Aswynn's book, she describes that once Odin received the runic language from Yggdrasil, he still needed knowledge of how to use it. Odin then sacrificed his eye to the well of *Mimir*, which holds the collective knowledge. Mimir is said to be the counsel of the gods, and once Odin gave him his eye, he was able to drink of the well, and thusly gain the knowledge of all.[73]

Although Norse originated in Scandinavia and Iceland, there are people worldwide who practice a form of Norse paganism. It is difficult to estimate the actual number of people following the ways of the "old gods," as there is no formal governing body or registration system, and followers of the faith usually work in small groups or solitude. However, with many New Age followers dabbling in Runic divination, blending Norse into their personal practices, and with popular television series and movies portraying historical Viking accounts, the number of people seeking interest in this tradition is growing.

As everything is cyclical, could we see a revival of the "Old Gods" and Norse making their way back up in the faith tradition list? Some say that the Norse mythological prophecy of *Ragnarök*, which predicted a series of catastrophic events, including a great battle, that ultimately leads to the destruction and subsequent rebirth of the world, is closer to reality than ever, and more of a reality than a myth. Others believe that Ragnarök, although foretold as a future prophecy, has already occurred in ancient times when the gods roamed the Earth alongside humans, and before our present time. One could surely make interesting arguments for either.

Why is this old religion our faith tradition for the final month of the Wheel of the Year?

The Norse religion's deep cultural resonance, regardless of precise age, suits December due to its enduring cyclical and communal themes, alignment with Yule (Old Norse: Jól, meaning "wheel" or "festivity"), and connection to Universal Consciousness, the 12th Chakra. Odin, the All-father, embodies the pursuit of enlightenment through sacrifice and wisdom-seeking, as seen in his hanging on Yggdrasil for nine nights to gain runic knowledge. His quest reflects the twelfth chakra's enlightenment, where the individual transcends the ego to align with universal truth. The Norse World Tree, Yggdrasil, connects the Nine Worlds, symbolizing the interconnectedness of all existence, from gods to humans and

---

[73] *Northern Mysteries and Magick* page 58

spirits. This mirrors the twelfth chakra's role as a conduit to universal consciousness, uniting all energies.

Besides, Vikings are cool.

Symbol: *Valknut*

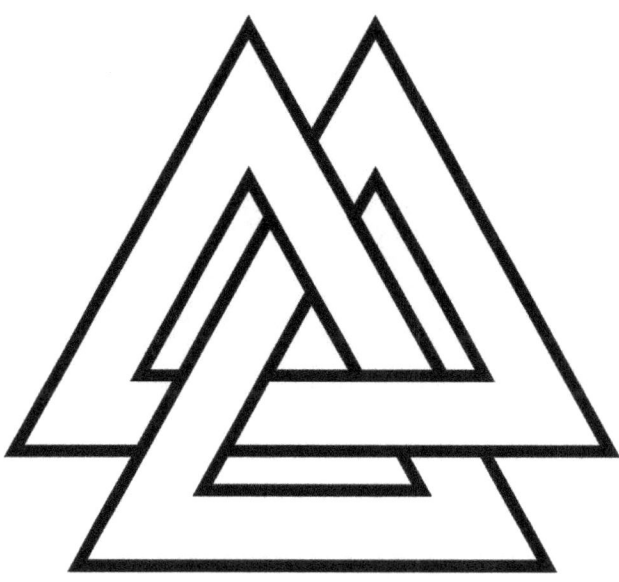

Valknut is the Norse symbol of three interlocking triangles, forming a complex, knot-like design with nine points. It is one of the most enigmatic and iconic symbols in Norse mythology, often associated with death, Odin, and the cycle of life and transformation. It is drawn as one, single, continuous line, creating a fluid knot found on runes, graves, and other artifacts. The name "Valknut" implies "knot of the slain," tying it to Odin's Valkyries, who choose the fallen and select them for *Valhalla*, the Vikings' heaven.

The Valknut's exact meaning is debated due to limited textual evidence in primary sources like the *Poetic Edda*. However, scholars and archaeologists interpret it through its artistic context, Odin associations, and triadic structure. It is likely to have been used for protection, as with many other knot symbols, and carried a promise that Odin would protect the spirit of the Warrior who had died as it made its way to Valhalla, the realm of the gods, where slain heroes are received.

As the symbol for December, and aligning with winter and the Solstice's promise of the coming of the light, the Valknut is a reminder that energy never ceases, yet instead changes form, continuing infinitely.

December Altar

- **Altar cloth:** Multi-faceted/Multi-colored or Opalescent/Iridescent cloth, the colors of the 12th chakra

- **Flowers:** Poinsettia

- **Candle:** White candle at the center of the altar to light whenever doing work, holding the energy of Spirit

- **Crystal/Stone:** Turquoise stone, prayer bead bracelet, or necklace, or Clear Quartz, a stone of overall positive energy, reflective of all colors

- **Symbol:** Picture of the Valknut

- **Essential Oil/Incense:** Balsam Fir, used in Norse Yule traditions, is a fresh, forest scent that symbolizes enduring hope in winter.

- **Herbs:** Ceremonial White Sage, pine needles, Juniper

- **Other items (optional):**
  - *The Modern Mystic's Wheel of the Year* Book, Workbook, and Oracle Deck
  - Any item that invokes the energy of Hope for you
  - Set of Norse Runes
  - Drum for trance
  - As hope rings this final month of the Wheel of the Year, infuse all that positive energy into your sankalpa, having had it as a repeated energy on your altar for the past year, it has become a staple for you. Honor it once again.

Angel/Ancestor: Seer

The Völva is a Norse term for a female prophetess and priestess who works with sorcery and the *seidr*.[74] Many reading this book have prophetic or journeying abilities and have relied on their own self as they explored these practices. For the Norse, the Seer was akin to the Shaman or Medicine Woman, connecting the community to the divine through visioning and prophecy, seidr magic (a magic linked to fate, allowing them to manipulate outcomes), and healing using various herbs and rituals.

As with all traditions, one should seek out a proper teacher for study and eventual initiation into the Norse rites. At the very least, studying *The Poetic Edda* and other complementary Norse and Viking texts is crucial in understanding the components of the Norse spiritual tradition.

Although there are some teachers of the old religion and its rites, it may be challenging to find a suitable guide in your area. A skilled Völva would take years of initiatory practice and training. However, as a "Seer," which is a more available term that crosses over into other traditions, there are practical steps that one might take to bring oneself into the fray should one find oneself available for such a thing.

According to Katie Gerrard, the first act of becoming the Völva requires a transformative initiatory process. In her book *Seidr: The Gate is Open*, she lists this Rite of Transformation to Becoming the Völva. We can borrow pieces of her steps for the average Modern Mystic.

1. Purify the space with incense
2. Cast a protective circle
3. Invoke your chosen deity, in this case, Freyja, who introduced Norse magic, seidr, to Odin. Invocation: "Freyja, Lady of the Vanir, Mistress of sorcery, Teacher of seidr and the *Aesir*, Golden lady of Brisingamen, you're welcome here now. Hail, Freyja!"
4. Use the incense to create a wall of smoke with a candle behind it
5. Create an altered state of consciousness through drumming (see December's ritual)
6. Step through the smoke wall, sit, and focus on the flame, drumming
7. Experience your journey, then step back through he smoke wall

---

[74] *Seidr the Gate is Open*, Katie Gerrard, 2011

8. Thank your deity, release the circle of protection, and thank them for their presence
9. Ground yourself[75]

---

[75] *Seidr the Gate is Open,* pages 38-40

December Ritual: Norse Seidr/Shamanic Trance

Norse traditions, not unlike many other tribal shamanic traditions, have no hard and fast rules. This can make ritual difficult or relatively easy, depending on how you wish to view it. Of course, we want to honor the tradition as much as possible, and the Norse tradition is one that most, whether of Germanic or Scandinavian descent or not, can embrace as their own. The term seidr refers to Nordic magic, so we work with this magical time of year in the shamanic tradition of trance to dive deeply into the subconscious to access the knowledge that we already have within us.

Shamans receive their knowledge from pathways to the subconscious realm. One of the practices that people can easily access for this is that of drumming. A regular rhythmic beat is produced either by the practitioner or another source, which allows one to enter into altered states of consciousness. The pace and the regularity of the beat are important, so if you are not well-versed in keeping a beat, you may want to enlist the assistance of a professional percussionist. However, moving into a trance state using your natural abilities can be a powerful technique.

Preparation:

- Drum or drummer to play for you
- Fire pit, fire pot, or candle and burner pot
- Herbs: Juniper, Pine, Heather, or other local herbs

Find a place with open space in which to perform your ritual this month. Ensure that you have everything in place before beginning. Turn off electronic devices and create a sacred space.

Steps:

1. Cast a protective circle: Freya Aswynn provides the list of directions in her book *Northern Mysteries & Magick*[76]:
   - *Dvalin (dwarf)*: Southern quarter/Fire
   - *Mimir (giant)*: Northern quarter/Earth
   - *Odin (god)*: Eastern quarter/Air
   - *Dain (elf)*: Western quarter/Water

---

[76] page 145

2. <u>Place Protection Around Your Space for Journeying</u>: The *Algiz* rune is for protection. It looks like an open hand. If you stand when calling in the directions, use this position, with your hands overhead. Once the circle is cast, keep the hands in the Algiz gesture and walk in a circle, envisioning that you are shielding and protecting your magical area from any lower vibrational energies that may be interested in entering. Ask that you are protected and guided to only interact with beings of the highest light and energy in your trance.

3. <u>Throw herbs into the fire</u>: Take your herbs and throw them into the sacrificial fire as an offering to Odin and the gods.

4. <u>Drumming</u>: When you are ready, begin by sitting comfortably with your drum and starting a simple rhythmic beat that mimics a heartbeat. Something as simple as "Boom-Boom, Boom-Boom" is considered perfect for moving into shamanic trance.

5. <u>Chant</u>: Once your beat is established as harmonious and being done unconsciously, you can begin to chant the rune *Perthro*, pronounced "Per-throw," asking for secret knowledge to be revealed.

6. <u>Trance</u>: You can choose to chant or not. You can allow yourself to move in whatever way that you are called to. You will want uninterrupted time to travel astrally and gain the knowledge you're asking for. Remain open instead of asking particular questions, so that Universal wisdom can be shared with me in whatever way it wants to come in.

7. <u>Close</u>: When it feels complete, put out any open flames.

After drumming, you may be tired and thirsty. Keep some water nearby and allow yourself to rest comfortably while you come down from your journeying. It is best not to have plans afterwards, as you may want to have a low-key evening to write and reflect on the visions that were shared with you.

Tracey's Personal Reflection

In October of 2019, I was introduced to a local group in New Jersey by a Shamanic practitioner that I knew. You needed to be invited to their annual Norse High Seat. The invitation read:

"The High Seat comes to us from the ancient Norse shamanic practice of seidr. It may be used by those seeking assistance from the spirit realm for healing, transformation, and wisdom. The community gathers with sacred staffs in hand and welcomes the wise Völva (Seer/staff carrier) and invites her/him to take the "High Seat" (also translated as the "Seat of Magic"). They sing the Seer out to the place of knowing, where she/he experiences a profound shift in consciousness. One by one, community members step before the wise one and ask a question from the heart. Answers are given and witnessed by the community."

The woman hosting this event was trained by Annette Høst, an expert on Scandinavian shamanic practices who co-founded the Scandinavian Center for Shamanic Studies in Denmark in 1986.

I went with a friend, open and excited to learn more about this old tradition. The vibe was inviting and mystical. The practice of the High Seat was professional and accessible. And the community was beautiful.

I continued to grow an interest in Norse traditions and picked up a copy of the *Poetic Edda*, along with other books on Norse mythology and religion.

In my ongoing research, I came across a woman named Imelda Almqvist from the Netherlands, who was coming to Philadelphia, PA, with a Völva training course. I was set to take the course when the COVID-19 pandemic put a stop to the training, and Imelda hasn't returned to the USA or done this training since. I connected with her on social media and have learned about the Norse tradition through her work, along with my own studies of the Futhark and runic divination—studies deepened by using my late friend's personally handcrafted set of runes.

I'm not going to lie, it's not easy stuff. It takes years to study and understand the detailed symbolism in a simple marking on a stone. We are always learning and growing, and as we age, we amass more knowledge and understanding. I remain a novice as a Seer and a rune reader. But I'm always open to diving deeper.

December Yoga Practice:
Connecting to the Energy Egg

This practice is for all levels, and no yoga experience is required. However, it is always recommended to consult a doctor before beginning any new physical program. Remember to modify anything for particular conditions that you may be experiencing, and to always follow your breath for the truth about a feeling that arises.

<u>Yoga Posture Sequence to Connect with the 12th Chakra's 32 "Secondary Chakra" Points</u>:

This practice is a full-body experience. It will take you through all the energetic components of the yoga practice, finishing with a meditation and relaxation. Allow yourself to go through all of the postures, feeling deeply into the energetic connections of these centers. If you need to stay longer in some areas to feel the connection, allow for that. There is no right or wrong way to practice connecting to these chakras.

Once the practice of the 32 points is complete, you will have time to feel into the end of the human self and the spheres that surround the body that attract energy towards what our Highest Self aligns with.

<u>Single Posture Practice</u>: Corpse (*Savasana*)

The most difficult posture to master is said to be the Corpse pose. While it appears easy, the difficulty lies in performing the stillness of a corpse, not just in the body, but in the mind.

It is best to have a blanket and other comforts. Some enjoy using lavender or balsam-scented eye pillows. The idea is to lie on the floor with your arms away from your body, palms facing upward, allowing the legs to rotate outward. The eyes should roll up towards the third eye or crown of the head. Then, the hard part: stop thinking, allow yourself to be in the flow with pure consciousness.

Breathing Practice: Full Body Breathing

In this breathing practice, we will come to the Corpse position, lying down. Whatever you need to be comfortable and relax your entire body, take the time to set up this pose. Once you are ready, begin by taking several deep breaths to center yourself in the present moment. With each breath, feel your body relaxing deeper into Mother Earth. Feel completely relaxed and supported.

When ready, begin with your inhale, and bring the breath from the abdomen outward in all directions, feeling the boundaries of your body expanding. When you exhale, feel your body releasing even more deeply. With each deep breath, you are simultaneously expanding and relaxing.

Pause between the inhalation and the exhalation. In that "pause," you will be able to feel into the boundaries of your human body, into the energy body, the auric field, and into the Cosmic Energy Egg.

Invite in Divine Consciousness to guide you in this practice of expanding your entire being beyond the boundaries of your human form—physically, energetically, and emotionally. Stay in this formless void for as long as you wish. If you fall asleep, that's okay. When ready to return, take a deep stretch to release the body, roll onto the right side, and gently press up to a seated position.

Once seated. Take several moments to feel into the boundaries of your being again. There's no rush. Be present and allow.

Mudra & Meditation:

Extend your time in corpse pose. Open palms facing the sky, lying in Corpse, feel energy move through the crown and down the central channel, then out the 1st chakra and into the Earth Star. From there, energy wraps around the body, above the head, meeting the 9th chakra, and then downward through all the chakras (8, 7, 6, 5, 4, 3, 2, 1, 10) and into the Earth Star again.

Visualize energy clearing issues in any parts/sheaths of the body. Imagine the life your Highest Self wants. Fantasize in detail about this and ask your Higher Self to harmonize your inner and outer beings to connect you to the people, places, and things most piscine to catapult you to vital, thriving, Creator-ship!

Hatha Yoga Sequence:

Seated Easy Pose for Energy Egg Meditation	(Pt 1 = Legs) Staff & Forward Fold	(Pt 2 - Buttocks) Cobbler with Butterflies	(Pt 3 = Coccyx) Seated Cat/Cow	(Pt 4/5 = Sacral & Lumbar) Table w/ Cat/Cow	(Pt 6 = Thoracic) Table w/ Twist for Cat & Cow
(Pt 7 = Cervical) Hero w/ Neck Stretches	(Pt 8 = Cranium) Hare Pose	(Pt 9 = Behind Neck) Interlace hands, bend elbows, look up	(Pt 10 = Feet) Cobbler for foot massage	(Pt 11 = Ankles) Ankle Rolls	(Pt 12 = Knees) Knee Massage, Point/Flex
(Pt 13 = Thighs) High Lunge	(Pt 14 = Hips) Lizard	Pt 15/16 = Naval, Sex Organs & Appendix) Squat	(Pt 17 = Kidney, Adrenals) 1/2 Locust	(Pt 18/19 = Lg.Sm. Intestines, Pancreas) Seated SpineTwist	(Pt 20 = Liver) Breath of Fire
(Pt 21 = Gallbladder) Side Bends	(Pt 22/24 = Spleen, Diaphragm, Lungs) Durga Pranayama	(Pt 23 = Stomach) Stomach Massage	(Pt 26 = Hands) Pranic Breath	(Pt 27 = Wrists) Stretches for Wrist	(Pt 28 = Elbow) Arms to Opposite Shoulders & switch
(Pt 25 = Arms) Making the Sun	(Pt 29 = Clavicle) Yoga Mudra	(Pt 30 = Throat) Lion	(Pt 31 = Upper Brain) Eye Exercises	(Pt 32 = Center of Earth) Meditation	Corpse

* Note that the pre-recorded practice may differ from the sequence above.

Short 15-minute Practice:

- Energy Egg Meditation
- Standing, "Making the Sun" (envision an energy egg around the body)
- "Pick a Pose"—one representing one of the 32 points you feel you need to focus on
- Full Body Stretch
- Corpse

December Recap

The Wheel of the Year has concluded, and we have a chance to start a new cycle soon. We close with the energies of hope as we align our energy, explore, and connect with our entire being, in the form of the Cosmic Energy Egg, to find our connection to our Highest Self and Oneness, reaching beyond the physical and to Consciousness.

Using the Norse tools of seidr and trance, we continue to move deeply into our being to remove obstacles in the path of being the best that we can be, and to discover the highest possibilities of where we can go.

Moving Forward

Ascension

Moving Forward

If you have spent this past year moving through the Modern Mystic's Wheel, thank you for your calling to dive deeper into the spiritual and mystical traditions of the world, to awaken and open to higher dimensions on your own spiritual journey.

So, what are we to do moving forward?

Much has been said about the times in which we are living. The idea that we are transcending the old and coming into a new "Golden Age" is a popular opinion among mystics. Energy has and continues to shift, moving into higher realms of consciousness, commonly referred to by names such as 5D Reality, the New Reality, and the New World. All of the major religions talk about a period of strife and pain on the planet that leads to one of bliss, love, and compassion. Hindus refer to us coming out of an age known as *Kali Yuga*, a time of war and suffering on the planet, and into *Satya Yuga*. This restores balance to the planet. So, when is this to occur – this Age of Aquarius?

Some say that this era began on December 21, 2012, at the end of the Mayan Calendar. Others believe it occurred in 2000. The phenomenon referred to as the Procession of the Equinoxes, scientifically says that around every 26,000 years, the Earth's wobble shifts the apparent position of the stars, and that a massive energetic event occurs at this time, which some say is now.

In David Wilcock's book *The Source Field Investigation,* he states that "The Hindus, the Mayans, and the Egyptian/Greek/Roman astrology tradition all appear to converge on the same two-year period—from 2012 to 2014—as the window in which major changes are predicted to take place."[77]

Spiritualist Steve Ahnael Nobel, creator of the Soul Matrix, feels, as do many other light-workers on the planet who are channeling higher light energy, that this portal of overcoming great spiritual darkness occurs between 1987 and 2030.[78]

---

[77] *The Source Field Investigations* page 114

[78] https://www.thesoulmatrix.com/about/

The truth is that scientists, historians, and religious scholars cannot agree on the exact time of the New Age. Varied evidence on planetary alignments, revised dating of sacred sites, and new translations of sacred texts do not give us a fixed time when the ascension process will begin. They do all, however, point to us being in that basic era of time presently.

This is exciting news. Staying away from news networks that foster fear and separateness is helpful at this time. These are the last days of duality, with Oneness and the Golden Age afoot. Naturally, any lower vibrational energies of darkness are going to stand up and rage to the very end. So, while many beings are awakening to ascension and higher light energy, there are still too many stuck in old ways of thinking and being. However, this is a temporary condition. Eventually, the souls of those who are not in alignment with the new age are going to have to choose to live in higher light or not. Either way, this is happening. And who gets to live a life of true peace on earth will be known soon enough. There are numerous speculations about what actually occurs and how this will all play out, and, most likely, there are many different ways it will. It's best to leave that "how" part out and concentrate on what we do know and can do in the now.

Contemporary voices in the realm of spiritual ascension proclaim that the era of rigid, dogmatic traditions has drawn to a close and the age of the guru has faded, giving way to a transformative epoch where we awaken to our innate gifts and inner wisdom. Within the cosmic tapestry of Oneness, we are understood to hold the Universe's boundless knowledge, realizing that true wholeness is discovered not through external seeking but by embracing the divine essence within ourselves.

This may cause some to ask what this means for world faiths and religions. Will there always be room for these traditions? Or is the time for them now over?

Let's not presume to answer those questions. One's spirituality and interconnectedness to Universal energies are personal. One person's experience may be uniquely different than another's, but at the end of the day, we will all be in the energy of Oneness together. Does this mean that some can find this truth through understanding Christ Consciousness? Yes. But if it doesn't resonate with you, then maybe not. Can one realize this through reading and living the virtues extolled in the Qur'an, Torah, or the Bible, all of which have multiple references to the ascension movement? Maybe that feels right for some of you. Or for a yoga teacher, will living the *yamas* and *niyamas* (the moral and ethical codes extolled in the Hindu text *The Yoga Sutra*) suffice? Yes, all possibilities, for sure.

The wisdom of the ancient ones, most of which is now lost or yet to be unearthed, could shed more light on how to reach Valhalla, the Otherworld, Nirvana, or the many other names Heaven goes by. Is it through an alignment and connection to astronomy and the stars? Many believe that this will be the way that we realign Oneness, as "Starseeds," realizing our True Selves, here on earth, to birth the new consciousness.

Mystical traditions such as the Jewish Kabbala, Tibetan Tantric Yoga, I-Ching, Norse Seidr, Egyptian Mystery Schools, secret societies such as the Freemasons and Illuminati, *ayahuasca* journeys, and many other neopagan movements working to revive the ancient polytheistic religions of the world could also all be valid methods in which to begin to align with these energies.

The underlying current or theme of our "Golden Age" is that of love. If we are thinking loving thoughts, performing loving deeds, and creating more flow of unconditional love in the world, then we are on the right path. When we are in service to others and the greater good, instead of solely in our ego's wants, then we will reach the pinnacle.

How do we work moving forward to stay in alignment with harmonizing our being?

Give yourself the freedom to explore what feels right for you. If certain paths and traditions speak to you, then use them. The mystics who have come before us offered much wisdom they experienced through these paths, and this will always be valid. Some of us will follow directly in their footpaths, as kin spirits, incarnations of the being, and sacred travelers in alignment with them. We modern mystics can offer fresh perspectives on these ancient practices, sharing them with the world.

If you feel called to visit the power places on the planet located along the famous ley lines, go to them, for the connections that you find there will astound you. Over the years, various individuals have explored diverse concepts of planetary energy gridlines. A scientist and photographer, Alfred Watkins, first recognized that certain straight lines or straight tracks helped our ancestors navigate the landscape and create sacred sites along them.

In 1921, he coined the phrase "ley line." But these lines were known in ancient lands for much longer. In the far East, these lines have been called "Dragon Lines," and the Aboriginals called them "Song Lines." Contemporary geologists such as Rory Duff employ dowsing—a technique using forked sticks—to detect these energy lines within the landscape. And then there are the visionaries like Robert Coon, who recognized that when multiple lines converge, they create what he called a Coon a planetary "Earth Chakra."

There is a hermetic principle: "As Above—So Below." It means that whatever exists in the heavens or on a vaster plane exists on earth or a smaller plane. If the rishis of India systemized the chakra system within the human body thousands of years ago, would it not stand to reason that this system came from a larger landscape?

Since Robert Coon many have explored the idea of a planetary chakra system. And while there is no consensus on what position on the planet directly aligns with the fifth chakra, all agree that the area around the Giza Plateau, the Sphinx, and the Great Pyramid in Egypt is most definitely one of the greatest planetary power places that exists.

Traveling to these "Earth Chakras" and their sacred sites is a way for Modern Mystics to align with the Earth, uncover deeper truths about who we are, and create reciprocal healing. When we travel to places like Mt. Shasta, Lake Titicaca, Glastonbury, and Anchor Wat with intention and reverence, we awaken dormant seeds within us that our Soul planned long ago. Each visit, each location, offers unique doorways to explore.

To learn more about these Earth Chakras, watch my documentary series:

Here's a link to the information on my website:
https://www.oneyogacenter.net/theearthchakras

The link goes to my website's free course, which shows the video series that is currently still in production, along with additional information, including the opportunity to travel with me to some of these planetary power places on a future retreat. If you prefer, you can search my YouTube channel: @TUlshafer or type in my whole name: Dr. Tracey L. Ulshafer.

Even though many feel aligned, not all are called to travel the world. That's okay. There is a pressing need to work with and heal the lands where we live and around our homes. Spending quality time there, the Modern Mystic can tap into the same energy as in other places, with focus and concentration. You can work with the natural phases of the sun and moon and the elements daily, using *The Modern Mystic's Wheel of the Year* and its companion Workbook as your guide. Just remember that the secret to any successful practice lies in our intention.

The influence of our thoughts should never be underestimated, as they generate powerful energy currents that shape our lives. Engage in continuous meditation, prayer, and the cultivation of positive intentions. The call is to transform your existence from the ordinary to the mystical by recognizing the inherent magic in all life, accessible to you, provided you remain true to the highest calling of love.

What will your daily or monthly rituals be? It should be based on what you attune and connect to.

What will your daily or monthly yoga practice be based on? You'll have to feel into that moment by moment.

When you are in alignment with your Highest Self, then you are capable of creating the rituals and practices that you need and that also honor the interconnectedness of all beings. And once you have ascended, there is no need for a teacher or a guide because you become the teacher, and the guide, and so much more.

My friend, Solara, in her book *The Star-Borne,* says that in our process of awakening, we move from horizontal patterning to a vertical one. Of this vertical alignment, she explains:

> *This is the realm of direct experience, receiving our guidance and knowingness straight from the ONE....This is how the great visionaries, mystics, and saints, as well as the founders of all world religions, received their Highest Truths. And it's readily available to us all!*[79]

If you have not yet awakened to your true vastness, seek out the truth. A vast amount of information flows through the world today. Not all will resonate with you, but you will soon find the ones that do. This book might have propelled you on a journey of seeking and understanding. That was certainly its intention.

---

[79] *The Star-Borne* page 37

Moving Forward Symbol: Metatron's Cube/*Merkabah*

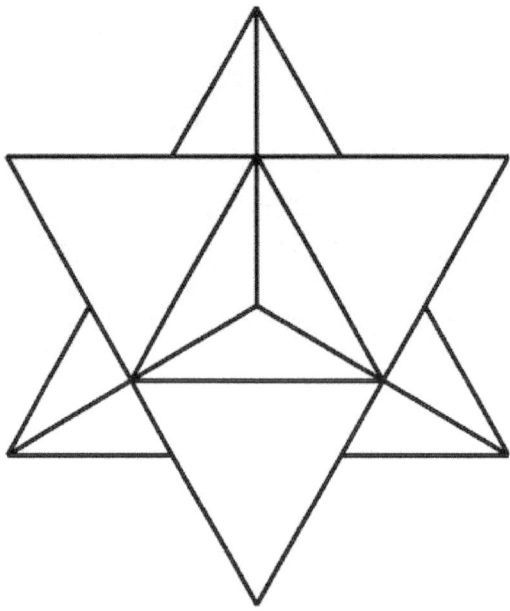

Archangel Metatron's cube, the Merkabah, is recognized for its mystical properties. Merkabah translates in Hebrew to mean light, spirit, and body. The Merkabah is described in Ezekiel as the "Chariot of God." The Book of Enoch describes how angels and Seraphim power this chariot with their flashes of light.[80]

The Merkabah is a timeless sacred geometric pattern said to depict a compilation of all of the Platonic solids that are the basis of physical matter. Energy workers agree that this pattern helps harmonize energy and can be used to clear away lower vibrational energy that exists at any time or space.

Kabbalistic sources say that Metatron created this cube from his soul, and that it is a powerful protective symbol, one that will serve us well as we move forward in our continued journey.

---

[80] *Angels 101* pages 77-88

Moving Forward Altar

- **Altar cloth:** Use an altar cloth that works for you, the energy you are working to cultivate, or one you want to return to and do again, or perhaps a simple, white cloth.

- **Flowers:** A bouquet of flowers or herbs that are naturally growing at the specific time of year that you're practicing, but the Glistening Starflower is said to assist in spiritual awakenings and ascension.

- **Candle:** White, gold, or magenta candle, or perhaps one of each

- **Crystal/Stone:** Some crystals said to aid in ascension energies or hold the vibration of 5D are: Herkimer Diamond (the master ascension stone), Selenite (to purify the auric field and amplify light codes), or Aqua Angel Aura Quartz (assisting in integrating cosmic wisdom).

- **Symbol:** Merkabah crystal or picture

- **Essential Oil/Incense:** Helichrysum, known for its properties of elevation, healing, and transcendence, and prized for its High Vibrational Energy

- **Herbs:** Ceremonial White Sage and any other herbs that align for you at the time.

- **Other Items (optional):**
  - *The Modern Mystic's Wheel of the Year* Book, Workbook, and Oracle Deck, or any oracle or divination items that you feel a connection to, and also a pendulum determining your energy, and associating with what you need on a particular day.
  - Any items that represent the feeling of ascension, heaven on earth, or 5D reality
  - Something to represent your current sankalpa

Moving Forward Angel/Ancestor: Archangel Metatron

Archangel Metatron is one of the two archangels whose name does not end in 'el, meaning "of God." He, along with Sandalphon, ascended to the realm of Archangel due to their piety. Some say the Metatron is the highest of all archangels, as noted in the Judaic book of Zohar.[81] And, since he was once human, it is felt that he serves as a unique bridge for humankind and God. Rooted in Jewish Kabbalah, he is referred to in the Talmud, the Zohar, and the Book of Enoch. He has also become beloved by many non-denominational, inter, and Intra-faith light-workers today.

According to the Zohar, Metatron records all events, thoughts, and deeds in the Akashic Records (Book of Life), a cosmic archive of universal knowledge. Metatron aids spiritual ascension, helping individuals release negative patterns and align with higher vibrations. Due to his strong connection with humanity, he is uniquely able to be a true bridge between humans and the Divine. One of these key roles is protecting the sensitive beings in our world.

Metatron's Merkabah is the symbol for "Moving Forward," and has been described.

Starseed, Steve Nobel, says to use Metatron in the vertical plane, and offers transmissions where Archangel Metatron and his cube are brought down from above and into the heart for such healing avenues. Our ritual in Moving Forward will also help you to connect more deeply with this archangel.

Like all archangels, calling in Metatron is simple and effective. Because he is our bridge to the divine, he is ready and willing to assist us in our spiritual journey of "Moving Forward."

<u>Metatron Invocation</u>:

> "Dear Archangel Metatron, be present in my life, guiding me to find a deeper connection to God/Universe/Spirit/Nature. Assist me in clearing out any lower vibrational energy that sits in the way of my understanding a deep and profound love of God/Universe/Spirit/Nature.

---

[81] *Archangels 101,* page 78

Moving Forward Ritual: Merkabah Meditation

Create a sacred space in whatever way feels appropriate to you.

Sit with your spine erect, aligning all of the chakra energy centers.

<u>Call in the Archangels of the Vertical Plane</u>:

>Eastern Direction: Archangel Raphael, the Healer, Green Ray
>Southern Direction: Archangel Michael, the Protector, Blue Ray
>Western Direction: Archangel Gabriel, the Messenger, White Ray
>Northern Direction: Archangel Uriel, Earth Angel, Red Ray

<u>Call in the Archangels of the Horizontal Plane</u>:

> <u>Below</u>:
> Archangel Sandalphon, Crystalline Grid of the Planet, Golden Ray
>
> <u>Above</u>:
> Archangel Metatron, Merkabah Cube, Magenta Ray

Feel yourself encased in a protective shield in all directions of time and space.

Begin with deep breathing, and allow your entire body, mind, and spirit to enter into a timeless trance.

Visualize that you are poised in the center of Metatron's Merkabah, the blueprint of the Universe. Raise your arms to the sides, bending the elbows while keeping the palms facing forward with all of the fingers touching. This gesture is what the Egyptians call the "Ka," and is the hieroglyph representing the part of us that is invisible. Say aloud with assuredness, "Here I am!" Feel your complete and Divine presence activated in the now. When you feel complete in this gesture, place your hands back down, touching your heart-center on the way.

Call upon your Archangel Metatron and any ascended masters and guides that you connect with to provide you with a working knowledge of how to proceed in your life moving forward, in the Highest Light, and for the greatest good of all.

Spend time cultivating the energy in the Merkabah to access anything that you need to know and understand at this time.

If you have no visions, experiences, or understandings, keep with it. Make it a daily practice to envision yourself in this sacred geometric pattern, therefore inclusive of all energy in the manifest and unmanifest realities.

As visions come, respond appropriately.

If you feel there is more work to be done for clearing, fine-tuning, and accessing this energy, go back to any previous month's work and go through the practices again. Otherwise, tap into your unlimited reserves of intuition and knowledge and multi-dimensional interconnections. Allow yourself to transcend the body and mind, move through time and space, and shift realities as needed.

Proceed immersed in love.

Tracey's Personal Reflection

In 2015, I took my first trip to Peru. This place wasn't even on my radar at the time, but a friend and fellow yoga studio owner suggested that we go together, and possibly guide others there on a yoga retreat. We went on a fact-finding mission that would forever change my life.

We had joined an Australian group led by a woman who works with Aboriginal Elders and had brought a group to Peru to dive deeply into the Shamanic traditions there. I knew nothing of those traditions and was receiving a crash course in all things Quechua, the indigenous peoples of the area, when we were told that she had a special surprise for us one day. A woman whom she had known from afar for many years lived in Sacred Valley, and we were stopping at her place to meet her. Her name was Solara Anani, and she was the "Visionary of the 11:11."

Gasps were heard around the bus. I sat in shock, knowing that there was something significant to me about the numbers 11:11. A quick check in my iPhone camera file showed 108 screenshots of that master number from 2015 alone, and I'd missed many opportunities to take them, so there should've been many more.

I became immediately emotional, and that heightened sense of homecoming remained with me throughout the visit and meeting with Solara. I couldn't speak because I was choking back tears the entire time.

When we finally left Solara's and came to the end of the dirt road in the village where she lives in Sacred Valley, the bus pulled over. More gasps came from the bus, and soon we all stepped outside to see a full rainbow, or "sunbow," around the sun. I knew that this was an auspicious symbol that today was a monumental moment in my life…

And then, I began to feel sick.

The sensitive, energetic souls on our trip recommended that I get grounded quickly. I began to feel lightheaded and weak. And by the time our bus arrived at the Incan site of Saqsaywaman, a major power place, I couldn't walk. The good yoga teacher in me squatted to get closer to the Earth, but it was not helping. Our guide, Jorge Luis Delgado, instructed me to lie down on Pachamama, spread-eagled, and breathe, releasing. I stayed here, breathing as many tourists walked around me until I felt that I could stand again. Time was lost on me, but our entire group was long gone.

My travel companion had to hold my hand as we walked through the Incan site because I was receiving an energy download that I have previously explained as a "Reverse Kundalini," where energy was traveling in and down from above the crown of my head, through my body, and then into Pachamama like thousands of thunderbolts, anchoring me into the Earth Star. The next day, I was physically sick as my body processed this intense energy upgrade.

When I returned home from our trip and walked into my yoga studio, I immediately knew that everything in my life was on the wrong path, and that I needed to make serious changes to simplify, downsize, and get more True. I was in the process of doing this when, in 2016, a deer ran into my car and hit me. Yes, the deer hit me.

It was a beautiful afternoon, and I was traveling to my father's house from an acupuncture appointment. I was feeling relaxed and blissful, having just pulled over to take a picture of the sun streaming down through the clouds into an open field. I felt the presence of Spirit strongly and an immense sense of peace. Not a quarter of a mile later, the deer hit my car.

Initially, I didn't feel that the hit was that bad. I called the police and my Dad, who promptly told me that they thought that the car might be totaled. I couldn't believe it. It was hardly a big hit, and from what I could see, little damage, and drivable. Well, it did need some repairs, but it was not completely damaged. The car had fared much better, however, than I had. A few days later, I found myself in the emergency room with Post-Concussion Syndrome.

And thus began my "Dark Night of the Soul."

For several years, I questioned everything that I had come to believe in. All of my spiritual beliefs and practices felt empty. And although I had a good life, a successful business, and was in relatively good health other than the concussion, I felt completely despondent and lost. There was one particular moment when I even considered death as a better solution than living in a state of vacantness in my heart. And that's when I found the archangels and began working with them through meditations, transmissions, and books by Steve Nobel and Doreen Virtue. Virtue has since denounced her angel work, but at the time, she was the most notable source on them, and Steve Nobel's extensive YouTube library offered many helpful resources that I partook of daily.

I eventually returned to Peru, hosting groups in 2016 and again in 2019. Both times I saw Solara and spent time at her home, which she calls "The Heart of AN." AN, she says, is the sun and moon as One Being. AN was the root civilization of all ancient cultures, like Egypt, the Druids, and the Incas. AN was part of the original planetary matrix, but on a different level. It is associated with the final Master Number 44 and the color magenta. The Heart of AN is where the New Reality was anchored on the planet for all.

I returned to The Heart of AN for ceremonies three more times in 2022 and 2023. Each time I went, I moved deeper into what Solara says is the "Timeless True Self." At the closing of our final ceremony, I felt a love so deep and true that it completed an eight-year cycle that began in 2015 of finding my True Self, my True Family, and my True Home—that resided in the last place that we often look—in my heart.

Deeply inspired by our ceremonies, the decision was shared with all to return home and channel this love toward healing immediate family members. I wanted everyone to feel the profound level of Pure True Love that I did. And, as usual in our spiritual journeys, this came with a few surprises.

First, my Grandmother died, and I spent her last night with her, holding her and opening a portal for her to move through, although it was not with complete ease as I would have liked. Next, old familial patterns arose for clearing. Then, my Mom got sick with a rare disease. And then, my Dad was diagnosed with Cancer. And the hits just kept on coming. As I write this final reflection, we are still moving through those stores. And I've had to dig really, really deep to keep in my heart's knowingness that all is revealing itself as it is meant to, and in Divine timing.

What is my spiritual practice today? I honor all traditions of the past, continue to pursue wisdom that may have been temporarily "lost" from ancient civilizations, feel more deeply into the invisible realms and dimensions, and am open to moving into something completely New and next-level that is still being born. I appreciate that the knowledge shared with us thus far in our written human experience is vast, with thousands of connections that should be valued. I also know that the time to move beyond some of the old ways and practices, in our evolutionary experience as spiritual beings, is now.

Tracey in the sacred Incan site, Raqch'i, Peru, where the 11 and 11 columns surround the massive stone structures. The location of our fourth and final AN-TAWA ceremony was conducted in 2023.
HERE I AM! HERE WE ARE!

As the Incas say, "In Love, In Service, and In Wisdom," ~ Dr. T.

* * *

Monthly Chart for *The Modern Mystic's Wheel of the Year—a Multi-Faith Path to Living in Harmony* by Rev. Dr. Tracey L. Ulshafer

Month	Theme	Tradition	Symbol	Ritual	Archangel/Ancestor	Chakra	Yoga Practice	Single Yoga Pose
January	New Beginnings	Shamanism	Spiral	Despacho Ceremony	Shaman	1 – Foundation/Rooting/New Beginning	1st Chakra for Grounding & Rooting w/Natural breath	Lotus
February	Harmony	Taoist	Yin-Yang	Feng Shui	Shaolin Master	2 – Flow/Joy/Happiness	2nd Chakra for fluidity w/Ujjayi Breath	One-Legged Pigeon
March	Rebirth	Islam/Sufism	Phoenix	Sufi Whirling Dervish/Sema	Archangel Gabriel	3 – Energy/Will/Ego/Sustain	3rd Chakra to Energize w/Kappalabhati breath	Seated Twist
April	Love/Devotion	Christianity	Rose	Anointing of the Feet	Archangel Raphael	4 – Love/Devotion	4th Chakra to open to love w/Durga Breath	Yoga Mudra & Cow Face
May	Fertility	Kemetic	Ankh	Festival of Wepet-Renpet	High Priest/Priestess	5 – Comm./Creativity/Detox	5th Chakra to open the Throat Center w/Surrender breath	Fish
June	Light	Native American	Medicine Wheel	Vision Quest	Medicine Man/Woman	6 – Intuition/Vision/3rd Eye/Seeing	6th Chakra to open the 3rd Eye w/Nadi Shodhana	Eye Exercises
July	Wisdom	Buddhism	Dharma Chakra	Vassa Retreat	Hermit (*Devas*) or Monk/Nun	7 – Wisdom/Spiritual Understanding	7th Chakra to channel wisdom w/Central Channel breath	Rabbit
August	Liberation	Hinduism	Lotus	Krishna Puja & Bhakti Yoga	Sage	8 – Soul Star/Life Purpose	8th Chakra Soul Star for Life Purpose w/Khumbukha breath	Making the Sun/Moon
September	Friendship & Community	Judaism	Star of David	Kabbala Tree of Life Meditation	Archangel Michael	9 – Stellar Gateway/Ascension	9th Chakra Stellar Gateway for Ascension/Descension w/Bellowsbreath	Headstand
October	The Harvest	Celtic/Druid	World Tree	Samhain Bonfire	Druid	10 – Earth Star/Legacy/Nature	10th Chakra Earth Star/Legacy w/Squat breath	Mountain
November	Remembrance	Meso-american spirituality	Sugar Skull	Oferanda	Elder/Ancestor	11 – Hands & Feet-Energy Transmutation	11th Chakra w/Pranic Ball breath	Downward Facing Dog
December	Hope	Norse	Valknut	Norse Seidr/Shamanic Trance	Seer	12th – Energy Egg/Ending or Pigeon Self	12th Chakra Energy Egg w/Full Body breath	Corpse
Moving Forward	Oneness	------	Merkabah/Metatron's Cube	Merkabah Meditation	Archangel Metatron	------	------	------

BIBLIOGRAPHY

Almond, J. & Seddon, K. (1999). *An Egyptian Book of Shadows - Eight Seasonal Rites of Egyptian Paganism*. London, England: Thorsons, UK.

Aswynn, Freya (1990). *Northern Mysteries & Magic, Runes, Gods, and Feminine Powers*, Llewellyn Publications, Woodbury, MN, USA.

Brockway, Laurie Sue (2002). *The Goddess Pages*, Goddess Communications LLC, New York, NY.

Bunker, Dusty (1987). *Numerology, Astrology & Dreams*, Whitford Press, West Chester, PA, USA.

Cabot, Laurie (1994). *Celebrate the Earth—a year of Holidays in the Pagan Tradition*, Delta Book Publishing, NY, NY, USA.

Clow, Barbara Hand (2007). *The Mayan Code*, Bear & Company, Rochester, VT, USA.

Coe, Michael D. (1966). *The Maya*, Thames and Hudson Inc., NY, NY, USA.

Crawford, Jackson (2015). *The Poetic Edda, Stories of the Norse Gods and Heroes*, Hackett Publishing Company, Inc., Indianapolis, IN, USA

Dale, Cyndi (2002). *New Chakra Healing*. Llewellyn Publications. St. Paul, Minnesota. USA.

Dale, Cyndi (2009). *The Subtle Body: An Encyclopedia of Your Energetic Anatomy*. Sounds True. Boulder, Colorado. USA.

Das, K. (2010). *Chants of a Lifetime*. Hay House. USA.

Delgado, Jorge Luis (2006). *Andean Awakening—an Inca Guide to Mystical Peru*, Millichap Books, Peru.

Delgado, Jorge Luis (April, 2018). *Inka Wisdom – Return to Joy*. Peru.

Feuerstein, Georg (2003). The Deeper Dimensions of Yoga, Shambhala Publications, Boston & London.

Frankl, Viktor (1959). *Man's Search for Meaning*. Beacon Press, Boston, MA. USA.

Gerrard, Katie (2011). *Seidr The Gate is Open*, Avalonia, London, England, UK.

Gimbutas, Marija (1982). *The Goddesses and Gods of Old Europe,* University of California Press, Berkeley, CA, USA.

Gray, Kyle (2018). *Angels and Ancestors Oracle Card Guidebook*, Hay House, New York, NY, USA.

Guttman, Ariel & Johnson, Kenneth (1998). *Mythic Astrology - Archetypes, Powers in the Horoscope*. Llewellyn Publications, St. Paul, Minnesota, USA.

Hirschi, Gertrud (2016). *Mudras Yoga in Your Hands*, Red Wheel/Weiser LLC, 2016, Newburyport, MA, USA.

Hope, Murry (1984). *The Ancient Wisdom of Egypt*, Thorns Harper Collins Publishers, Hammersmith, London, UK.

Iyengar, B.K.S. (2001). *Light on Pranayama*, Crossroad Publishing Company, NY, NY, USA.

Iyengar, B.K.S. (1966). *Light on Yoga*, Schocken Books, NY, NY, USA.

Jenkins, John Major (2002). Galactic Alignment—Transformation of Consciousness According to Mayan, Egyptian, and Vedic Traditions, Bear & Company, Rochester, VT, USA.

Judith, Anodea (1996). *Eastern Body Western Mind—Psychology and the Chakra System as a Path to the Self,* Celestial Arts Publishing, Berkeley, CA, USA.

Judith, Anodea (1987). *Wheels of Life—the Classical Guide to the Chakra System*, Llewellyn Worldwide, Woodbury, MN, USA.

Mason, Nicole (2011). *The Little Book of Angels*, Chronicle Books LLC, San Francisco, CA, USA.

Mayo, Jeff, *Teach Yourself Astrology*, NTC Publishing Group, Chicago, IL, USA.

McCoy, Daniel (2016)., *The Viking Spirit—An Introduction to Norse Mythology and Religion*.

Mitford, Miranda Bruce (2004). *The Illustrated Book of Signs and Symbols*, Dorling Kindersley Limited, London, UK & Barnes and Noble Publishing, Inc., USA.

Morgan, Marlo (1994). *Mutant Message Down Under*, Harper Collins Publishers, New York, NY, USA.

Morter, Dr. Sue (2019). The Energy Codes, Simon & Schuster Inc., NY, NY, USA.

Muktibodhananda, Swami (1993). *Hatha Yoga Pradipika*, Bihar Yoga School of Yoga, Munger, India.

Myss, Caroline (2001). *Sacred Contracts*, Harmony Books, NY, NY, USA.

Nozedar, Adele (2008). *The Element Encyclopedia of Secret Signs and Symbols*, Harper Collins Publishers Ltd, London, UK.

Piggott, Stuart (1975). *The Druids*, Thames and Hudson, Inc., New York, NY, USA.

Robins, Gay (1993). *Women in Ancient Egypt*, Harvard University Press, Cambridge, MA, USA.

Rochat de la Vallée, Elisabeth, translated by Sandra Hill (2008). *Wu Xing: The Five Elements in Chinese Classical Texts*, Monkey Press, London, England, UK.

Rochberg, Francesca (2004). *The Heavenly Writing: Divination, Horoscopy, and Astronomy in Mesopotamian Culture*, Cambridge University Press, Cambridge, England, UK.

Samuel, Geoffrey (2008). The Origins of Yoga and Tantra, Cambridge University Press, Cambridge, NY, USA.

Satchidananda, Sri Swami (1978). *The Yoga Sutras of Patanjali—Translations and Commentary*, Satchidananda-Ashram-Yogaville, Buckingham, VA, USA.

Silk, Linda (2012). *Survival Manual for the Modern Mystic*, Balboa Press, Bloomington, IN, USA.

Skye, Michelle (2009). *Goddess Aloud!—Transforming your World Through Rituals & Mantras,* Llewellyn Worldwide, Woodbury, MN, USA.

Smith, Huston (1991). *The World's Religions*, Harper's Collins, NY, NY, USA.

Solara (1992). *11:11*. Charlottesville, VA: Star-Borne Unlimited. USA.

Solara (2012). The Star-Borne. N*Visible Publishing, USA.

Studa, Tamara L. (2007). *The Ancient Egyptian Prayerbook,* 2nd Edition, Eschaton Publishing, Wiltshire, England, UK.

Stryker, Rod (2011). *The Four Desires*, Delacorte Press/The Random House Publishing Group, NYC, USA.

Tobin, M. (2018). *The Magdalene - Temple of the Divine Feminine*. Self-Published. USA.

Various Authors (1993). *Our Religions*, Harper Collins Publishers.

Virtue, Doreen (2010). Angels 101. Hay House, Inc., USA.

Wentz, W.Y. Evans (1958). *Tibetan Yoga and the Secret Doctrines,* Oxford University Press, Oxford, NY, USA.

Wilcock, David (2016). *The Ascension Mysteries*. Dutton-Penguin Random House, NY, NY. USA.

Wilcock, David (2011). *The Source Field Investigations*. Durron, Penguin Random House, NY, NY. USA.

OTHER BOOKS BY TRACEY

Sh!t Yogis Shouldn't Say

<u>The Accidental Yogini Series</u>:
The Accidental Yogini: Kristin
The Accidental Yogini: Padma
The Accidental Yogini: Ruth (Coming Soon, along with others)

<u>The Tia Brooks Trilogy</u>:
Butterfly
Wolf
Raven

<u>Co-Author Books</u>:
The Magdalene Oracle: Awakening the Power of the Rose
Love Initiation: Learning the Language of Soul
Stories from the Yogic Heart
Yoga in America

Tracey's Amazon Author Page:
https://www.amazon.com/stores/Tracey-L.-Ulshafer/author/

Contact Tracey directly to purchase an autographed copy of her books or to host her for your event:

www.TraceyUlshafer.com
www.OneYogaCenter.net

"THE VAULT" YOGA

"The Vault" holds treasured, curated yoga classes taught by Rev. Dr. Tracey. You can practice her many themed yoga classes for all levels with a small monthly subscription. With a simple internet connection, you can practice yoga anywhere, anytime. Inside The Vault, you'll find these types of classes with modifications and variations for all levels:
- Gentle Yoga
- Hatha Yoga
- Vinyasa Yoga
- Meditation
- Short Practices

Other Specialty Playlists on The Vault:
- Wheel of the Year
- Chakra Yoga Classes
- Sun/Moon/Stars
- The Goddess (Divine Feminine)
- Yoga for Precarious Times (also a live class that began in October 2025, meeting online). Yoga for Precarious Times is free to The Vault subscribers.

Subscribe to The Vault today:
https://www.oneyogacenter.net/yoga-classes

* Free 12-Step Chair Yoga Practices to assist those in ongoing recovery can be found on Tracey's "Ministry" page.

ABOUT THE AUTHOR

Rev. Dr. Tracey L. Ulshafer is the founder of One Yoga and Wellness Center, which operated as a physical studio in New Jersey until 2022. Dr. Tracey now continues to offer her unique brand of Hatha Yoga, trainings, and workshops on Thai Yoga Bodywork and other yogic principles, both virtually and in person. She hosts international yoga and healing retreats, along with local offerings on yoga and other holistic healing modalities.

Her self-published, award-winning fictional book, *The Accidental Yogini*, continues to be praised as an easy read with digestible yoga philosophies spread throughout. The book was rebranded as a series in 2024, as *The Accidental Yogini: Kristin and The Accidental Yogini: Padma*, with additional books planned for the series. She published the highly praised *Sh!t Yogis Shouldn't Say* in 2025, which utilizes satirical humor to interpret yogic concepts into modern-day understandings.

With a Doctorate in Ministries, she has studied world religions, and as an Interfaith minister, she designs ceremonies and rituals that ring of Timeless

Trueness. She is currently working on Chaplaincy units through The New Seminary.

Since closing the studio, Tracey has devoted more time to her passions of writing and producing her documentary series, *The Earth Chakras*, which is available for free on her YouTube Channel: https://www.youtube.com/@TUlshafer

Connect on Facebook & Instagram: @TUlshafer
One Yoga & Wellness on Facebook: www.facebook.com/oneyogawellnessctr and on Instagram: Onewellness1111

www.ingramcontent.com/pod-product-compliance
Lightning Source LLC
Chambersburg PA
CBHW080834230426
43665CB00021B/2838